Out of the Alleyway

Nakagami Kenji and the Poetics of Outcaste Fiction

Harvard East Asian Monographs 290

Aerial photo of Shingū, Wakayama Prefecture, 1948.
Photo by U.S. Far East Air Forces. 米軍撮影の空中写真 (昭和 23 年撮影)

Out of the Alleyway

Nakagami Kenji and the Poetics of Outcaste Fiction

Eve Zimmerman

Published by the Harvard University Asia Center
and distributed by Harvard University Press
Cambridge (Massachusetts) and London, 2007

Printed in the United States of America

The Harvard University Asia Center publishes a monograph series and, in coordination with the Fairbank Center for Chinese Studies, the Korea Institute, the Reischauer Institute of Japanese Studies, and other faculties and institutes, administers research projects designed to further scholarly understanding of China, Japan, Vietnam, Korea, and other Asian countries. The Center also sponsors projects addressing multidisciplinary and regional issues in Asia.

Library of Congress Cataloging-in-Publication Data

Zimmerman, Eve.
Out of the alleyway : Nakagami Kenji and the poetics of outcaste fiction / Eve Zimmerman.
p. cm. -- (Harvard East Asian monographs ; 290)
Includes bibliographical references and index.
ISBN 978-0-674-02603-2 (cloth : alk. paper)
1. Nakagami, Kenji--Criticism and interpretation. 2. Buraku people in literature. I. Title.
PL857.A3683A99 2007
895.6'35--dc22

2007034819

Index by the author

♾ Printed on acid-free paper

Last figure below indicates year of this printing

17 16 15 14 13 12 11 10 09 08 07

To Seth, Emma, and Zoe

Acknowledgments

This book took shape in dialogue with others. Beginning with those in Japan, I would like to express my gratitude:

To the Nakagami family who generously gave me their time in Tokyo and Shingū. In particular, I extend thanks to Kasumi Nakagami whose most recent book, *Yume Kumano* was published in 2002 under her penname, Kyō Kiwa.

To Kōjin and Naoko Karatani in appreciation for their company, particularly for a walk around Walden Pond one winter's day. To Kōjin, whose work "affects the quality of the day."

I couldn't have written this book without the friendship and inspiration given by Inuhiko Yomota and Chie Tarumi Yomota.

Fūki Nakamura, fellow traveller, for her generosity over two decades of friendship.

Riki Suzuki and Shūji Takazawa for sharing their thoughts on Nakagami.

The Nakagami Research Room at the Shingū Library, which provided the historical photos in this book and pointed me in the direction of research about Shingū.

Yūji Morimoto and his family for warm receptions in Shingū, beginning in 1993.

In Great Britain, Canada, and the U.S., I would like to thank:

Paul Anderer, my Ph.D. advisor at Columbia University, for inspired teaching about Japanese literature and for support that never wavered.

Tomi Suzuki of Columbia University, who got me on the right track.

Jay Rubin, scholar and friend, who was willing to teach me about the mysteries of translation, even really tough ones, over the phone.

Hosea Hirata, for help with bringing the poetry across languages

Charles Inouye, who makes Boston a better place to work.

Atsuko Sakaki, who pushes me to see further.

Melissa Wender, for breaking new ground.

Ted Goossen, for penetrating suggestions that I simply had to act on.

Sumiko Otsubo, for help with the history.

Mark Morris of the University of Cambridge, who invited me to be a visiting scholar in the summer of 1999.

My colleagues at Wellesley College, where I have taught since 2000: Ann Huss, Margery Sabin, Lawrence Rosenwald and Tak Matsusaka for their support, their integrity, and their helpful suggestions on this manuscript.

The faculty of the Japanese program at Wellesley for their help with the book: Carolyn Morley, Yoshimi Maeno, Kazuko Ozawa, Kyoko Takahara, and Eiko Torii. Special thanks to Janet Rubenstein, our administrator, who keeps us on an even keel.

Natsuko Fujimaki, Wakaba Yonaiyama, and Erika Meltzer, my student researchers/editors, for their help and their optimism that the work would get done.

Brittain Smith and Shawn Maurer, my former colleagues at Boston University, who gave me incisive comments on my work, and more importantly, their friendship.

The Bunting Institute at Radcliffe for a grant in 1999–2000 to work on this book, and to members of my writing group: Mako Yoshikawa, Ikumi Kaminishi, and Gretchen Shultz.

Northeast Asia Council of the Association for Asian Studies for a short-term travel grant to Japan in the summer of 1999.

Peter Goodman, editor and founder of Stone Bridge Press, for his foresight in shaping a body of Japanese literature in translation.

Heather Bowen-Struyk for a talk she gave on the importance of keeping it "real."

William Hammell, my editor at Harvard, for having insight into what we should and shouldn't do.

Finally, I give my thanks to my family. My mother, Rachel Phillips Belash, who knew what it would take to finish this book because she had done it herself, and who helped me throughout the process.

Alexis Belash (in memory), my stepfather, who provided tangible and intangible forms of support for the completion of this project.

Bob and Sue Lloyd, my parents-in-law. Special thanks to Sue, historian of education, who edited the first draft of the manuscript and who took the children on many a "brook walk" in Vermont.

Judith and Lawrence Smith, who took me to Japan in the first place.

My father, Franklin B. Zimmerman, a model of scholarly perseverance and a great storyteller.

My siblings, Guy, Claire and Grace, who kept in constant touch while I was working on this project and who are always part of the story.

To my two daughters, Emma and Zoe, who once thought that "tenure" meant that I only had to teach for ten years; who have now grown up considerably and give me editorial advice; and who are the best company a person could have, whether writing a book or not.

Last but not least, to my husband Seth who patiently supported me every step of the way during this project; who hiked the old road of Kumano with me in the heat of summer in 1992; and who came back in 1998, this time with a toddler in one hand and a baby on his back. This book really would not have been written without you.

Contents

Figures

Frontispiece

Photo Insert (following p. 146)

Out of the Alleyway

Nakagami Kenji and the Poetics of Outcaste Fiction

INTRODUCTION
Nothing but Words

Empty hills
No one in sight
Only the sound of
Someone talking
—Wang Wei, "The Deer Park Hermitage"
(tr. Burton Watson)

Nakagami Kenji (1946–1992) rose to fame in the mid-1970s for his vivid stories about a clan scarred by violence and poverty on the underside of the Japanese economic miracle. Wrung from his own experience growing up in a provincial city in southeastern Wakayama, Nakagami's writing burst apart stereotypes of a serene, precious, and exotic Japan. Possessing a highly sensitive ear, he wrote a rhythmic, kinetic prose that in the early years of his writing career scans in short poetic breaths and in his later work winds into great streams of words. In this prose, Nakagami captured his characters' sudden widening of vision, depicting moments when physical experience transforms into knowing and knowing can be reduced to simple physical acts. Despite its deep roots in the real world, Nakagami's writing nevertheless transcended realism. He experimented widely with narrative voice and hewed plots out of the bedrock of old tales, myths, and local legends. Even at its most experimental, however, Nakagami's language sustains its living tissue, breathing immediacy into his writings, and linking disparate works across boundaries of time and genre.

Nakagami, Japan, and Beyond

In the years since Nakagami's death in 1992, interest in his work continues to grow around the world. We read Nakagami because we cannot go around him. Through Nakagami, our perceptions of Japanese literature and culture are subtly, but indelibly, transformed. His brief but eventful life spanned the key years of the postwar Shōwa era and his work opens up those years to view. Nakagami's early fiction, for example, traces Japan's postwar recovery from the viewpoint of the underclass—in such portraits as a rogue father trading goods on the black market, an elder brother committing suicide, a family's early poverty. The later work, which mines the myths and stories of Kumano (an old name for Wakayama and Mie prefectures), reflects a resurgent interest in nativism in the late 1970s and early 1980s, when writers turned away from urban culture, searching for a rough folk edge.

During these decades, literature was serious business for Nakagami, who once stated that he had "nothing but words" at his disposal to effect change.[1] Simply in the way that he formulated his arguments did Nakagami follow in the footsteps of a long line of Japanese writers who shouldered the burden of engagement with the world. His funeral in 1992 was held in Tokyo and open to the public. It drew 800 people, including such prominent intellectuals as Karatani Kōjin and Yasuoka Shōtarō, who lamented the void that Nakagami's early death had left in Japanese intellectual circles. Coming on the heels of the 1989 death of the Shōwa Emperor, the funeral itself bracketed the close of an era, particularly for older writers such as Yasuoka who had seen the future of serious and engaged writing in Nakagami Kenji. Younger writers, too, remarked on his significance. In an oft-quoted adage, the young writer Shimada Masahiko described Nakagami as Japan's "last author" (*saigo no sakka*).[2]

We read Nakagami because he so clearly illuminates the literary scene of the 1970s and 1980s, which he largely helped to shape. During those years, he stood out as a master of the *taidan*, the published "conversation," a genre that captures, if not drives, the vicissitudes of Japanese intellectual life.[3] By exploring Nakagami's dialogues with contemporaries such as Karatani Kōjin and Tsushima Yūko, we gain not only a fuller picture of Nakagami himself but also a taste of the rich print culture that filled the pages of monthly journals: *Bungei shuto, Bungei shunjū, Bungakukai, Yurīka, Subaru, Shinchō*, and others. Indeed, Nakagami's willingness to experiment as a writer cannot be divorced from his sustained engagement with others, whether writers, critics, editors, or friends; he was a thoroughly social being who took a passionate interest in the issues of his times, and who argued, even wrangled, with those around him.

We read Nakagami because he transforms our understanding of the "edifice" of modern Japanese literature. For example, Nakagami offered incisive comments on the work of the influential critic Kobayashi Hideo—and after Nakagami's reading of him, we do not see Kobayashi's ideas in quite the same way. Indeed, Nakagami's Shingū fictions serve as a barbed response to Kobayashi's notion of the "lost home," a metaphor for the modern intellectual, adrift in the anonymous space of the city, forever severed from the roots of the local home. In contrast, Nakagami shows the "lost home" to be the source of nagging anxiety and self-loathing, a home that never held out any prospect of comfort. During the late 1960s and early 1970s, Nakagami took Ōe Kenzaburō's project to its logical extension, mining the subversive possibilities of the mythic, the local, and the spoken. If we look across the political spectrum, we can see that Nakagami's public life also resonates with the image projected by Mishima Yukio, another revealing example of how one's life becomes one's favorite text, and vice versa, how one's texts transform one's life. In a manner similar to Mishima, Nakagami showed great passion for telling his own idiosyncratic life story, using himself as the model for *buraku* discourse.

Nakagami also takes us beyond the borders of Japanese literature entirely. Like other writers before him, Nakagami read widely in French, American, and Latin American literature, revealing a global frame of reference that links Japanese writers dating back to the Meiji period. But from the beginning, Nakagami did more: he envisioned his own place within Japan by cultivating a view from outside, stressing his affinity to writers from other minority cultures. Cleverly, Nakagami hides a reference to Richard Wright's *Native Son* in an early story; he coins the term "*buraku* is beautiful" in reference to the American black power movement of the 1960s. Repeatedly he draws the figure of the committed young tough from the *buraku* on a collision course with middle class values. Witness the titles of a few of the early stories: "Arakure" (Tough Guy, 1975); "Ja'in" (Snake Lust, 1975); "Jūkyūsai no chizu" (Map of a Nineteen-Year-Old, 1973); "Ore jūhassai" (I'm Eighteen, 1966). As time went on, Nakagami expanded his frames of reference on a larger scale by forging relationships with Korean writers, discovering Latin American magic realism, and shading the narrow alleyways of the *buraku* or *roji* as ubiquitous spaces that one finds in the poor neighborhoods of every city. Nakagami not only cultivated his liminal identity but he parodied it: in copies of the novel *Sennen no yuraku* (A Thousand Years of Pleasure, 1982), for example, Nakagami chose the beautiful, bisexual character named Hanzō, signing, "Hanzō was me," an ironic reference to Flaubert's identification with Madame Bovary ("Madame Bovary c'est moi"). Through such playful gestures, Nakagami revealed his familiarity with the literary canon and his sense that he too belonged on the world stage.

Nakagami and the Alleyway

Last, but not least, we read Nakagami because he challenges our preconceptions about minority identity in Japan. Nakagami was born and raised until the age of seven in the *buraku* or outcaste neighborhood of Shingū, Wakayama, a small city in southwestern Japan (pop. 35,000). Nakagami's open admission in 1977 that he was from the *buraku* marked a turning point in Japanese literary history, as I shall discuss in the first chapter of this book. Yet his *buraku* origins were a complicated matter for him, as we shall see below.

Burakumin or "people of the village," a seemingly neutral term, refers to a class of people in Japan who have long been viewed as a group apart from the majority of Japanese. Historically, outcaste status was linked to jobs that were considered to be defiling or demeaning: leather worker, undertaker, slaughterer, shoemaker. In premodern Japan, such status was relatively flexible, but under the rule of the Tokugawa shogunate (1600–1868), outcaste status became linked with bloodline rather than simply with occupation.[4] Gradually, *burakumin* were pushed to the margins of towns and prohibitions against them were codified. In a historical novel entitled *The River with No Bridge* (Hashi no nai kawa, 1958), Sumii Sue details discriminatory practices against the *burakumin* in the late Meiji period (1868–1912): these include refusing to hand money directly to *burakumin* farm workers, breaking cups that had touched workers' lips, and forcing dress codes on *burakumin* (such as leather badges) in order to identify them.[5] Discrimination did not necessarily abate with the Meiji government's Liberation Edict of August 1871, which legally abolished the caste system. In Wakayama prefecture, for example, fears of equality spurred local farmers to go on violent hunts for *buraku* residents (*eta-gari*). It would take many years of struggle on the part of the *burakumin* themselves, coupled with government policies, to combat the most oppressive aspects of discrimination.

Although such blatant practices are not visible in Japan today, discrimination against the *burakumin* has remarkable staying power. In fact, *burakumin* do not differ ethnically from other Japanese yet they continue to be construed as somehow of different origin: ethnic Korean or Ainu or simply "other." Given the lack of ethnic difference, the disappearance of many traditional *buraku* occupations, and the growing mobility of the Japanese population, contemporary *buraku* status is somewhat mystifying. Its survival testifies to lasting discriminatory cultural attitudes and to the power of place in constructing Japanese identity: one's legal identity lies in the local family register (*koseki*) of one's birthplace. According to the Diène Report on Discrimination and Racism in Japan, which was issued by the United Nations in January 2006, the lack of a national law against discrimination has hampered positive change. (The Law on Special Measures for Dōwa ["assimilation"] Projects, which targeted specific reforms for *buraku* living conditions, expired in 2002.) The Japanese still tend to construe poverty and difference in distinctly ethnic and unfavorable terms.[6] Even *burakumin* population figures are the subject of controversy. Depending on whether one consults government figures or the figures of the Burakumin Liberation League, an advocacy group, there are between 1.2 and 3 million Japanese who are either of *buraku* ancestry or who live in *buraku* today.[7] Mirroring these intangible *buraku* population figures, the Shingū *buraku* had disappeared by 2004, its narrow alleyways erased and its people moved to other parts of the city. But even without a geographical location, one's surname could still be used as an indicator of *buraku* status, and discrimination in marriage and employment persists. In 2004, a cheerful sign adorned the Shingū city office (*shiyakusho*), testifying to stigmas that outlast urban transformations: "Starting with discrimination against the *buraku*, let's get rid of all kinds of discrimination (*buraku sabetsu o hajime, arayuru sabetsu o nakusō*)."

As a former resident of the Shingū *buraku*, Nakagami turned his gaze on his own community, transcribing a record of *buraku* culture in fiction and nonfiction that remains unmatched in scope and content to this day. Nakagami left Shingū for Tokyo in 1965, but he returned periodically, broadening his circle of acquaintances in the *buraku*. From the mid-1970s to his death in 1992, Nakagami remained active in Shingū, holding symposia with Tokyo intellectuals, staging his own play, collaborating on the 1986 film *Himatsuri* (Fire Festival) for which he had written the screenplay, and producing dozens of essays about aspects of Kumano culture. In 1977, for example, he spent months traveling around the Kii Peninsula, interviewing and recording the stories of people from scattered *buraku,* a work that became *Kishū: ki no kuni ne no kuni monogatari* (Tales of Kishū: Land of Trees, Land of Roots, 1986), a polished work of nonfiction that had important repercussions in his fiction writing. In these activities, Nakagami clearly worked against the fact that Tokyo had become the center of cultural production; he meant to shift the balance.

Although Nakagami openly discussed his views on the *buraku,* he was highly skeptical of political orthodoxies and fiercely independent in his opinions. He himself was the subject of controversy, much of it his own making. For example, Nakagami found himself on uneasy terms with the formal *burakumin* organizations such as the Burakumin Liberation League (BLL), once calling them the "secret police of words."[8] Even after his death, the BLL sent a representative to a 1993 symposium in Nakagami's honor to monitor the use of discriminatory language among its participants. Nakagami also seemed prone to making sweeping statements about the *buraku* that at times shaded toward rhetoric: he once criticized the label of "minority writer" because he equated it with a position of weakness.[9] In addition, although his own writing contains references to African American literature, he would not delineate a category of *buraku* writing in Japan that paralleled African American writing in the United States. Referring to the challenges that he had faced in achieving mainstream success, he stated about *burakumin* writers, "I am the only one."[10] Finally, his literary practices rendered his *buraku* identity elusive, at least in his early work. Nakagami uses the term *roji* or alleyway to describe the small streets that once zigzagged through the Shingū *buraku;* for many readers, however, *roji* does not necessarily connote *buraku* but simply a common space in Japan.[11]

Nakagami's skepticism about his own position as "minority writer," though at times awkward, seems prescient today of our increased consciousness of issues around representation and voice, or who speaks for whom. First, we should simply be grateful for Nakagami's pioneering example when we view the literary landscape of contemporary Japan, where such "minorities" as the Okinawan writer Medoruma Shun and the Japanese Korean writer Yū Miri flourish. Second, we should be grateful for Nakagami's tough skepticism because it forces us to reexamine our notions of minority literature as shaped by the West. Nakagami prompts us to ask what are the strands that intertwine to create a status "on the margins" in Japan? Rather than the term "minority" writer, perhaps we need to use different categories, depending on geographical origin (Okinawan), socioeconomic class (*burakumin*), or ethnic identification (Japanese Korean [*zainichi*]). Or perhaps we need a binary model based on the slippage and the tension between standard and regional Japanese. Given that the production of print culture is based in Tokyo, how do writers "on the margins" (loosely conceived) navigate between their own communities and the literary world of Tokyo without succumbing to its numbing pull? How do writers in Japan work simultaneously in different modalities and different tongues?

Nakagami's ambiguous stance on these issues—his insistence on maintaining his own independence—is replicated in critical discourse. Critics take issue as to whether Nakagami was properly authentic, or whether his *buraku* origins figure prominently enough in his writing. Hirano Hidehisa, for example, a critic from the *buraku* himself, questioned whether Nakagami's literature should even be included in the category of *buraku* writing, and if so, how.[12] More recently, in his assessment of how the *buraku* has been used and abused in twentieth-century Japanese literature, Edward Fowler compares Nakagami with Hijikata Tetsu, the *burakumin* writer and activist, and finds Nakagami lacking: "Unlike Nakagami's mythologized landscapes, in which the characters' identity as *burakumin* is almost inconsequential, Hijikata's work presents a visceral sense of marginality and characters who wrestle head-on with their *burakumin*-hood."[13] Seen from the perspective of a century of *burakumin* writing, however ignored and reviled, Nakagami does not dovetail seamlessly with other *buraku* writers.

There has also been resistance on the part of critics to tie Nakagami too closely to the actual *buraku* of Shingū. For example, Nina Cornyetz breaks the link between the Shingū *buraku* and Nakagami's fictional map, stating: "the *roji* in Nakagami's texts must be recognized as a *narrative* [*sic*] topos; it is not a mimetic representation of the "real *buraku*," and there should be no assumption that there exists a transparency or interchangeability between the two."[14] Curiously, Fowler and Cornyetz display quite different agendas when reading Nakagami: Fowler bemoans the lack of social realism in Nakagami, while Cornyetz challenges an overly literal reading of Nakagami and stresses the primacy of the text. Both critics make undeniably important contributions to their respective areas of interest—Fowler to creating a wider picture of *burakumin* writing in Japan, and Cornyetz to gender studies within the Japanese literary field. But neither adequately appraises Nakagami's poetic vision, in which the actual *buraku* and the imaginary topos function not as opposites but as mutually determining elements of an equation that lies at the heart of Nakagami's creative process.

We sacrifice something if we fault Nakagami for not being engaged enough, or if we deny the link between the real *buraku* of Shingū and Nakagami's *roji*. Simply stated, we lose the story of Nakagami Kenji himself and his connection to history. For example, Nakagami's texts are dotted with the names of people whom he knew. On one trip back to Shingū, he was introduced to Tabata Ryū, an old woman who kept the genealogy of the community in her head. Tabata's stories make their way, however indirectly, into *Sennen no yuraku* (A Thousand Years of Pleasure, 1982), a collection of tales about six beautiful young men named Nakamoto, a common *roji* name.[15] Kinoshita Katsuichirō, the first husband of Nakagami's mother, had once gone by that same name.[16] The name of Mon, the barkeeper in *Chi no hate shijō no toki* (The Sublime Time at the Ends of the Earth, 1983) came from a woman who kept Nakagami's books over her bar in Shingū even though she herself could not read; a photo of Roku, a lumberman in *Chi no hate*, appeared in the pages of a local magazine.

I do not mean to suggest that these people served as literal one-to-one models for Nakagami's characters or that we can explain the complexities of fiction through reference to "real" life. Rather, the correspondences reflect Nakagami's own interest in and passion for the concrete details of experience and for the people whose lives intersected with his. Most importantly, these fragments of names and places illuminate Nakagami's predilection for stitching together "this and that" in his making of a fictional world. The world ebbs and flows outside the text, but the world also bleeds into it. Names and places of the world spark connections in the mind so that Nakagami's reader exists both simultaneously in the world and inside the text. Or, as filmmaker Aoyama Shinji expressed in a discussion about his 2001 documentary film, *Roji e: Nakagami Kenji no nokoshita fuirumu* (To the Alleyway: Nakagami Kenji's *Roji* Film), when we visit the *roji* or alleyway of Nakagami's fiction, we embark on a real journey to a non-existent place (*nai basho ni iku*).[17]

How do we read Nakagami's *buraku* origins? Rather than attempt to judge whether Nakagami's texts accurately reproduce the alleyways, or whether Nakagami overplayed or betrayed his origins, we might instead read his fiction from the outside in. If we look at what Nakagami said and did in relation to the Shingū *buraku* during his lifetime, his words (re)create voices that stir up other voices and these in turn reverberate until we find ourselves awash in a sea of language. Dialogic and multifaceted, Nakagami's *roji* consists of words that rise from speech acts—stories and accents and dialects—that occur "out there" in the world. To use M. M. Bakhtin's terms, Nakagami's fictional *roji* arises from heteroglossia—different modes of discourse that jostle one another on the page.[18] To Nakagami alone, perhaps the *roji* was simply the space of memory or was merely the beginning of an impulse to write. But to his readers who get on the train to Shingū, or to those who come from the *buraku*, Nakagami's *roji* bursts out of its narratological dimensions. Nakagami began a discussion about writing and difference that continues to this day, spilling out of Shingū, out of Tokyo, out of Japan, into classrooms, bookstores, libraries, and rooms around the world. In this *roji* that drifts free, we hear the sound of voices talking.[19]

Presenting Nakagami Kenji

In this book, I address the triangular relationship between a body of texts, an author, and the world outside. Given the contemporary nature of the material, I take an "ethnographic" approach, sketching out certain elements of Nakagami's life and drawing on four long interviews that I conducted with the author himself; with his mother, Nakaue Chisato; with his friend and mentor, Matsune Hisao; and most recently, with his widow, Kasumi. The book grew organically out of these conversations and a Ph.D. thesis that I completed at Columbia University under the supervision of Paul Anderer. As time passed, my goals for the book shifted, moving away from a straightforward academic study. Instead, I decided to incorporate more of Nakagami's story. I had translated a few pieces of Nakagami's early fiction in 1999 and my views on the import of his work changed considerably during this process. The history of the project, which unfolded over time, thus shapes my approach in this book. Rather than account for Nakagami's work *in toto*, I present Nakagami in various stages of transformation, each stage emerging from his dialogue with the voices around him. Instead of a writer's strategies, I highlight a writer's responses, for the writer, like the rest of us, lives in time.

To create a tighter narrative, I focus on Nakagami's work of the 1970s and 1980s. Each chapter takes up a period of his writing life organized around a single topic, whether it focuses on a genre (poetry), a formal concern (literary style), or a theme (violence and narrative). I have also chosen the works that I believe were Nakagami's most innovative, from the early short story "Ichiban hajime no dekigoto" (The First Thing that Happened, 1969), to the tales in the late collection *Jūryoku no miyako*

(City of Gravity, 1988). Frequently, Nakagami would come up with a new idea, which he would work and then overwork with time. For example, *Chi no hate shijō no toki* builds on the earlier work *Karekinada* (Withered Tree Straits, 1977), drawing upon and developing certain plot threads; however, it suffers from an overly ambitious scope, a lack of internal cohesion, as if Nakagami did not know when to stop. I include *Chi no hate* in this book because I believe it to be one of Nakagami's most daring works of realism despite its flaws. But I have skipped over the works that struck me as weak or repetitive, and I leave it to other Nakagami readers to explore the later works, *Sanka* (Hymm, 1990), *Keibetsu* (Scorn, 1992), and the unfinished work *Izoku* (The Tribe, 1993).

Chapter 1 explores the literary persona of Nakagami Kenji, or how he created himself as a writer, beginning with his childhood in Shingū, moving through his literary career in Tokyo and abroad, and touching on the ways in which minority identity is encoded in the early fiction. It highlights Nakagami's extraordinary rise in the mid-1970s, focusing on the overlap between Nakagami's fiction and his activities as a public intellectual. Admittedly not all of Nakagami's critical work is of the same caliber, but Nakagami's identity as a writer stretched beyond pure fiction, and we need to draw on the criticism, if selectively, to create an accurate picture of a social writer. As stated earlier, Nakagami was extraordinarily responsive to his environment; he had an ability to identify the key issues of the times, to engage in debate with others, and to shape his fiction accordingly. Chapter 1 puts Nakagami in the context of his times, highlighting the sudden conjunction (or disjunction) of events, voices, and discoveries that propelled his writing forward from the mid-1960s to his death in 1992.

Chapter 2 explores Nakagami's early experiments with poetry, particularly his discovery of the French symbolist Arthur Rimbaud. The poetry written between 1965 and 1969, even more than the early fiction, offers a clear glimpse of Nakagami's struggle to choose a writerly language for himself. In 1959, when Kenji was 13 years old, his elder half-brother Ikuhei committed suicide. This death stirred ripples of incomprehension and despair in the younger brother. It also served as the starting point for an extended rumination on *buraku* male identity and its intersection with sexuality. The poems obsessively repeat the figure of a young man dying or dead, who floats on water, inspiring fear and desire in the speaker. Referred to variously as "Icarus," "brother" or "me," the speaker explores the spectacle of male death, linking the fate of the young man to the "expendable" males of his community, and using poetic language to mark himself off from his brother. In the early poems, Nakagami spins the tale of the family saga, his words bursting out of the abstract contours of the poem. He would stop writing poetry in 1969, but he carried his poetic interests into his fiction, particularly through his use of mythic tropes and symbolism, his poetic sense of closure, and his interest in birds, grasses, and exotic (even invented) flowers.

By the early 1970s, Nakagami had moved decisively into the writing of fiction. Between 1975 and 1983, he wrote three works that transformed modern Japanese realism: *Misaki* (The Cape, 1975); *Karekinada* (1977); and *Chi no hate* (1983). In these works Nakagami explores the character of Akiyuki, the brooding laborer with a tragic family history and a streak of violence. Working within the parameters of the *shishōsetsu* (the semiautobiographical form of modern Japanese fiction), Nakagami creates a rich narrative dotted with identifiable characters and places, a facsimile of Shingū. However, by plotting a different kind of family romance that spins on the dynamic of brother-sister love, Nakagami veers away from the oedipal plot of many *shishōsetsu*—the archetypal story by which the son defines his identity in opposition to his father. In underlying plots of brother-sister love, Nakagami explores the son's struggle to break free of the mother's realm, the locus of abjection and death, which is identified with the alleyway itself. Through the brother-sister plot Nakagami expounds upon the complexities of *buraku* identity and empties out deterministic notions of the blood. Chapter 3 uses the trope of incest to read Akiyuki's story of maturation as a new kind of *shishōsetsu*, one that unfolds at some distance from other Japanese works of the modern period.

Chapter 4 turns to Nakagami's fiction of the 1980s. The stories of this period incorporate the myths and legends of Kumano, and foreground the grotesque, the uncanny, and the unseen. During this period, Nakagami once again combined the roles of fiction writer and public intellectual. In particular, Nakagami and other critics took up the term *monogatari* as they assessed the state of modern Japanese literature. The term *monogatari* simply means "tale" (as in *Genji monogatari*, or *The Tale of Genji*), but the critics were not urging a return to a premodern tradition. Rather, they used the term *monogatari* in a number of diverse—and at times contradictory—ways. Perhaps most importantly, Nakagami took in his fiction a far more open-minded approach to the literary past than his critical essays might suggest. During the 1980s, for example, he engaged in an examination of different types of *monogatari* that might provide new directions for his fiction. In place of high-culture literary *monogatari*, Nakagami turned to popular religious folk tales (*sekkyōbushi*), fantastic stories of foreign lands (*Utsubo monogatari*), and local folktales and legends. He then began to write what we might call newly conceived *monogatari*, tales that drew on mythic tropes and experimented widely with point of view and narrative voice. The titles of the 1980s speak to Nakagami's fascination: *Sennen no yuraku* (A Thousand Years of Pleasure, 1982); *Kii monogatari* (Tales of Kii, 1984); and *Kumano shū* (Tales of Kumano, 1984). However, Nakagami's goal was not to preserve a disappearing rural culture but to forge a new literary art form—a facsimile or approximation of oral *buraku* culture that would alter the cadence of written Japanese prose. Not all his experiments succeeded, but during this period, Nakagami made his most daring contributions to modern Japanese literature.

Nakagami transformed Japanese modern prose radically through his experiments with language in the tales of the 1980s. Chapter 5 explores the mechanics of his texts, or how he used language to subvert and transform existing norms.

The local dialect of the alleyways, for example, with its grotesque and hyperbolic characteristics forms what Henry Louis Gates in his study of African American literature terms a "point of consciousness," a binding of communal energies for the alleyway people that resists the homogenizing powers of the culture of the center.[20] Nakagami drew on this local language to disrupt the highly subjective style of Japanese prose, creating not only an amalgam of voices (the old women of the alleyways, for example) but also experimenting with sudden switches in subject, wandering, disjointed passages, and other forms of stream of consciousness writing. Nakagami's numerous experiments with style serve as the focus of this chapter.

The final chapter of the book breaks with the chronological pattern of earlier chapters, addressing a topic that has received much attention in Western academic circles: the prevalence of violent spectacles, often with erotic content, in Nakagami's work. Certain critics read violence as the continuation of Nakagami's assault on the modern literary canon. Violence is thus equated with subversion, a direct blow to discrimination itself. Chapter 6 asks a different question of Nakagami's fiction: what ends does violence serve? Does violence dismantle discrimination when its object is a woman, or a weaker younger brother? A recurring theme in Nakagami's work concerns a tough young laborer who meets a beautiful and mysterious woman, often a female shaman. Unsettled by her beauty, the man secludes himself with the woman but passion soon turns to violent blows. In 1993, the critic Watanabe Naomi stated that violence against women in Nakagami's work springs from his desire to overturn the Japanese literary canon.[21] But a close reading of these scenes reveals the intense need of Nakagami's protagonists for domination and their palpable misery and alienation in the aftermath of such violent encounters. Nakagami's protagonists return from their encounters with female shamans broken, weary, and defeated. Can we read violence in Nakagami's fiction as an allegory for his own eventual hopelessness vis-à-vis literature itself?

At the end of *Chi no hate,* the alleyway of the outcastes explodes in flames and Akiyuki disappears from Nakagami's work forever. In subsequent years, Nakagami's fiction moved into new locales; his fiction literally "took to the road." One example of this shift is *Nichirin no tsubasa* (Wings of the Sun, 1984), the story of a group of old women from Shingū who travel around Japan in a refrigerated truck visiting sacred sites. In the early 1990s, Nakagami began to experiment again, searching for the next mode. He wrote about the Tokyo underworld in *Sanka* and *Keibetsu.* He started *Izoku,* a work with a pan-Asian theme now counted among the eight "unfinished" works so classified in the *Nakagami Kenji zenshū* (Collected Works of Nakagami Kenji, 1996). Before his death, Nakagami also dabbled in the graphic novel form, publishing four installments of a work entitled *Nankai kisen* (The Nankai Ferry, 1989–90) with artwork by Tanaka Akio.[22] Even when his health began to fail, Nakagami continued to write, experimenting with form and voice. In a short conclusion to this book I explore Nakagami's legacy to young Japanese readers at the time of the memorial service in 2004 that marked the thirteenth anniversary of his death. Recent films, lectures, and fiction reveal an ongoing process of remembering and sorting that continues to this day. How is Nakagami being remembered? How is his legacy being shaped? We might also put the question in reverse: how do we reconcile current-day Japan—with its seeming eradication of marked differences, its dominant urbanism, and its consumerist proclivities—with the stories of Nakagami Kenji?

Before we turn to Nakagami's fiction, however, we will first consider a portrait of the author and his times—or, more accurately, we will separate out the polyphony of critical and creative voices that held sway in the 1970s and 1980s when Nakagami Kenji stepped forward. We begin with an overall picture, a birth, a place, a name, like a patchwork of fields seen from above, a shifting but indispensable view.

ONE

Roots and Branches

In 1988, Nakagami sat down to do a taped interview with me in a noisy restaurant in the Chelsea area of New York City that offered a "gospel brunch." At that point, little of Nakagami's work had been translated into English, and he was known mainly in academic circles in the United States. We talked for over an hour before conversation was cut short by the arrival of the gospel choir. In the interview, Nakagami covered some familiar ground, such as his views on Japanese literature; but he also shaded his remarks for a Western audience, reminiscing about aspects of growing up in the postwar *buraku* in ways that he might not have done for Japanese readers. This interview stands as an example of one of Nakagami's many brilliant oral performances, whether he was in Tokyo, or Shingū, or on one of his many trips abroad.

Early Life, 1946–1965

A talented storyteller, Nakagami Kenji spoke of his life as if it were a confluence of dramatic historical events: a world war, an upheaval in family circumstances, the obliteration of a local neighborhood. Moreover, Nakagami stressed his sense of himself as unique or different. First, he was a *burakumin*, having been born in 1946 next to the railroad tracks in the impoverished outcaste neighborhood of Shingū, Wakayama, to a widowed mother of four. In order to help a married sister in a fish shop, Nakagami's mother, Chisato, had come to Shingū in her teens from a *buraku* in Koza, a town further south on the Kii Peninsula. Already as a child Chisato had known dire poverty. By her own account, her father had once been a successful cattle dealer who had managed to build his family a home; but he died tragically, soon after Chisato was born and the family lost their house.[1] In Shingū she met and married Kinoshita Katsuichirō, with whom she had five children, one a little boy who died of a childhood illness at the age of three. In 1944, Kinoshita himself died at the age of 35, leaving Chisato a widow with four children to support in hard war-stricken times; she sold everything she could and eked out a living as a peddler.[2]

Nakagami also felt different because he was the only child who did not share a father with his siblings. Chisato's sixth and last child, Kenji was the product of a brief liaison between Chisato and Suzuki Tomezō, a resident of the *buraku* in Arima, a town to the north, who had drifted to Shingū looking for work after the war. Matsune Hisao, a long-time resident of the Shingū *buraku* and a relative of Nakagami's father, described Tomezō: "He was born in Arima, and after the war, everybody was short of food so he came here. We had a black market that sold lots of stuff. Well, he wasn't a gangster (*yakuza*) but he was pretty extreme. A tough fighter . . . strong in his fights with men, and strong with the women, too—he could get his way with them."[3]

Nakagami would not formally meet his biological father until he was an adult. In 1954, at the young age of eight, he was separated from his older siblings when his mother took him to live with Nakaue Shichirō, the man who later became his legal stepfather. The older siblings remained behind in their house in the Kasuga district, except for one younger daughter who was still in middle school and who shuttled back and forth.[4] As he himself frequently mentioned, Nakagami Kenji, before the age of thirteen, had gone by two different family names, neither of which came from the man who was his biological father. His pen name, Nakagami, is a different reading of the characters of Nakaue's name, a reading he adopted only after his arrival in Tokyo at age nineteen.

The Kasuga district, which spills out behind the central train station in Shingū, is still the *buraku* to this day, although very few of the original houses remain. In my 1993 interview with Matsune Hisao, he stressed that discrimination against the *burakumin* in Shingū had been intense in the prewar era. Nagayama, the original outcaste enclave, was located near the feudal castle, nestled behind a small hill named Garyū-san that separated it from the rest of the town. (During the Tokugawa Period, a gate further segregated the people of Nagayama from the town). Isolation thus exacerbated the already poor living conditions.[5] Families could not afford an education beyond primary school. The young men, some hardly more than boys, were sent out to work at a limited number of arduous, unskilled jobs. They served as day laborers (hauling earth or timber in the mountains), construction workers, or butchers in a nearby slaughterhouse. The work could be dangerous: pulling logs through the mountains (*kinmahiki*) had caused numerous casualties in the *buraku*. The young women were shipped off to work in factories or pressed into domestic service in Nagoya and Osaka. Matsune Hisao even remembered young women being sold to the local brothel whenever times got hard.[6]

The end of World War II marked a sea change for the Shingū *buraku*, ushering in an era of land reform, urban renewal, and educational opportunities. Nakagami himself ascribed change to the wave of democratic ideas of equality and freedom that swept through Japan on the heels of the American Occupation:

> If Japan hadn't been defeated in the War, Nakagami Kenji wouldn't have become what he is today. I was the first one to get letters. Education finally got here for the first time. When I said that I could read my own name, they'd say, "What?" as if I were some kind of prodigy. They'd praise me for being smart because I could do that one thing. Just getting an education was a revolutionary change. I was on the first wave of that change.[7]

Change in the outcaste neighborhood can be traced to developments on the national front; but equally important was the fact that the *burakumin* themselves began to fight assiduously from within to better their lot. In 1946, the year of Nakagami's birth, a group of young *buraku* activists formed the National Committee for Burakumin Liberation, which lead eventually to the founding of the Burakumin Liberation League (BLL) in 1955. The BLL concentrated primarily on bringing egregious health and human rights violations into the public eye, demanding physical improvement of schools and neighborhoods, and fighting discrimination through a policy of denouncement (*kyūdan tōsō*).[8] Takazawa Shūji, Nakagami's biographer, notes the importance of the grassroots *buraku* movement in readying the young Nakagami to receive an education. In 1952, a nursery with books opened in the Kasuga *buraku* community center (*kodomo no kai*), and the six-year-old Kenji went there while his mother peddled her wares. In Takazawa Shūji's words, "Nakagami Kenji was the first literary youth (*bungaku seinen*) of the alleyway."[9]

In addition to the influx of democratic ideals nationwide in Japan, and to the advent of activism within the outcaste community itself, the overall growth in prosperity during the 1950s contributed to the improving quality of life in the Shingū *buraku*. New types of machinery and tools, along with ever-increasing construction contracts, improved the life of the Shingū worker.[10] General economic expansion exerted a direct effect on Nakagami's new family. His stepfather, Nakaue Shichirō, previously a day laborer, was now able to build a successful contracting firm and to grow relatively prosperous. From the age of eight, Nakagami knew the security of a steady income. As his mother stated in our interview, "I had no money worries once we came to Noda to live with [Shichirō]; he'd buy me whatever I needed."

Despite this recently acquired financial stability, however, Nakagami's family was not immune from trouble. Nakagami himself described the move to the Nakaue house as a major upheaval in his life. His older siblings resented being left behind by their mother and having to fend for themselves. In sharp contrast to Kenji's relatively comfortable childhood, his elder half-brother Ikuhei had gone out to work in his early teens, like many before him, and had never attended middle school. With a tendency toward alcoholism already apparent, Ikuhei began to behave erratically after the move. He appeared drunk in his stepfather's house, issuing threats to the members of the newly combined family. In 1959, when Kenji was thirteen years old, Ikuhei hanged himself with a leather strap from a scaffold in a Shingū tatami factory. This death is inscribed repeatedly in Nakagami's early writing. Trouble also broke out in the extended family: in a domestic dispute named the Ohama Incident, the brother of Nakagami's sister's husband was fatally stabbed by another brother-in-law in a knife fight.[11] The details of the murder—down to descriptions of the fatal leg wound—are replicated in such early works as *Misaki* (The Cape, 1975).

If Kenji's childhood experience differed from that of his siblings in terms of money and paternity, the differences were magnified by his superior education. Of the five children, he was the only one to receive a complete secondary education. The local Education Bureau offered incentives after World War II to keep *buraku* children in school. Nakagami himself remembered receiving aid in kind, not in cash, as local officials were afraid that the money would be misspent: "They told me, when I was in primary school, if you need a pencil, ask the teacher, she'll give it to you. . . . But it was hard to ask for things. When it rained, I needed rubber boots so I had to go and ask for them (laughter)."[12]

Nakagami often related the story of his mother's distrust of literature, repeatedly stating how he had grown up in a house without books. But his mother did know the value of a good education. In her words: "This is Noda. We used to live in Kasuga. Even though we had a house there, papa [Shichirō] asked me to come live here and we came when Kenji was in first grade. He wasn't put into some rural school, it was Midorigaoka school, a little better than the others."[13]

Nakagami's childhood differed from his siblings in one other crucial respect. Being younger, he grew up in a *buraku* that was no longer the target of the harsh and overt discrimination it had suffered before the war. Discrimination had not been eradicated in postwar Shingū, however; it had simply been driven underground.[14] According to Matsumoto Iwayo, a classmate who later became a *sake* merchant, certain parents of Kenji's classmates did not invite Kenji to their homes.[15] In addition, *burakumin* names could be recognized easily by those in town. Matsune Hisao, for one, immediately recognized the Nakaue name when he saw one of the young writer's poems in the local newspaper.[16] Describing the contrasts between his home in the alleyways and the other neighborhoods of Shingū, Nakagami waxed inventive and said:

> The air was different, the air inside the alleyway and out. The atmosphere was different. Imagine a boy who says, "Ah, I'm different. Around here I'm the same but when I go to school I go out, right? I play with other kids, I make friends. The minute I leave home it feels different." In the summer all the houses along the alleyways are wide open, in the evening everybody comes outside to enjoy the cool air, and they talk up a storm. But when you go out there, all the houses are shut up tight, everybody's locked up inside their houses, they don't hang around outside together. . . . In the old sense of the word, Japan's old communal system survived in the alleyway.[17]

The architecture of Kasuga, the heart of the fabled Shingū *buraku*, no longer exists in its previous form, having been knocked down in two stages of urban renewal. The first dates to the period immediately after the war and included improvements in infrastructure (streets and sewage) as well as the construction of new housing units in Kasuga (157 between 1954 and 1969). The second stage of redevelopment, dated to the late 1970s, destroyed the Kasuga of Nakagami's early childhood. Facilitating the obliteration of Kasuga was the gradual leveling of Garyū-san, the hill that had segregated the original enclave. By 1977, the hill was gone and the real work on Kasuga began. The city razed 56 houses and built 54 new two-story concrete buildings in their place. Many residents took cash payments and left the area for good. During this phase, the public bath, the communal well, and the family's original house in Kasuga were all destroyed. The alleyway was no more.[18] In 2004, nothing marked the spot where Nakagami's house once stood; even the two-story concrete buildings that had been put up to house the displaced people of the earlier wave of development were gone, with one exception. Ironically, the site of Nakagami's house is marked only on tourist maps that commemorate the birthplace of the town's second famous writer, the first one being Satō Haruo. A new shopping district has replaced the alleyways, anchored at one end by a large department store. The old Kasuga architecture remains on a single street in Shingū where, in 2004, a smell of gas pervaded the air.

Nakagami began to write in his early teens. In Midorigaoka Middle School he entered the class of Yamamoto Ai, a teacher who prompted her students to write poetry and compositions. By his own account, Nakagami got poor grades but showed talent in music and writing.[19] Tamura Satoko, a classmate of Kenji's who became a poet and a translator of Latin American literature, remembers the teacher telling them to "keep a record of your feelings every day and show it to me."[20] It is amusing to consider that Nakagami's writing career might have been, in part, a function of habit—a compulsion to record the world to show one's teacher.

Even at this early age, however, Nakagami's writing stirred up controversy. When he and Tamura competed for who would represent the class in a school literary contest, Tamura was chosen. Later she discovered that Yamamoto had preferred Kenji's story about a boy lying to his mother but could not recommend it because of the last line: "The end justifies the means." Tamura remarks on the incident: "At that moment I realized for the first time (as well as I could at that age) that Kenji was fashioning his own unassailable space."[21] What Tamura suggests here is that Nakagami was not simply writing for pleasure or accomplishment: writing was a means of coping and coming to terms with a harsh environment—a way to ensure survival.

Discovery of Tokyo, 1965

In February 1965, Nakagami made an exit from Shingū, gathering whatever cash lay at hand and boarding a train to Tokyo with a friend. Although he was the only member of his family to complete high school, he missed his March graduation. He would never live full time in Shingū again. Once in Tokyo, he pretended to study for the entrance exam to Waseda University on a generous allowance from home.[22] But in reality he wandered around Tokyo with friends, some who were connections from Shingū; he experimented with drugs; and he discovered jazz. Much has been made of Nakagami's early experience of jazz, particularly how it shaped his writing.[23] In fact, Nakagami had shown musical talent early, participating in his school choir. His music teacher had even suggested a training course in Tokyo, a suggestion his mother did not act on. But jazz, as he put it, was different; it was an escape route from Shingū, from his experience with Western classical music, from his family itself. Nakagami's discovery of jazz coincided perfectly with his discovery of Tokyo:

> In the beginning I loved classical music. There [in Shingū] I was suddenly reading books, writing words, and listening to music. Even listening to classical music on our cheap radio thrilled me. I didn't like the world I lived in. Classical music was like news coming over the radio from another place. I loved it and opera, too. I was good at singing. When I graduated from middle school, the teacher came and said that I had musical talent and my mother should send me to a high school in Tokyo. We were a family in construction. My mother. That mother of mine. She'd turn off the radio when I was listening to it, just like that. The teacher came to say, put your son in a high school in Tokyo, there's a special music school. What kind of ridiculous idea is that, she told him bluntly. . . .
>
> I started high school feeling down, and I just read books. I didn't study or do anything else, I just read. When I graduated I came to Tokyo because of a friend's older brother. The friend didn't come, but his older brother showed me around. Me and one other guy, we packed these rucksacks with almost nothing inside them. Underwear, one change of clothes, a sweater, a brush, we grabbed a bunch of money and literally flew out the door. I didn't go to my high

school graduation. Then, the guy we knew put us up, and that night he took us to Shinjuku. I went to my first modern jazz place, a place called "Live," behind Nikkō. Going there and listening to that music, it was great, really, I was in shock. The next day the older guy had to go somewhere so he said you go wherever you want, I'll give you a key. I had the key, it was cold, I was bored in the room, so I went out. I thought this is where I got the train yesterday, this is where I bought a ticket, this is Shinjuku where I got off the train. I walked off in what I thought was the right direction but I didn't get to the back of Nikkō, I got to Kabukichō. I got to a place called Jazz Village. I could hear music, and it was the same modern jazz, so I went in. I met a bunch of people, I got in with them. I didn't have any plans to go to university, I listened to jazz every day. Why did I like jazz so much? Why did I go so crazy over it? To me, classical music beautified my lower class world, I mean the world of laborers, the world of the alleyway, or you could even say that pleasurable existence where life is the same day in and day out. Music was my own forbidden pleasure. But jazz smashed everything—the pleasure, the alleyway, classical music. It enfolded it, too. It was destruction and creation. That's jazz, destruction and continuation. I drank it up. Every day I listened to jazz, from morning till night. Jazz was me.[24]

Once again, Nakagami's life becomes his favorite text, one that he polished and re-polished with each telling. The equivalencies shine: Tokyo equals jazz, which in turn equals freedom from home.

Although Nakagami immersed himself in music, he was also hard at work at his writing in the mid-1960s, producing both poetry and fiction. In 1966, he joined *Bungei shuto*, a *dōjin zasshi* (magazine circle), which anyone could join for a small monthly fee. Nakagami published poetry and fiction in the *Bungei shuto* journal, rising through the ranks from member, to associate, to editor. At this time, he met the woman who would become his wife, Yamaguchi Kasumi, the well-educated daughter of a businessman who had been writing poetry and stories since her teens. According to Kasumi, Nakagami was already a celebrity (*yūmeijin*) in the *Bungei shuto* group when they met. At their first joint meeting, she remembered being struck by his "unique opinions" rather than by his looks or by his charm.[25]

Kasumi and Kenji married in 1970. Nori, their eldest daughter, was born in 1971 and two more children followed: a girl, Naho, in 1973; and a boy, Suzushi, in 1978. When the money from home ran out in 1970, Nakagami got a job with International Airport Utility (IAU), a subsidiary of All Nippon Airways (ANA), based in Haneda Airport. He cleaned airplanes and moved baggage for the Flying Tiger Line, a major air cargo carrier. It was physical labor in often demanding conditions. His employers, thinking that Nakagami could not read or write, offered to fill in the company forms for him. In the meantime, Nakagami wrote fiction during breaks to the toilet. After a heavy piece of luggage fell on him and injured his foot, Nakagami spent a week in the Kamata Hospital. There, in 1973, he finished a final draft of "Jūkyūsai no chizu" (Map of a Nineteen-Year-Old) and asked Kasumi to take it to the publisher, Kawade Shobō.[26]

In the early days of their marriage, Kasumi played the role of the supportive spouse, acceding to Nakagami's request that she not write for three years—although this was a point of contention between them. While Kasumi raised the children, Nakagami wrote the fiction that brought him his first taste of success. Kasumi read, commented, and copied out his manuscripts, tasks she would continue up until *Chi no hate shijō no toki* (The Sublime Time at the Ends of the Earth, 1983). He also drank. During these years Nakagami began to spend evenings out in the Tokyo bars with other writers and critics. Kasumi described how alcohol and intellectual life were linked in Nakagami's circle:

> His life in the bars, all that debate (*ronsō*), was part of life in the literary world (*bundan*). He'd get drunk and then he'd get into trouble. He'd fight with people he cared about. He didn't have any trouble with people he didn't care about. You know the expression "*karamizake*"—picking fights when drunk. He was known for that. But he was also very logical (*rikkutsu poi*). He wasn't nice when he was drinking. In the 1970s, that's the way the *bundan* was.[27]

Kasumi describes a masculine, cliquish environment in the bars, where partnerships were forged, enemies made, and women rarely intruded, except for those female proprietors who served as confidantes or lovers to the men within. Real business was done in these places and a writer would go to the same establishments night after night. In fact, much of the Tokyo publishing world seemed to operate after hours, editors' paths converging on the drinking establishments of Shinjuku and Shibuya. Editors would track Nakagami down to his favorite haunts. Once at an Okinawan restaurant in Shibuya, two editors arrived, demanding work that Nakagami had promised them. At Nakagami's invitation, they joined the party but kept a close eye on him until they got what they had come for—a couple of pages of copy for a fashion magazine.

Stories of Nakagami's exploits in the bars of Tokyo have lasted long after his death; as one anonymous reader of this book wrote, "everyone has a Nakagami story." In particular, I can attest to the fact that Nakagami often got into fights late at night in the heat of drinking and discussion. There were also occasions where his fury was turned on himself, as in New York in 1988 when he kicked a garbage can on the way to a party, injured his foot, and had to be carried piggyback to the hospital. But often it was turned on others, including younger members of his entourage, and other writers and editors who worked with him. More striking than Nakagami's violent temper, however, was the level of his remorse afterward and the extent to which those around him, even his victims who suffered physical injury, forgave him. Through 20 years of drunken exploits, Nakagami was quick to apologize and colleagues and friends were inclined to overlook faults, as if they recognized that they could not have one Nakagami without the other. To this day, Nakagami's former editors speak of him with great fondness and a good measure of forbearance and humor.

The stories that circulate about Nakagami do more than fuel gossip; they reveal the collective nature of the literary enterprise in Japan. Nakagami enjoyed the support of a group of editors and critics who were deeply invested in his work, whisking him away to hotels and vacation homes where he would write alcohol-free. In the late 1970s and into the 1980s, Nakagami's professional acquaintances felt themselves to be participants in a unique moment in Japanese literary history, or as Suzuki Riki, a well-known editor who had worked on Nakagami's mid-career fiction, stated: "It was a time when something special was happening in Japan."[28] Nakagami stood at the center of a burst of grassroots literary and cultural activity.

Nakagami knew people from all walks of life, from the Hell's Angels of Yokohama, to local prefectural officials in Wakayama, to academics, translators, and artists abroad. Given the activity that Nakagami fomented wherever he went, we might read his violent outbursts along a continuum. The same impetuous nature that led him to create happenings that drew Shingū locals and Tokyo intellectuals together also fueled his drinking bouts and his irascibility. It was as if Nakagami could not tolerate what he himself had created. On a personal level, he was overtly social, but he lacked a sense of boundaries, and he was too easily drawn in and agitated. He did not conform to the model of the removed intellectual nor could he show restraint. Kasumi herself remembers the two sides of her former husband: "He was gentle and delicate on the one hand, and violent on the other."[29]

The birth of the Nakagami's first daughter, Nori, in 1971 marked a turning point in Nakagami's life, according to Kasumi. Nakagami had long felt cut off from Shingū because he felt that he did not have a home to which he could return. But suddenly he had his own family in Tokyo. In Kasumi's words: "Having a family (*katei*) really changed his perspective, I think. He thought about what it meant to be a father once he became a father. He could see himself that way."[30] Although home life was certainly never peaceful, Nakagami began to experience a small measure of success in the early 1970s. In 1974, he quit his job at the airport and began to support his family on the proceeds of his writing and on various part-time jobs. One year later he published *Misaki*, the work that would first bring him mainstream critical success. Before we move to Nakagami's sudden rise in the mid-1970s, however, let us briefly consider his early fiction written in the late 1960s and early 1970s, a body of work that reflects Nakagami's early experimentation with words.

Early Fiction, 1967–1975

The early stories take place in two locales: the underside of Tokyo, along the paths of newcomers like himself, or in a rural locale that Nakagami openly names "Shingū." No matter the location, Nakagami's protagonists evince a fascination with criminality, or more accurately, they reveal both dread and longing for the moment when a "crime" will be revealed. Both the Shingū and the Tokyo stories tend to employ first-person narration, using *boku*, or "I," the word used by younger men and boys; but the stories set in Tokyo experiment more with form and narrative voice. "Ai no yō" (Something Like Love, 1968), for example, features *boku* and his alter ego, *aitsu* (that guy), his hand that masturbates incessantly. With its split character and its self-mocking asides about politics and pleasure, the story approaches the tone of Ōe Kenzaburō's satirical early work, particularly his portrait of a right-wing terrorist in "Sebuntīn" (Seventeen, 1961).

By 1973, however, Nakagami had further developed the portrait of a sociopath in "Jūkyūsai no chizu" and had drawn the attention of critics. "Jūkyūsai" depicts a newspaper delivery boy who spends his days in his room, marking Xs on a map as he makes plans to punish customers along his paper route. Occasionally, he emerges to make anonymous prank phone calls. Akiyama Shun wrote that such stories of alienated youth had been done many times before, but here was something new: "It's violent, it's subversive, but it opens up a new space of a liberated, fresh sensibility."[31]

The "liberated sensibility" described by Akiyama can be seen in the odd mixture of bravado and reticence that characterizes the protagonist's actions—and also infuses Nakagami's language, which veers between abstract poetic metaphors and violent curses. We never learn much about the protagonist (except for the fact that he is a student who never attends his preparatory school) but we do discover his dark fantasies. Trapped in a cheap boarding house that is permeated with the smells of his roommate's sweat and semen, the newspaper boy feels like a slug coming apart from the inside. His only recourse is to mark Xs on his delivery map to assert control over his world. He also plays games with another alter ego, a yellow dog that slinks around town in the early morning, and he engages in light-hearted meditations on how he will punish his clients with death. Here, near the end of the story, the newspaper delivery boy has what for him is a typical revelation:

> I pushed a newspaper into the crack of the door and I was struck by the ordinary fact that the people in the house were sleeping in their warm futons, and that this had no relevance to me. I guess 5 in the morning is my time of day. Dawn still hadn't come. The gray sky was still spattered with black splotches. The rain hit my face. I breathed deeply into my nostrils for sheer pleasure. Then, as though I had received a revelation from the gods, I knew that I would do whatever I wanted until I was 20, and then I would die. I'd made a momentous discovery. Somehow, I would get to that year but after that I didn't know. Hey Matsushima family, this house has never had an X before but to commemorate the place of my discovery, I sentence you all to death. I don't know how I'll do it, I can decide that later. A rightist sheds no tears. A dog spirit loose on the town doesn't feel a thing.[32]

Standing in the liminal moment between night and day, the newspaper boy firmly repudiates middle-class life. He tries on the mask of the rightist, dismissing the students who join the radical student movement Zengakuren (All-Japan Federation of Students' Self-Governing Associations) as children of privilege who can afford university. But he does not fit the profile of the right-wing zealot either; later in the story, the boy discusses how he cannot stomach mythical accounts of Japanese history. Even the revelation from the gods gives him no indication of what route to take. Through this portrait, Nakagami creates a sliver of displaced, angry youth, newly arrived in the city. Rather than create a three-dimensional character, however, Nakagami's interest lies in how the psyche boldly harnesses language to forge a map of reality, in this case a map belonging to a nineteen-year-old. Here is the self that wills itself into being through language:

> As I walked toward the station on the main road, I tried on the words as if I were reciting a lover's name, "I am a rightist." The effect wasn't bad at all. Taking a right around the corner, I passed the factory. Okay, listen up, this is what I want to say! You are filth, you can't run barefoot through a field of grass where stalks poke up like spears, you're fat, grotesquely fat like a river work horse, hung grossly low. I am pure, without sin, I shine, just cut open my chest and watch my blood flow. Taste the sperm that comes out of my dick. I thought of all the things I would shout at Takayama Nashinoichirō, but then a line of poetry came to mind: I am a dog, a beast who will tear out your soft insides given the chance. It came from some poem in my college prep textbook, but I felt happy, it fit my current mood perfectly. . . . (*NKZ* 1: 387–88)

The newspaper boy's declaration begins and ends in a flow of disjointed language; he is a pastiche of images, fragmented quotes, and random thoughts. The story ends with the boy slipping further into fantasy, getting down on all fours and running loose, a dog on the town. In "Jūkyūsai no chizu" Nakagami keeps the reader at bay, refusing to give a logical or satisfying ending to a series of bizarre happenings.

In contrast to the isolated newspaper boy with his delusions of grandeur, the early fiction set in Shingū is concerned with a gang of boys. *Boku*, the central character, participates in the activities of the gang even as he marks his distance. But here, too, crimes are committed and secrets are kept. Set in a small provincial city, the stories ruminate more directly on the problem of identity and of trying to pass oneself off as one of the others. In fact, no direct mention is made of the *buraku*, although the topography of the stories suggests how space reflects social hierarchies. In 1969, for example, Nakagami published the story "Ichiban hajime no dekigoto" (The First Thing That Happened, 1969) in *Bungei shunjū*. In this story, the plot unfolds around a double of the hero, a young boy named Shirakawa, who comes from a Korean hamlet outside of town.

The Korean hamlet thus serves as a suitable cover or decoy for the main character's *burakumin* heritage and his feelings of shame over his own family.

As Faye Kleeman points out, Nakagami could not have afforded to reveal his *burakumin* origins at the time, even if he had wanted to, for it would have exerted a negative impact on his literary career.[33] But the early stories spin many variations on the theme of identity. In "Ore jūhassai" (I'm Eighteen, 1967), a gang of boys borrows a car and runs down a policeman. In the end, the boys laugh when they discover that the man was an imposter, and the joke is on the adult world. To further the concern with truth and lies, sly hints surface about the main character's own secrets. He slips a love letter from his girlfriend into the pages of Richard Wright's *A Native Son,* wondering how his girlfriend would like the sex scene between a black man and a white woman. Subsequently, a gang of boys from another school beats up the main character when they see him with Yuri, the girl. No mention is made of whether the boys punish him for dating someone from a different social class or because he goes to a different school. But the former theory takes precedence when the main character forbids his gang to exact revenge on his behalf, as if he alone must bear the brunt of being bullied. Even at this early date, Nakagami explores the violence that can accompany the simplest social transactions: an outing with friends, a date. A dark message lies beneath the surface of what appears to be a comical portrait of growing up in postwar Japan.

"Ichiban hajime no dekigoto" further turns on the power of buried secrets. Kōji, the central character, compares himself to Shirakawa, the Korean-Japanese boy whose family resides in the hamlet that the boys mock in the beginning of the story. What links Kōji and Shirakawa are the lies that they both tell, Shirakawa about his place of origin, and Kōji about his stepfather, who he claims to be his real father. Nakagami suggests that the lie has greater implications:

> Shirakawa and I were always going to be big liars, and we weren't going to change unless some red demon from hell came and ripped

out our tongues. Like me, Shirakawa would always be a big stubborn liar. Shirakawa, who claimed not to be Korean, even though he was, and who said he hated Koreans, was just like me living with my fake father, my mother, and the others. (*NKZ* 1: 253)

The repetition of the words "big liar" links Kōji and Shirakawa in the act of masking their own family backgrounds. In Shirakawa's case, the desire to pass as a non-Korean is made explicit by his lies. But Kōji's deception is further encoded through the figure of the stepfather, a "fake" father whom Kōji uses to represent both conventional middle class status and "normal" family life. In this early story, Nakagami not only represents the psychological mechanism of the desire to pass, but also the ways in which minority identity is encoded, displaced, and literally projected onto the body of the other. Kōji also notes that Shirakawa's real crime is not to like his own group—a hint of the main character's own buried self-hatred?

Kōji shrinks from having any contact with his elder half-brother, who raises chickens and believes that a god in the sea sends him personal messages. In order to avoid encounters with this big brother, Kōji tells further lies. One day, to Kōji's horror, the older brother discovers him with his gang of boys as they build a secret tower in the mountains. On the one hand, Kōji imagines that his tower will be a haven for his family in case of a natural disaster, but he feels deeply ashamed when his brother appears at the site. The mad but affectionate brother eventually commits suicide, and after the wake Kōji climbs into the mountains above the town:

Still lying prone, I grasped some eulalia leaves, tugging hard at them as I tried to get up. I felt a hot searing pain, and when I examined my hand, blood oozed from the spot where a leaf had cut me. Feeling the pain tickle, I stared at the blood beading in red droplets on my hand, and then I got up slowly. . . . Tear everyone to pieces, I thought, with the sound of the wind whistling in my ears. Tear up the sky, the sea, the mountain (with the secret tower), tear up XX Yasuji, Pest, the Takenaka River, my dead brother, the light that dazzles my eyes, tear everything apart! (*NKZ* 1: 261)

In the blood that oozes from his hand, Kōji suddenly confronts the immutable condition of his own existence, the blood that links him to the brother, his own hidden identity. The shame Kōji felt when the brother appeared at the tower becomes more comprehensible in light of Kōji's fear that his own origins might be revealed. At the same time, the trickle of his own blood provides a release from the riddles that haunt him, a sign of identity made apparent—witness his sudden fantasy to destroy the world, a mirror reflection of the newspaper boy's fantasies in "Jūkyūsai no chizu." Nakagami is making a point about writing itself: to identify secrets and lies in words; to reveal them, if obliquely, is to recognize and at once confront their power. We see the continuation of the process that Nakagami began in middle school, when his classmate Tamura Satoko recognized his writing as a means to create an "unassailable space." Nakagami's early fiction shows hesitation, repeatedly addressing the question: do I declare myself in the face of complete exposure, or do I run and hide? In the stories secrets invariably emerge—a hidden life as a proto-terrorist, a false cop unmasked, a group of boys who choose a scapegoat—suggesting that secrecy is impossible. At the same time, Nakagami's protagonists strive to perfect their disguises, striking a posture of defense. Riddles of identity and problems of difference loom beneath the surface of Nakagami's early works, and these themes reemerge with a vengeance in the mid-1970s when Nakagami created the character of Akiyuki. We now turn to the moment of Nakagami's rise during the early and mid-1970s when the chorus of voices, both his and others, grew louder.

Nakagami's Literary Rise, 1975

In "Shōwa gojū nendai no bungaku" (Literature of the Shōwa 50s, 1984), the critic Isoda Kōichi writes, "The debut of Nakagami Kenji was akin to an incident [*jiken*]. With the publication of *Karekinada* [Withered Tree Straits, 1977], Nakagami . . . became the flag bearer of a new generation. Nakagami appeared, overthrowing the postwar framework, the process of postwar modernization in which nature was being lost through continued development."[34]

Isoda reveals the high expectations placed on the young Nakagami, even as he expresses a measure of anxiety through the use of words such as "incident" (*jiken*) and "overthrow" (*kutsugaesu*). In the course of his essay, Isoda mentions Nakagami three separate times, but Murakami Haruki, arguably the most famous Japanese writer in the world today, receives no more than a couple of sentences—"he creates a unique literary world."[35] Isoda then places Nakagami's achievement into the old opposition between a rural folk Japan and an "Americanized" urban Japan. To Isoda, Nakagami celebrates, even preserves, the mythical landscape (*shinwateki na fūdo*) that floats behind postwar Japan even as the landscape itself disappears.[36]

Isoda's statements also reveal the patent bias of the critic of serious highbrow literature (*junbungaku*). As in other periods of Japan's modern era, literature serves as a medium through which one mulls over issues of state and self, questions of history and national identity.[37] Isoda, born in 1931, still reads fiction for its seriousness of purpose. Radical though Nakagami may have seemed to Isoda, he addressed the important issues of his day: postwar growth, *fūdo* or landscape, and urbanization. Would Japan move toward Nakagami Kenji, Isoda asks indirectly, or in the direction of Murakami Haruki and Murakami Ryū, products of a thoroughly urban sensibility?

Isoda chose 1975 to mark a new era in Shōwa literature, the year that Nakagami published *Misaki*, the novella that would bring him the Akutagawa Prize for new young writers, in the October issue of *Bungakukai*. Did Isoda begin his new period in the year 1975 because of Nakagami? Or, as he mentions in his introduction to the essay, did Nakagami simply number among the many young men who came to the cities in the late 1960s and early 1970s, flush with the proceeds of postwar wealth?

Whatever motivated Isoda to mark the start of a new period, the early 1970s proved to be crucial years for Nakagami. Not only was he becoming known for his fiction, but he also was gaining momentum as an essayist and critic. He was practicing to be a public intellectual. In the exemplary essay "Sakka to nikutai" (The Writer and the Flesh, 1976), published in *Bungei shunjū*, for example, Nakagami asks: what is the relation between writing and flesh (*nikutai*), between the life of the body and the life of the mind? Nakagami equates a degenerate life in Tokyo, filled with drugs and jazz, to the life of a laborer in his hometown. Both serve the flesh, and by doing so, destroy the self (*jiko*). Nakagami discovers that he cannot live without words; coming from a laborer's home without books, he compares words to flowers. Eventually, Nakagami quits his job as a baggage handler at Haneda Airport, but when he gives up physical labor, he turns to alcohol in order to write. He concludes, "I don't know how I'm going to live my life. For a little while, I'll drink to keep my balance."[38]

Nakagami's gritty evocation of his rural origins in "Sakka to nikutai" might first be read within the context of an upsurge in grassroots nativism during the 1970s. According to the writer Tsushima Yūko, a contemporary of Nakagami's, many young writers, herself included, were engaged in a search for their folk roots at this time.[39] Was Nakagami simply riding a wave, parading his rural origins to get attention?[40] In fact, the critical interest in such terms as *nikutai* and *jiko* dates back even earlier. In its immediate postwar manifestation, *nikutai* signified a release from wartime ideologies and systems and a return to a simple, material life of the body. Nakagami also sets the flesh up in opposition to the self (*jiko*), another key term from the postwar period when intellectuals were frantically trying to redefine the relationship between the individual and society in the aftermath of war. In the work of Honda Shūgo, for example, the term *jiko* refers to an ethically engaged concept of self, one that measures itself in relation to others. Or, as Honda declared, "To know the self is to fight with one's internalized image of the world, to break one's world image that is based on ordinary crimes and laws, and make a new image of the world wrung from the depths of the self."[41]

In his use of the terms *nikutai* and *jiko*, Nakagami works within the parameters of postwar discourse and demonstrates that he has done his homework.[42] At the same time, Nakagami critiques the terms from the viewpoint of one who was born into a family of laborers. In typical fashion, the moment he sets up the old categories (flesh and self), he collapses the argument and reformulates it dialectically. We cannot have flesh without writing nor writing without flesh, he suggests; the question is how to mediate between the two in order to write. In fact, Nakagami does not espouse a nativist argument; the flesh cannot be made into material for the pen, because it will not submit. But Nakagami also refuses to idealize the *nikutai;* no matter how much he feels the flesh, he cannot go back to a house without words. Finally, Nakagami makes his point in a personal vein: the debate, after all, is being played out through his body. By candidly admitting to a lack of certainty that seems compelling even today, Nakagami gets the reader on his side.

In 1975, Nakagami put his ideas of flesh and self to the test in *Misaki,* a story about a family of laborers in a rough, provincial coastal town. *Misaki* also stands as the first work in what has often been read as a series of three works that are linked in time and space by Akiyuki, the central character. *Karekinada,* the second work in the series, brought Nakagami real fame. *Chi no hate shijō no toki* further explores the history of the outcastes as well as traces the eventual destruction of the alleyways. With the emergence of the central figure of Akiyuki, Nakagami's work attains lyrical intensity, replicating the shades of light and dark, the sounds and voices of the neighborhood where the laborers live. Though not explicitly identified as *buraku,* this neighborhood, the *roji,* or alleyway, constitutes a world in itself. The language of "Ichiban hajime no dekigoto," published six years earlier, with its polished tone and deliberate imagery, reads like a studious attempt to write literature. In contrast, *Misaki* flows seamlessly forward, a series of discrete utterances that build to small crescendos, then scatter and regroup. The difference is Akiyuki. Through a third-person narration, Nakagami achieves the necessary distance to shape his materials with a firm hand. For the first time, too, through Akiyuki's eyes, Nakagami draws a map of his fictional world in all its scale and complexity, including the threads of a genealogy that will stretch from work to work like trade routes across a sea.

In recognition of *Misaki*, Nakagami was honored early in 1976 with one of two Akutagawa Prizes for Literature, the debut prize for young writers.[43] *Misaki* was his fourth submission in ten years. In hindsight *Misaki* dazzles, but the discussion by the Akutagawa committee was so tendentious that the deliberations were mentioned in the popular press. One journalist took Nakagami's side in the *Asahi Journal*, first asking, "Nakagami-san, are you happy with the way you were chosen?" He then exhorted: "Please don't write fiction that is too easy to understand because the media expects it of you. . . ."[44] The main argument against *Misaki* was that the number of its characters made the plot hard to follow. As Takii Kōsaku, one judge, stated, "*Misaki* seems to be the story of a laborer's family in Shingū in Kishū, but the characters are all mixed up, there's no realism, I couldn't make heads or tails of it."[45]

The Akutagawa Prize committee of 1975 itself reads like a Who's Who guide to postwar Japanese literature [with high representation of the second wave of postwar writers, oddly named the "third group of new writers" (*daisan no shinjin*)]: Yoshiyuki Junnosuke, Niwa Fumio, Nagai Tatsuo, Inoue Yasushi, Nakamura Mitsuo, Yasuoka Shōtarō, and Takii Kōsaku.[46] Even as they grumbled about the number of characters, however, the judges came to a consensus on one thing: Nakagami's mimetic power. To varying degrees, all the judges commented on this ability: "This writer has got a powerful style when it comes to bringing out one kind of people" (Nagai Tatsuo), or "If you go through it patiently, the bedridden mother and the clique of middle-aged women are crisply drawn. The appearance of this family, living with old-style emotions against a backdrop of earth and labor, rises up in the mind's eye"[47] (Nakamura Mitsuo). Like Isoda Kōichi, these judges align Nakagami with the native landscape (*fūdo*) and the body (*niku-*

tai), repeating the refrain of "earth, blood, and sweat," as if Nakagami were a diamond in the rough.

One year later, Nakagami published *Karekinada* in book form, another watershed for him. Etō Jun, the postwar critic, penned an extraordinary review of *Karekinada* in the *Mainichi shinbun*. Etō was obviously writing for popular consumption, but in contrast to the cerebral, abstract style that characterizes his essays, he waxes poetic:

> The prose in this longer work pulsates from beginning to end with the tingling (*uzuki*) of the writer's heart. . . . Reading *Karekinada*, I couldn't help feeling that perhaps after seventy years Japanese naturalism had finally fulfilled its promise. However, Nakagami's is not a borrowed theory of naturalism; he creates characters through the beat of his own heart as he breathes in earth and blood. He captures what the "physics" of naturalist theory could not . . . he sings about the sorrows that people feel in this world.[48]

Most important to Etō is Nakagami's language, which pulsates and sings. Etō compares it to a folksong that he heard two young women singing on a train on his way to Princeton University. The song "penetrates his heart" (*shimiiru*), which he believes good fiction should do, too. Given Etō's view of the many failures of Japanese writers over the course of the modern period, his positive view of Nakagami stands out sharply. In an essay entitled "Seishun no kōhai" (The Desolation of Youth), for example, Etō charts the pitfalls of modern Japanese writing:

> It is already common knowledge that the naturalists attacked literary style (*buntai*). It was further eroded, little by little, by the proletarian writers and the New Sensationalists (*Shinkankakuha*). Postwar literature tried to experiment with prose style (*bunshō*), but in the end it didn't at all break away from the habit of scorning it. Isn't it time to reflect on the fact that such scorn signaled the weakening of our spirit (*seishin*)? When it comes to the issue of how we have imitated the language of translated novels, if the critics had been more aware of prose style (*bunshō*), they could have engaged in the job of analysis rather than in roundabout debates.[49]

Etō launches a spirited critique of the postwar writers who, caught up in the bad habits of the past, did not use the moment of defeat to contemplate the situation in which they found themselves. Like architects charged with rebuilding the nation, postwar writers should have taken a hard look at what effect the influx of Western languages in translation had had on Japanese writing and focused on the rejuvenation of prose style (*bunshō*). Instead, they made no progress. Thirty years later, Nakagami, on the other hand, has created a *pure* naturalism, not a borrowed one. His characters rise from the pulse of his heart, he forges links to the landscape (*fūdo*) through earth and blood, and he creates a language that fulfills a mimetic promise: to sing of the pain that people feel in this world. How interesting that Etō makes this discovery first in an airport and then on a train listening to an American folksong—as if he can only envision the *fūdo* from the perspective of "somewhere else."

Conversations with Noma Hiroshi and Yasuoka Shōtarō, 1977

Between the years 1975 and 1977, Nakagami achieved great literary success after years of relative obscurity. How did he respond to his ascendance? Or, more accurately, how did he respond to being positioned as a writer of "earth, sweat and blood," particularly in light of his *buraku* origins? Characteristically, Nakagami's response varied according to context. One particularly dramatic forum in which he expressed his views was a public discussion on the topic of discrimination in Japan with the fiction writers Noma Hiroshi and Yasuoka Shōtarō. The text appeared in printed form in the *Asahi Journal* in March 1977. Nakagami publicly declared his *buraku* origins on a national stage for the first time, a brave step for a young writer. Even more bravely, he openly disagreed with Noma Hiroshi on many matters pertaining to the *buraku*.

Nakagami was in good company that day in 1977. Noma Hiroshi, the author of *Kurai e* (Dark Pictures, 1946), a central work of postwar fiction, had worked in a *buraku* for the improvement of social conditions before the war. Yasuoka Shōtarō, one of the "third group of new writers" (*daisan no shinjin*), first began to think about the problem of discrimination in Japan during a visit to the American South. The conversation began with a discussion of the Sayama Case, the conviction of a young *burakumin* man for rape and murder on circumstantial evidence.[50] It would end with Nakagami praising the oral culture of his mother, stating that his mother's storytelling had inspired him to become a writer.[51]

If Noma and Yasuoka expected Nakagami to express the orthodox viewpoint of the oppressed group that they themselves were championing, they had a surprise in store for them. As we have noted, Nakagami rejected the label of minority writer because of its connotations of victimization; he criticized the BLL; and he even made the claim that the *buraku* should remain in Japanese society because it is beauty itself (playing with the phrase "black is beautiful").[52] He also invited the disapproval of Noma by stating that sexual mores in the *buraku* were looser than in majority society owing to a dearth of property with which to cement marriages. Noma countered Nakagami sternly at this point, stating that conditions vary greatly from *buraku* to *buraku*. Farming communities, points out Noma, can be deeply conservative. There is no universal *buraku* in Japan.[53]

On the surface, Nakagami plays the role of the young upstart challenging his elders. But Noma and Nakagami are not merely quibbling over facts. Rather, they are arguing about the writer's place in the world. Noma, who had spent time in the *buraku*, sees the *buraku* as a serious social problem that needs fixing. Nakagami, on the other hand, disputes Noma's reformist agenda; he views discrimination as a structural issue, an element that saturates the very fiber of Japanese culture. According to Nakagami, a humanist preoccupation with the *buraku* merely feeds the fires of discrimination. He makes a direct appeal to Noma:

> It's useless to view the *buraku* simply as a communal system. In the case of the novelist, in contrast to the politician or the intellectual, first you have to realize that people don't live by ideals alone. The problem of passing, it's tied up with people's lives, there's nothing

to be done about it. I want to keep my eyes on that kind of reality in Japan. Noma-san, I'm saying this to you openly as a young writer, but as long as you're writing a novel you must not avert your gaze from the *burakumin* problem or the Korean problem. I think that it's absolutely essential. Looking at the history of Japanese literature as a novelist, the oppressed and excluded dreams of the people wouldn't have come into being without the untouchables (*hinin*), the weak point in society. . . . Mostly, I want to pin down Japan—that's the ambition I have—the special condition of Japan, the Japan that bleeds if you cut it. There's a saying about the *nō* theatre, it lies between the gods and the outcastes. As a novelist working now, I want to capture that.[54]

Despite Nakagami's exhortation, Noma holds his ground. He refuses to back down on what he perceives to be the role of the intellectual—namely, to fight the pernicious problem of discrimination at all costs and in any way possible. Eschewing Nakagami's notion that art and discrimination are inextricably linked, Noma counters:

The *buraku* is like a wound on the Japanese. Concepts of the "individual" (*ko*) or the "self" (*jiga*) in Japan make me think of a gash running down someone's back. That is what I always write about. Not many people notice this. But that fact too is deeply interwoven with the existence of the *buraku*. The establishment of the individual is relevant, but when we think of the Japanese "self" (*jiga*) that is struggling to make its place, the *buraku* serves as the gash running down the back.[55]

What appears to divide Noma and Nakagami is nothing less than history itself. Noma, who has come through World War II and dedicated his writing to what he perceives to be a social and political agenda, clings tenaciously to the notion that something can and must be done. Nakagami, on the other hand, raised on the disaffection of the 1960s, refuses the position of writer as humanist. Suddenly, he states that if he thinks too much about discrimination, he has no choice but to throw a bomb.[56] The writer in the post-1960s era cannot accept Noma's methods. In spite of the impasse between them, however, Noma praises Nakagami's writing, and Nakagami makes a sincere effort to explain his position to Noma. Noma and Nakagami would meet for another discussion in 1981 during which Nakagami would report that he had been severely criticized by the *burakumin* of Shingū for contradicting Noma the first time around.[57] By this admission, was Nakagami showing his respect, however obliquely, for an elder statesman?

Although Nakagami expressed unorthodox, even radical views to Noma and Yasuoka, he nevertheless craved understanding. During 1977, Nakagami was experiencing the destruction of the Kasuga district in Shingū. That year he quit the BLL and formed his own group named the Buraku Seinen Bunkakai (Buraku Youth Cultural Group). To Nakagami, the threat was complete assimilation, a process he saw occurring before his very eyes. In Kasuga's gradual disappearance from Shingū, Nakagami was viewing the *roji,* his own recent literary discovery, expunged from the world. As he told Noma, "I feel longing in my heart, I feel love."[58] At this time he also embarked on his journey around the Kii Peninsula recording the stories of people from various *buraku* in the area. Nakagami later told Karatani Kōjin that the discussion with Noma and Yasuoka had inspired him to research and write the nonfictional account of his travels, *Kishū: ki no kuni ne no kuni monogatari* (Tales of Kishū: Land of Trees, Land of Roots, 1986).[59]

Before turning to a more detailed discussion of Nakagami's writing, however, I want to consider a final context in which Nakagami's work flourished throughout the ensuing decade: his friendship with Karatani Kōjin and his rediscovery of the *monogatari* (tale) as narrative form. Within the framework of this collaborative relationship, Nakagami and his contemporaries usher out the era of "earth, blood, and sweat" and move toward a more dispassionate form of criticism.

Conversations with Karatani Kōjin, 1979

Nakagami Kenji met Karatani Kōjin, writer and critic, in 1968, when Karatani was 27 and Nakagami was 22. Neither had yet achieved success.[60] As always, Nakagami transformed the mundane into a story: he entered a room where he saw a young man talking with Endō Shūsaku, the postwar writer who read Japan through a Christian lens and who at the time was serving as editor of the literary journal *Mita bungaku*. Listening to this unknown figure announce his opinions in a loud voice as he crunched on a rice cracker, Nakagami felt tempted to reach out and snatch the cracker. But the conversation went on in his presence without interruption. "He was full of himself," Nakagami writes. When he turned to go, however, to his surprise, the man came with him. It was Karatani Kōjin. The two went to a coffee shop in Shinjuku and began to talk. Later Karatani reported his first (deplorable) impression of Nakagami directly to him: "Your clothes looked hideous, the shirt at both elbows torn and what should have been a white shirt was brown with stains."[61]

Karatani Kōjin and Nakagami Kenji embarked on a friendship that would last for nearly a quarter of a century. Nakagami's account of their first meeting is redolent with symbolism: two young men strike out on their own, leaving an older generation behind. Their dialogue was unique in the 1970s and 1980s because it ebbed and flowed beside the first stirrings of what has been called a postmodern movement in Japan, one thread of which was a complete revision of how Japan "got" modernity. In fact, Karatani published very little formal criticism about Nakagami during his lifetime, a number of essays that can be counted on the fingers of one hand. But each piece delivered a fatal blow to the "earth, blood, and sweat" school of Nakagami criticism. In a 1974 review of "Jūkyūsai no chizu," for example, Karatani states that Nakagami finds his style in this work, but that in the next work "Katatsumuri" (Snail, 1974) he mocks it. Drawing out the opposing principles in Nakagami's work would be Karatani's signature. Or, as he wrote, "I watch him to see him get out of the spaces that he's written himself into."[62]

In 1979, Nakagami invited Karatani to sit down and discuss Kobayashi Hideo, the critic whose work is part of every literary education in Japan. The discussion was later printed with what turned out to be the apt title, "Kobayashi Hideo o koete"

(Beyond Kobayashi Hideo). To some extent, Kobayashi served as a straw figure. In fact, both Nakagami and Karatani had read Kobayashi voraciously at one point in time but now expressed ambivalence. Nakagami no longer cared about the path of restraint and civility that Kobayashi represented—the "middle way," a phrase that Nakagami borrowed from an essay by Kobayashi.[63] In contrast, Kobayashi represented the blueprint that Nakagami intended to erase and eventually reconfigure.[64] Karatani, too, expressed a feeling of alienation (*iwakan*) that would overwhelm him—not when he thought of Kobayashi ("It's not that I have any interest in analyzing Kobayashi per se," states Karatani)—but when he thought of the grandiose role played by the highbrow Japanese critic.[65]

The full extent to which both Nakagami and Karatani had been thinking about the "domain"of modern Japanese literature becomes apparent in their discussion of Kobayashi. In 1979, Karatani had just published "Kokuhaku to iu seido" (Confession as a System) in the winter edition of *Kikan geijutsu*. This essay would later comprise one chapter of *Nihon kindai bungaku no kigen* (Origins of Modern Japanese Literature, 1980), an examination of the underpinnings of Japan's modernity. Rather than read the "modern" as the result of transplanted Western ideas, Western books, or Western ships, Karatani turns to the transforming power of language itself. For example, the confessional narrative (*shishōsetsu*) did not emerge because the Japanese had imported a new notion of "self"; rather, it emerged in tandem with a new type of written language, *genbun itchi*, a style of writing that approximated transcribed speech. This vernacular style in turn brought "interiority" into being, or in Karatani's words, "a sense of the presence of one's voice."[66] Suddenly, there was a psychological self that had secrets to confess.

Karatani gives the name "inversion" (*tentō*) to random shifts in the phenomenological landscape that are consequently read within a causal framework and assigned teleology. Many markers of modernity he interprets the same way: spirit (*seishin*), genius (*tensai*), and style (*buntai*).[67] What Karatani seeks to do is to strip such events of their causality, and, like the scientist, to view them as random fluctuations in nature. He tells Nakagami: "I do not affirm. The present is built on the inversions of the past. Everyone mistakes the effects with the causes. As for the nature of the inversion, it is to think of random deviation as a necessary event. Once this happens the past is forever a process of making random or arbitrary events inevitable and giving them teleology."[68]

Because we do not recognize the random nature of inversions, we create fixed narratives that draw causal links between how we got from our past position to our present one. With the monolithic West situated on one side, we then posit the East on the other: a fixed and essential "Japan," that in its pristine isolation produced the cherry blossom, the samurai, and the geisha, and then submitted to the inevitable march of modern civilization while still secretly preserving its own unique roots. Karatani's embrace of randomness cuts Japan loose from the myth of its own modern birth. In a discussion of Kobayashi's wartime writings, Karatani puts his ideas on an "essential Japan" to work. On the one hand, Karatani states, Kobayashi had the brains to realize the coincidental nature of "Japan"; yet in his writings on Motoori Norinaga, the nativist eighteenth-century scholar, Kobayashi "inverted" Japan so that he could believe in it for a time. Most Japanese, however, lacking Kobayashi's sophistication, took him at his word: Japan *was* sacred.[69] In fact, Karatani states that Kobayashi Hideo and Motoori Norinaga resemble one another because they both share an "optimism that comes before nationalism."[70] No matter what invades from the outside (whether in the form of the Western philosophy or Chinese learning), the root that is Japan will not wither or die.[71]

Karatani's notion of "inversion" galvanized Nakagami. What could have been more liberating than the idea that the traditional space—*fūdo*—with which one has always been aligned—is no more saturated with culture or history than any other? It, too, is a product of a random shift that has been misconstrued. All spaces to one extent or another are simply scribbles on the map. At the same time, Nakagami did not simply follow in Karatani's theoretical footsteps. In the late 1970s, Nakagami initiated his own critical leaps that emerged from his dialogue with Karatani but were not limited to that dialogue. Typical of his writerly tendencies toward attention to detail, Nakagami elected to examine the products of inversion rather than analyze the overall process. The material at hand in this case was local—the *monogatari* or tale, a major form in the history and development of Japanese literature. At the time of the 1979 discussion with Karatani, Nakagami was publishing sections of his most extended piece of critical writing, "Monogatari no keifu: danshō" (The Genealogy of the Tale: Fragments, 1979), ideas on the *monogatari* that are central to his critical thought.[72]

Nakagami does not intend the term *monogatari* in its thematic or descriptive sense, a topic that will be fully developed in Chapter 4 of this book. Instead Nakagami focuses on the most basic definition of *monogatari*—that which stands in opposition to *shōsetsu* or to realistic prose narratives. Appropriately, Nakagami began his discussion of *monogatari* that day in 1979 with a nod to Karatani's essay on confession. According to Nakagami, literature (*bungaku*) arises from the same inversion that produced notions of the self; it is simply a result of translation. But what disturbs Nakagami is that confessional writers do not recognize themselves as products of translation; rather, they believe in the myth of an authentic, unique self. Because the confessional writers are blind, Nakagami declares that he can only work with *monogatari* writers who recognize the fact that they are at the mercy of the languages that they use and who also recognize the existence of a law/system (*hō/seido*) that controls them.[73] Nakagami holds up the example of Tanizaki Jun'ichirō, a writer who pragmatically admits through his unbridled masochism that he is a creature of the system. The *monogatari* at least recognizes its own ideological and rhetorical underpinnings whereas "literature" (*bungaku*) feeds on the fallacious myth of its own authenticity.[74]

Ironically, baring the roots of "Japan" with Karatani allowed Nakagami to move on to the next period of his writing life—fixing his eye on the "Japan" of tradition as reflected in the form of the *monogatari*. Suddenly, Nakagami could turn the *monogatari* to his own advantage, using it to transform his own writing. Like a collage artist, Nakagami worked with preexisting materials, tearing them apart and reassembling them while still holding the pieces in his hands. He would never write the clever, urbane fiction of Murakami Haruki or Takahashi Gen'ichirō. Given how Nakagami positioned himself, we might view him as a writer who stood on the cusp between a national discourse and a global one, or as one who represented a moment in time that was fast disappearing. Witness how Isoda placed Nakagami in such a critical position in the 1970s. And, as Nakagami himself told Etō Jun in a discussion in the late 1980s, "As representatives of contemporary literature, other writers don't think about how to cross swords with the classical tradition. I often do."[75]

In the late 1970s and early 1980s, Karatani and Nakagami stood in the middle of a current of new ideas, a moment of critical and even writerly intoxication. Not coincidentally, these were Nakagami's most productive writing years. We might label this current "postmodernism," or we might simply read it along the continuum of Karatani and Nakagami's developing train of thought. Recently, Hosea Hirata has suggested that the term "postmodern" might not even do justice to Karatani's project. Referring to one of Karatani's essays, Hirata writes:

> Here Karatani seems to be criticizing a postmodernist posture that too facilely claims the death of the subject "I." But more precisely, he is pointing to an "ironical" twist built into a supercilious attitude named postmodernism. For this and other reasons, we need to be wary of labeling Karatani a postmodernist thinker. His criticism is also in a sense directed at his own thinking, at his own milieu. There is no doubt that he rejects the essentialist notion of the subject. Yet at the same time, he is not content with a vacant critical discourse that "boasts that there is no 'I.'"[76]

If we search for the thread that links Nakagami and Karatani, perhaps it would be this self-critical, self-reflective stance. We see once again how the two men formulated their positions with one eye on the other. In a 1981 essay styled as a "letter to Nakagami Kenji," Karatani mentions his interest in Gödel's 1931 theorem, that famous proof in mathematics that shows that within any system of logic there are certain statements which cannot be proved, and which can be taken to be true or false without contradiction. Gödel's theorem can also be stated in the form of the Cretan Liar's Paradox: All Cretans are liars; I am a Cretan. In the essay/letter, Karatani explains Gödel's theorem to Nakagami not because he advocates nihilism but because he means to urge upon Nakagami the importance of maintaining one's uncertainty and one's ability to question.[77]

In light of Gödel's theorem, a moment of crisis in the West that produced modern mathematics, we might read Karatani and Nakagami's dialogue as a pivotal moment in postwar literary history—a moment when the notion of a purely indigenous literary form was declared dead and was buried forever. From the point of view of the literary historian, however, we are also left with the artifacts of a conversation that ebbed and flowed over the course of 25 years. During the 1979 discussion, Nakagami and Karatani also talked about jazz. Nakagami stated that his attraction to modern jazz was rooted in the fact that musicians recognize the existence of the code and then search for ways to blow around it. What more fitting metaphor for a discussion (*taidan*)—two musicians working side by side, listening and responding to one another, improvising. That day Nakagami and Karatani paused for a moment to explore their respective motivations for working. Nakagami admitted tongue in cheek to having "ambition." Karatani, at first loathe to reveal himself, offered, "I have no desire, it's probably ambition [*laugh*] or maybe it's just excessiveness, I don't know."[78] The exchange revels in the rhythms of repartee, the joy of statement and response. Over the years, Karatani read and talked to Nakagami outside the boundaries of "Japan." And what did Nakagami do for Karatani, the most original and incisive thinker of his day? In one review of Nakagami, Karatani remembered Sakaguchi Ango's statement that "a work isn't something just to be written, but something to be lived."[79] To Karatani, perhaps Nakagami simply represented the messy, engaging, and unfinished business of life itself.

The Discovery of Kumano, 1980–1988

Although Nakagami left Shingū in 1965, his connection to Shingū and to Wakayama only deepened with time. In 1980 he bought a condominium in Katsuura, a nearby resort town in Wakayama, where he spent weeks at a time and stored many of his books. As discussed earlier, he gave lectures and sponsored events beginning in the mid-1970s, formalizing these activities with the founding of the Buraku Youth Cultural Group in 1978 and then later with the founding of Kumano Daigaku (Kumano University) in 1990. Kumano Daigaku is a "school without walls," its motto being, "no walls, no entrance exams, graduate at death." In Shingū today, Kumano Daigaku is best known for the yearly events that it sponsors, including concerts with celebrities such as Miyako Harumi, and symposia that draw major writers and intellectuals, including Asada Akira, Karatani Kōjin, Suga Hidemi, Tsushima Yūko, Watanabe Naomi, Yomota Inuhiko, and others. Today Kumano Daigaku continues on a shoestring budget under the able leadership of local citizens such as Hibi Kazuichirō, Matsumoto Iwayo, and Morimoto Yūji.

One event that occurred before the official founding of Kumano Daigaku in 1990 and before Nakagami's death provides a useful example of the ambitious nature of the group's mission. In the summer of 1986, Nakagami staged his own play, *Kanakanuchi*, in Hongū, a town in the mountains above Shingū. Early in 1986, Nakagami had scouted the area around Hongū to find a location for the outdoor production. He chose Ōyunohara, the former site of the Kumano Hongū Shrine, which had been washed away by the flooded Kumano River in the nineteenth century. Characteristically, Nakagami showed his fascination with spaces that had been effaced or erased, this time by an abundance of rain. *Kanakanuchi,* an amalgam of tales about a godlike mountain robber, was produced in collaboration with Kumano Daigaku and various prefecture officials. The storyline was thin, but the emphasis was on dramatic acting and staging; lit by torches at night, the play exploited the possibilities of the site of the old shrine, including a scene in which the main actor flew across the sky on a wire and burst into flames. Particularly successful was Nakagami's depiction of the origins of the *nō* theater: a group of lowly wandering actors performed a rendition of an early spirit dance complete with masks and robes.

The *Kanakanuchi* play revealed Nakagami's ability to galvanize those around him and to bring the cultural worlds of Tokyo and Wakayama together. In attendance at the event were local officials and audience members, the Hamidashi Theatre Group of Tokyo, filmmakers, journalists, and editors from Tokyo, and, of course, Nakagami himself. The play ran for three performances, one of which was plagued by technical difficulties, as Tobayama Bunmei, the actor who played the role of Kanakanuchi, burst into flame too early on his flight across the wire. But Tobayama survived under his heavy costume and the play went on. Watching from the audience by the side of Kumano River, one soon realized that Nakagami was not simply producing a boutique event for Tokyo visitors. He stated that his toughest audience was the local one, particularly the older women. Fortunately, in the audience, there were audible sighs of awe and appreciation when a Chinese dragon crossed the outdoor stage and when Tobayama made his fiery flight overhead. Nakagami had succeeded in taking old stories, reinterpreting them, and offering them back to the Kumano audience in a form of new theatrical art. *Kanakanuchi* later played in Yokohama, but according to Nakagami, urban audiences lacked the necessary sophistication that would allow them to respond properly to the spectacle.

Last Years, 1988–1992

In the late 1980s and early 1990s, Nakagami was hard at work again. Once he had exhausted the vein of the *monogatari*, Nakagami's writing had moved back to the underside of Tokyo in works such as *Sanka* (Hymn, 1990) and *Keibetsu* (Scorn, 1992)—this time to explore characters such as the male prostitute, the gangster, and the topless dancer. By this time, Nakagami had formally separated from Kasumi; after the family house in Hachiōji burned to the ground in 1988, Nakagami made his Shinjuku office his home. There he continued to make his round of the bars, including one gay bar where, according to the bartender, he sat quietly watching customers rather than drawing attention to himself.

During these years Nakagami also traveled extensively, remaining in Japan barely longer than a few months at a time. His wandering reveals that he had set his sights on an international reputation and was cementing connections in Europe, the United States, Korea, and the Philippines. In 1988, Pierre Aubry, a French literary agent who briefly held Nakagami's international rights, made a documentary about Nakagami with the backing of European television in a series entitled, "Writers on the Border." In the late 1980s and early 1990s Nakagami traveled the world in a dizzying pattern, with frequent stops in Hawai'i where his children attended private school. In 1990, Nakagami attended a symposium in San Francisco, went to a literary meeting in Paris, gave a lecture in Frankfurt, and moved on to New York. Translations of his work into French appeared, beginning in 1988, and a Dutch translation of *Misaki* was published in 1986. Full-length English translations of his work would not appear until 1999, but Nakagami had been notoriously choosy about the English rights.

In addition to his ambitions for his future, Nakagami expressed his growing sense of constriction at home. In the 1988 interview in New York, Nakagami sounded a note of disaffection with both Shingū and Tokyo, and suggested that he had begun to align himself with an international community of writers, declaring:

> From the first, Nakagami Kenji has been a stranger in the world outside. A stranger in regular society (*ippan no shakai*). Not because I'm a writer, mind you, but because I'm *burakumin*. Because I come from there. But if you ask me how it is for me in the *buraku*, in the *roji* . . . I'm literate, I read and write books, right? That makes me a stranger there, too. I have no place of my own (*ibasho ga nai*). I don't have a place of my own anywhere. I'm two things at once. I can't escape it. . . . This not having a place of one's own, it means you can exist anywhere, you can be anywhere, I don't try to escape it. If I had tried to stay there, I would have suffered greatly, an excessive kind of suffering—well, I do suffer that way all the time, but that's what links me to the American Indian writer or the South African writer born in the ghetto, staying in the ghetto. We have that in common. . . . For example, if the writer returns to the ghetto and settles there, he becomes a small painted bird, that's what others think of him in the *roji*. Books and writing, that's what they are. He's a painted bird. . . .[80]

In his reference to Jerzy Kosiński's *The Painted Bird* (1965), Nakagami again views himself as different or unique, but we also see his move to link himself to a global minority experience, a connection he had been polishing in numerous essays in the 1980s. This portion of the 1988 interview is clearly shaded with a Western audience in mind. At the same time, Nakagami had certainly been disappointed by not being awarded the Tanizaki Prize even after he had continued to publish at a prodigious rate through the 1980s. His disaffection vis-à-vis Japan and the literary establishment was genuine. In the late 1980s Nakagami was actively searching for an established English translator who might secure his international reputation the way that Edward Seidensticker had done for Kawabata Yasunari. His statement above suggests that he meant to travel even further from home in future.

Unfortunately, early in 1992 on a trip to Hawai'i, Nakagami fell severely ill. All his adult life, he had suffered from liver problems and from exhaustion. But this time his doctors discovered that he had advanced kidney cancer and the diagnosis had come too late to halt the progress of the disease. Kasumi returned to nurse him; she would remain by his side until the end. In March 1992, Nakagami gave Watanabe Naomi a final interview, entitled, "Shijifosu no yō ni yamai to tawamurete" (Jesting with Illness Like Sisyphus), in which he discussed the work that he would do when he got well, including the possibility of Akiyuki making another appearance.[81] Perhaps the last time he was seen in public was his appearance, while very ill, at the wake of the Korean-Japanese writer, I Yanji (1955–1992), who died under mysterious circumstances in May 1992. Nakamura Fūki, a friend and former editor, describes seeing the frail Nakagami weeping over I Yanji's glass casket; it was the last time she would see him alive.

After chemotherapy treatments in Tokyo, Nakagami returned to Shingū in July 1992 and entered the Hibi Memorial Hospital which was run by Hibi Kazuichirō, a school friend and long-time personal physician of the writer. There, in the hospital, attended by his wife, Kasumi, and his family, he died on August 12, barely half a year after his diagnosis. He was 46 years old. Of all his friends in Tokyo, he had allowed only Karatani Kōjin to see him in the last days of his life. The funeral in Tokyo on August 22, 1992, was a public event that drew a crowd of nearly 800 people, many of whom were Nakagami's readers. Karatani spoke:

> All of you who have come today knew Nakagami Kenji. Of course, some of you have probably only read his books, but in his case, that means you knew him. If his books made a strong impression, so did he. Even those who don't read—who, bluntly speaking, are illiterate—were left with a strong impression. This was surprising. Nakagami was a more intellectual writer than most. In fact I don't know any writer who was more of an intellectual. But I also don't know any writer who made such a deep impression on people just for being who he was. It is not only those in the narrow literary world who mourn his death. It's the same for non-Japanese. . . . A few days ago I received a fax from a professor in an American university. It said, "Nakagami brought weight to a nearly weightless environment. . . . Nakagami has died and I have lost my sense of gravity."[82]

Nakagami's voice fell silent in 1992. But, as is true when someone dies, mourning occurs through speech; and in the first few years after Nakagami's death, many voices began to rise and to fill the gap. One voice stands out in the chorus of those speaking about Nakagami—the voice of the writer Tsushima Yūko. A true contemporary of Nakagami's, she was born in 1947 and had belonged to the *Bungei shuto* group in the early 1960s. Tsushima had watched Nakagami as their respective reputations grew. She described being aware of his talent when she herself was struggling to become a writer in the face of opposition from her mother.

In 1995, Tsushima recorded her memories of Nakagami in an article entitled, "Ani Nakagami Kenji no yume" (My Older Brother Nakagami Kenji's Dream) in the September edition of *Shinchō*. The title was deceptive. In the essay, Tsushima expressed a sense of exasperation over Nakagami's confrontational style. But Tsushima could not help comparing herself to Nakagami. Both had suffered suicides in their families as children (Tsushima's father, Dazai Osamu, killed himself in 1949), both came from matriarchal stock, both had grown up with stories of the war. Tsushima suggested that Nakagami's fascination with criminals spoke to what they saw around them as children: veterans straggling back from the war, horrendous crimes committed, those who had been reported dead suddenly appearing at home.

Tsushima also carefully charted the differences between herself and Nakagami, particularly their different backgrounds: Tokyo versus Shingū, a literate family versus an illiterate one. The biggest difference between them lay in their attitudes toward words. Tsushima grew up in a house where words were abundant. Even after her father had committed suicide, "words crowded around, and continued to be stirred up by many readers and the interpretations of critics."[83] Nakagami, on the other hand, came from what Tsushima calls the silent ones (*mukoku no tami*), a reference to how the *burakumin* have been silenced by majority Japanese society. Tsushima suggests that Nakagami's eagerness to put everything into words, on the page and in person, came not from a desire to reproduce the world but from a compulsion to create a world apart—a black hole that would "suck in the reader."[84] What Tsushima implies is that coming late to words, Nakagami did not properly dread their power. Tsushima's vision of a black hole echoes Tamura Satoko's notion of an "unassailable space." Both women refer to Nakagami's insistence on his own vision, his stamina, and the sheer will that flows through his pages. Their dense spatial metaphors also sound a note of opposition. The violence in the work proves daunting as if Nakagami's vision is one that they cannot or do not want to explore themselves.

Writing on Nakagami, Tsushima's tone changes when she turns to *Karekinada,* the 1977 work that brought Nakagami such fame. To describe Nakagami's achievement in this book, she finds that literary terms are not adequate. She thinks of a theme in music or a cinematic technique, such as the pillow shot that appears repeatedly in between scenes but does nothing to advance plot. Finally, Tsushima turns to poetry, writing that "from the time of *Karekinada,* Nakagami was no longer a prose writer but a poet singing a heroic epic poem, or a blind priest-musician (*biwa hōshi*) accompanying himself on the *biwa.*"[85] Tsushima's references to things outside the domain of what we know as modern prose—epic poetry and musical recitation—suggest how far Nakagami had pushed known literary boundaries. With Tsushima's statements echoing in our ears, we tune out all the competing voices and turn to a single, compelling figure—the young poet, Nakagami Kenji.

TWO

Icarus Descending: Expendable Males and the Poetry of Nakagami Kenji

In those days I had my own words
Brother wore a white suit
And played with the girls
A tragic hero, like Icarus,
He flew through a blue sky
—Nakagami Kenji, "Umi e"

In August 1966, Nakagami Kenji published a handful of poems in *Michi*, a local Shingū literary magazine. Soon after publication, he attended a gathering in Shingū to celebrate the tenth issue of the magazine in hopes of hearing comments on his poetry. Unfortunately, the audience asked only a few questions about specific words in the poems, waiting patiently for the author to explain his own work. Asamori Mizuho, the editor of the magazine, reported that people had complained about the difficulty of the poems even as some declared that they must be masterpieces.[1]

The silence in the room that day in Shingū echoes down to the present; ultimately, Nakagami's poetry would be read as a footnote to his fiction. Of the many scholars working on Nakagami, only Yomota Inuhiko has written about the poetry at some length, work that we shall consider presently.[2] In total, only 24 poems survive, the earliest one dating back to 1964. Through the 1960s, however, Nakagami wrote both prose and poetry simultaneously, and he made his formal debut with a poem in the mainstream literary journal *Bungakukai* in September 1968. Nakagami's attendance at the *Michi* gathering further reveals that he was simultaneously making a name for himself on two fronts, submitting material to journals in both Tokyo and Shingū. In the summer of 1965, Asamori remembered that Nakagami had first come to see him to submit poetry in person, stating awkwardly, "My poetry is wasted on a magazine like yours, but here you are. . . ." —a comment that had made Asamori smile in spite of himself.[3] Even after his dramatic exodus to Tokyo by train, Nakagami had not cut his ties to home.

Takazawa Shūji states that by 1969 Nakagami Kenji's poetic flame had burned out.[4] Like Kafka's Gregor, one morning, the story goes, Nakagami awoke to find himself transformed into a writer of fiction. Nakagami himself put little emphasis on this aspect of his early career. During a discussion with Karatani Kōjin in 1979, he stated simply that he had written poetry before becoming better known as a writer of fiction. Prose had not supplanted poetry; he had simply stopped writing poems.[5]

Given Nakagami's own nonchalance and the scant number of extant poems, what can be gained from a consideration of the work? First, the poems reveal a young writer's encounter with European literature, specifically the writing of Arthur Rimbaud (1854–1891), the French symbolist poet. Like many Japanese writers before him, Nakagami claims his own literary credentials through his reading as a *bungaku seinen*, a literary youth. But given that Nakagami came from a house without books, we might imagine that the discovery of Rimbaud was more dramatic for him than for his middle class companions. Nakagami relates his discovery in his own words:

> I went to high school with a guy named Nakamori Morio. At first he was writing lyric poetry and showing it to me, but after awhile he started to write this modern stuff filled with big words. I think it had something literary about it, but for me, coming from a background that had absolutely nothing to do with literature, I was

drawn to him because of his slightly menacing air, which came from the fact that he was over 1 meter and 80 centimeters tall. I encountered Rimbaud at Nakamori's house. I borrowed a collection of the poems. Somehow I understood them. . . . Once I told Nakamori that I'd translated Rimbaud. He looked surprised. You mean, you understand French? . . . I explained that I had translated it in my own way [*ore no ryūgi ni kakikaeta*]. Nakamori just laughed.[6]

To the young Nakagami, "literature" is not only poetry but words writ large in a language that he does not understand. It exists at a double remove from himself—in the higher intellectual echelon of Nakamori and in a foreign tongue altogether. Interestingly, Nakagami's lack of French proved no obstacle to his "discovery" of Rimbaud. He could read and translate Rimbaud "in his own way." In this description from his early life, Nakagami chronicles his transformation into writer, a willful act of self-creation that began in the slippage between a mysterious original and his own translated words. Nakagami's Rimbaud story also neatly illustrates the history of modern Japanese literature, a tradition deeply invested in the act of producing and consuming translations. By his twenties, the poems suggest, Nakagami was reading widely if spottily in world literature. References abound to classical Greek tragedy and poetry; to French writers such as Stendhal, Céline, and Arthur Rimbaud; and to modern Japanese poets such as Tanikawa Shuntarō and Irisawa Yasuo, to name a few.[7]

Second, Nakagami's poems reveal how he attempted to bend poetic form to suit his own purposes even as he submerged himself in others' voices. As a poet, Nakagami translates even when he writes in Japanese. In 1966, for example, Nakagami published a poem entitled "Rirekisho" (Record of a Life, 1966), which borrowed the form of a similarly titled poem by Tanikawa Shuntarō, "Seichō" (Growth, 1952). The second half of the earlier poem by Tanikawa reads:

age eleven
my past went back to dinosaurs

age fourteen
my past agreed with the texts at school

age sixteen
I look at the infinity of my past with fear

age eighteen
I know not a thing about time[8]

With simple, concise phrases, Tanikawa maps the course of "growth," suggesting that one arrives at adulthood with a growing sense of wonder and incomprehension about how one has moved through time. When Nakagami writes about growth, on the other hand, he struggles to control his medium, practicing a poetic style that ranges from simple lines to great mouthfuls of words. His message is also quite distinct from Tanikawa's. An excerpt from Nakagami's "Rirekisho":

> age eleven: I knew a life that should be sung
> even though it was crushed by the long mountain range.
>
> age thirteen: the people sent a secret murder plot in marriage to a dream, dressing it in showy robes. It was 1959, a young man, ignorant of heroic excess and the proper songs to sing, killed himself at the absurd sight of the moving van. The body, piled with dewy chrysanthemums and brimming over with human anger, burst into flames.
>
> age sixteen: time became something that should stop forever. (*NKZ* 14: 29)

In the simple but dramatic language of the "age eleven" stanza, Nakagami follows Tanikawa's model to some degree. But in the next stanza, Nakagami uses dense, unconventional language that stymies any single reading. We surmise that a young man commits suicide in despair over the marriage of a woman he loves. The "secret murder plot" suggests that the people who planned the marriage are fully aware of the possible consequences of their action, which will result in the young man's death. The "showy robes" conjure up the figure of a bride who is being married off to satisfy social convention. When the moving van passes by, the young man breaks down, not understanding "heroic excess and the proper songs to sing." The implication is that rather than fight back, armed with heroism or poetry, the man simply turns his anger on himself, and in the fires of the crematorium, the body burns with anger toward the living. Unlike Tanikawa who meditates on life from a detached, even bemused perspective, Nakagami records his desire to short-circuit pain: time "should stop forever." We move from a playful, even endearing poem, into obscure tragedy.

Finally, and perhaps most strikingly, these poems offer a glimpse into how Nakagami Kenji, then and later, would negotiate the explosive material of lived experience. In order to understand the poem "Rirekisho," we need to remember a biographical fact: in March 1959, when Nakagami was thirteen years old, Kinoshita Ikuhei, his 24-year-old half-brother by his mother's first husband, hanged himself at a tatami factory. When the brother's body was discovered, the local newspaper merely reported, "Kinoshita had been suffering from mental illness."[9] The "age thirteen" stanza embroiders on the brother's death, searching for an explanation for the suicide. As we shall see, the theme of young male death threads through the poems. And, gradually, through his exploration of the brother's death, Nakagami begins to triangulate from the particulars of his own life and his complex family drama the situation of a minority community. He first creates the portrait of the vulnerable young *buraku* male.

It is this last facet of the poetry—its relation to the blunt facts of a life—that intrigues Yomota Inuhiko, who analyzes the early poems for their relevance to the later fiction. Yomota discusses a poem entitled, "Kokyō o hōmuru uta" (Burying the Hometown, 1968), in which the speaker mentions family members by name and calls for their deaths. According to Yomota, the experience of poetry, filled with desire, violence, and nihilism, allowed Nakagami to confront the unspeakable and essential thing (*iishirenu honshitsuteki na mono*) and begin to move past it. Through poetry Nakagami exorcised his demons and then turned his hand to fiction.[10]

Yomota views Nakagami's poetry as a way to master what had previously been unspeakable, even taboo, imaginings. But I would put it a little differently. Unable to master his demons,

Nakagami turned away from poetry to the firmer ground of fiction. Without the mediation of character, plot, and dialogue, poetry proved to be too raw and direct a medium for Nakagami. This rawness is replicated in the experience of the reader: the poems provide a clear view of the room, the figures passing unobstructed back and forth behind the glass. In fiction, on the contrary, with its formal demands, its concrete topography, and its molding of memory to service plot, Nakagami could visit and revisit the old traumas, but from a safer distance. He could tell many tales and from multiple points of view. Witness the cycle of stories about the brother's death in the early fiction, each told from a slightly different angle. By 1969 Nakagami had made his choice as to genre. But before we move into the 1970s, we pause before the spectacle of a young writer who was consciously fashioning himself in the image of the poet in the 1960s.

The Road to Hell

Two young men led Nakagami to poetry in his early years: Nakamori Morio, the Shingū schoolmate, and Arthur Rimbaud. Throughout the early and mid-1960s, Nakagami wrote a series of poems that showed him to be an enthusiastic reader of Rimbaud, or as he stated later in an essay on poetry, "in those days, Rimbaud was my life" (*NKZ* 14: 461). Of the 24 poems published in the collected works, nine have the word "season" (*kisetsu*) in the title. In a cryptic note appended to one of the season poems, Nakagami himself referenced Rimbaud's work, *A Season in Hell* (Une saison en enfer, 1873), a long narrative poem that traces the links (and the disjunctures) between travel, selfhood, and writing in rich, symbolic, and at times, paradoxical language.[11] Nakagami also reveals the element that brought him to poetry—the lure of a close intellectual friendship with the tall and slightly menacing Nakamori. Nakamori himself and Arthur Rimbaud were tied to the person Nakagami wanted to become. Or, as Nakagami would later sum up his interest in "translating" Rimbaud (and in an echo of Rimbaud's own words), "I thought I was creating my own language" (*NKZ* 14: 461).

In extraliterary terms, Rimbaud also provided a good biographical model for Nakagami. Not only did Rimbaud himself leave provincial roots for the city, where he practiced a bohemian life (drugs, absinthe, a protracted and at times turbulent affair with the poet Paul Verlaine), but he had also been raised by a single mother who expressed open hostility to literature.[12] In addition, Rimbaud's move to Paris in 1871 to meet Verlaine for the first time reinforced Nakagami's own intuition that writing was not something done in isolation but in close collaboration with other men. Most importantly, however, Rimbaud occupied a special niche in Japanese literature because he had been celebrated by a few of the great literary figures of the early twentieth-century, including the critic Kobayashi Hideo and the poet Nakahara Chūya.[13] In an essay on poetry written in his thirties, Nakagami hinted at another route by which he might actually have discovered Rimbaud—through Kobayashi Hideo. Nakagami writes that he may have abandoned poetry, but that he had not outgrown the poetry of Rimbaud, whose words still "detonate words inside him" (*NKZ* 14: 461). This remark echoes the language of Kobayashi Hideo, who describes his own discovery of Rimbaud:

> Not even in my dreams did I imagine how powerful an explosive charge had been set inside that shabby, compact volume of *A Season in Hell*—the Mercure [de France] edition—which unexpectedly caught my eye in the shop window of a certain bookseller. . . . This small book exploded in the most marvelous way so that years later I still remain in the vortex of the event.[14]

Kobayashi Hideo enflamed Nakagami's interest in Rimbaud as he had done to other "literary youths" before him. In fact, Nakagami's (and Nakamori's) encounter with modern literature was filtered through Japanese writers who had been raised on a diet of symbolist poetry, French drama, and European naturalism. Following this route, Nakamori and Nakagami both undertook a common form of modern Japanese literary apprenticeship indeed.[15]

Nakagami's most obvious hymn to Arthur Rimbaud is a poem entitled "Itsutsu no boin kara naru kisetsu" (A Season in Five Vowels, 1967), which follows the conceit of Rimbaud's more famous poem, "Voyelles" (Vowels, c. 1870). In this poem, Rimbaud creates a string out of the vowels, A-E-I-O-U, each with its own color and associated images. The poem reads like shorthand, a cryptic code that we try in vain to break. First, Rimbaud's original, followed by an English translation:

> A noir, E blanc, I rouge, U vert, O, bleu: voyelles,
> Je dirai quelque jour vos naissances latentes:
> A, noir corset velu des mouches éclatantes
> Qui bombinent autour des puanteurs cruelles,
>
> Golfes d'ombre; E, candeurs des vapeurs et des tentes,
> Lances des glaciers fiers, rois blancs, frisson d'ombelles;
> I, pourpres, sang craché, rires des lèvres belles
> Dans la colère où les ivresses pénitentes;
>
> U, cycles, vibrements divins des mers virides,
> Paix des pâtis semés d'animaux, paix des rides
> Que l'alchimie imprime aux grands fronts studieux;
>
> O, suprême Clairon plein des strideurs étranges,
> Silences traversés des Mondes et des Anges:
> O l'Oméga, rayon violet de Ses Yeux!

> A black, E white, I red, U green, O blue: vowels, I shall one day
> tell your hidden births: A, black hairy corset of bursting flies
> that murmur around cruel stenches,
>
> shadowy gulfs; E, candors of mists and of tents, lances of
> proud glaciers,
> white kings, umbels' shiver; I, purples, spit blood, laughter of
> fair lips in anger or in frenzied penitence;
>
> U, cycles, surge divine of glaucous seas, peace of fields strewn
> with animals, peace of furrows that alchemy imprints on large
> studious brows;
>
> O, supreme Clarion full of strange shrillness,
> Silences traversed by Angels and by Worlds:
> —O the Omega, violet ray of Its Eyes![16]

Rimbaud teases the reader with the vowels, suggesting that, as in concrete poetry, their shape *is* the story. Many critics have tackled this poem trying to find the definite correspondences between shapes, letters, and images. René Etiemble, for one, expresses his exasperation with the poem in 1968, describing it as "incoherent."[17] In the 1970s, Robert Greer Cohn also disparages "Vowels," but he goes on to perform an erudite exegesis of its imagery, suggesting that the "A" stanza represents Rimbaud's peasant mother, "a dark pit of maternity," and that the "O" stanza sings a hymn of praise to a divine male spirit through its use of the color violet.[18] Finally, in the 1990s, James Lawler takes a formalist approach to the poem, reading it as a particularly dense sonnet whose origins he traces back to Baudelaire's line, "perfumes, colors and sounds correspond."[19]

Given the plethora of critical readings of "Vowels" and the dissonance that surrounds the poem even today, it is hard to imagine a better poem for Nakagami's own ambitious experimentation. The cryptic "Vowels" pretends to create its own grammar and syntax, even a universe of meaning, but in fact the poem resists the hand of the translator. In 1967, Nakagami Kenji, newly arrived in Tokyo, wrote his own version of "Vowels" and published it in the July 2nd issue of Shingū's *Sunday Journal*.

Season in Five Vowels

I

I'm yours—
Cola overflowing with sadness in the white coffin of your glass, anger spilling out like chalky lime, Icarus falling, hope dissolving in the sea, I'm yours. Yours, yours, yours—
me.

O

A missing finger
Like a paring knife opening on to the future
The poet's chest has a lid that opens freely,
Monologue of a boy who ejaculates to divine revelation
The magnolia petals won't reveal the séance between a snapped-off match and water trembling in the oilcan.
Light beginning to walk
Won't you loosen your clothing and slip out your breasts?
(The hall reeks with cheap sake,
so begins the Greek tragedy of the girl with one eye)
A sparrow on the wet road looks for aborted-fetus love

and then like a gas pipe that can't find its opening
the man in room 6 performs the oratorio
Suddenly my lust rises

U
Morning
Branches sparkle
a cat's corpse floats down a muddy ditch
The revelation no longer taps on the glass
Hey, look at that, here comes
The blind king of Thebes

E
Wet us, rain
Wet my shoulders, Yukiko's soft breasts
Wet us
nape of my neck, numb with Dororan,
poppy flowers, wet us, gentle rain,
night street,
a song, scattering in splinters

A
Piercing the spring
my heart
my useless heart—
the rose I stole and put in a vase
is
dying. (*NKZ* 14: 34–35)

In contrast to Rimbaud's tightly structured verse, the stanzas of Nakagami's poem read like a series of discrete poems rather than parts of an integrated whole. Like Rimbaud, Nakagami at first aims for abstraction. The "O" stanza, for example, lingers on images of the male artist—the poet with the lid on his chest, a boy who receives divine revelation, an oratorio singer. To bolster the air of mystery, Nakagami employs vague echoes of the classical Greek poetry that he had been reading. The woman slipping out her breasts, for example, suggests Ariadne on the beach at Naxos after Theseus has abandoned her. The lost sparrow harks back to an erotic poem by Catullus in which a young woman plays with a sparrow on her lap that subsequently dies.

For all its abstract trappings, however, Nakagami reads his letter "O" literally, bringing it back to earth and using the shape of the letter to explore the forms of desire. The overall tone of the stanza is anticipatory, brimming over with libidinous agency. The speaker stands caught in a posture of waiting—for an act of telepathy, a woman to undress, or a performance to begin. In addition, the speaker feverishly urges the woman to slip out her breasts, and the sparrow seeks aborted love. Finally, the oratorio itself remains trapped in the room like gas expanding inside a tube. Against this backdrop of connections missed and pressure building, the speaker concludes with an assertion of his own lust.

Beneath the speaker's assertion of lust, a note of anxiety sounds as if the speaker cannot quite identify the object of desire or perform with confidence. The stanza opens with an image of a disembodied phallus—"a missing finger like a paring knife opening onto the future"—that suggests fear of castration or lack of potency. The poet's chest with the "lid that opens freely" suggests the writer struggling to resist clichéd or facile expression. Finally, the man who performs the oratorio in "room 6" does so without any certainty of release or recognition. Nakagami draws a portrait of the precocious young artist whose struggle to perform linguistically is represented in concrete, physical, even sexual terms.

A similar note of anxiety characterizes the "I" stanza, but this time the speaker fears breaching boundaries and falling into the sea. The letter "I" refers both to the speaker himself—*boku* ("I" in English) and to the fallen angel Icarus, whose wings melt because he flies too close to the sun. The images in the "I stanza" point to the gradual dissolution of "I": cola overflowing the edges of its glass; the wings of Icarus melting in the hot sun; and finally to hope itself melting into the sea. Finally, the "I" dissolves irrevocably into "you," an action that is emphasized by the repetition of the word, *omae* (you) in the phrase, "I'm yours, yours, yours—me." But the prospect of merging is not blissful; rather, with its reference to Icarus and the sea, dissolution stirs grief and anger, and finally results in death. In its reference to young male death, Nakagami transforms Rimbaud's austere symbolism into narrative form, creating a stanza that hums with a tale of mythic decline.

In both stanzas, Nakagami reads the shape of the letters literally to illustrate the poet's dilemma. In other stanzas, we see more fragments of stories: the shape of the ditch and Oedipus (U); the walk in the rain with Yukiko (E); the speaker's own disgust with himself and with poetry (A). In its exploration of poetry, desire, and danger, Nakagami shows an affiliation with Rimbaud, who, in Nakagami's eyes, insisted on the primacy of his own desires, nonconformist though they were. At the same time, Nakagami's poems sound a more tentative note as if he were still formulating exactly what shape his own desire might take. A childish myopia characterizes the poems as the speaker both longs for and fears blissful merging. We might well pursue a little further what Rimbaud's poetry, particularly with its focus on water, meant to Nakagami.

Before we turn to Nakagami's next poem which is replete with bodies of water, we will briefly consider Rimbaud's *A Season in Hell*. Rimbaud wrote *A Season in Hell*, his only published book, during two short stays at his rural home, the latter of which occurred after his violent breakup with his lover, Paul Verlaine, who had wounded him with a pistol. Closeting himself away in his room at the family farm while relatives and workers did chores around him, Rimbaud finished his manuscript (emitting shouts as he wrote) and sent it to Paris. Rimbaud's "poetic notebook" focuses on the author's own wanderings, both literal and metaphysical. The text depicts a descent into hell, but it nevertheless lurches forward with the rhythm of self-discovery and utopian dreaming. Toward the end of the work, the speaker describes his impulse to move: "I had to travel, divert the spells assembled in my brain. Over the sea, that I loved as though it were to cleanse me of a stain, I saw the comforting cross arise. I had been damned by the rainbow. Happiness was my fatality, my remorse, my worm: my life would always be too enormous to be devoted to strength and to beauty."[20]

The sea delivers the speaker from madness and cures him of defilement. In literal terms, it provides an escape from home—a way to pass through from here to there, from the everyday to the exotic, from the settled cities of Europe to a place where "strange climates will tan my skin."[21] At the same time, the journey becomes a metaphor for Rimbaud's excursions into poetry, from whence he emerges weary and defeated. Or, as the speaker concludes: "I created all fêtes, all triumphs, all dramas. I tried to invent new flowers, new stars, new flesh, new tongues. I thought I was acquiring supernatural powers. Well! I must bury my imagination and my memories! An artist's and storyteller's precious fame flung away!"[22]

On every page of his "poetic notebook," Rimbaud expresses his desire for spiritual transcendence and bodily escape. Let us now turn to what Nakagami does with the sea and travel in the next poem, entitled, "Kisetsu e no teigen oyobi hika" (A Proposal and a Lament for the Season). The speaker, an old man (as is made clear by his dialect) climbs to the top of a hill and looks down over the sea off the Kumano coast.

> Climb up Kumasaka Hill and you'll see
> the sea bubbling white at Kumano River's end
> That sea is angry, it chafes our skin,
> the gods whisper a curse
> in young men's ears—
> "Come to us, board a boat, swim, walk here"
> You can see from here, can't you? Kasuga Mountain and
> the town the color of flayed skin,
> spinning in a whirlpool of fire
> the town is rotting,
> it breathes smoke and it rots away,
> Once a swindler came and bought mountain land,
> bought young men, too.
> Then a clown came, playing the flute and dancing,
> preaching about the victory of our race
> he bought young men, too.
> Do you see them?
> Those sold mountains and those young men,
> tongues protruding as they die in agony.

Do you hear the words of the gods?
"Come to us, to the sea, to the sea!
They'll sell you off somewhere
Don't follow swindlers and clowns."
Climb Kumasaka Hill and you'll see
the fields past a fingertip, and beyond
the sea breathing blue
"Don't be fooled, don't be bought out"
Can you hear the never-ending curse of the silver-scaled sea?
Can you hear their whispers—
"Come to us, board a boat, swim, walk here"?

Envoy: Lament for the Season
Warm, shallow-eyed bird-thistle
prickles shaved my finger
burned to bits—the tiny resume of my life, with its 15 feelings,
Morning
The light strikes the soft leaves of the persimmon
Wind fluttering the black handkerchief in my hand
Seabird that struck the window and died,
Sick old woman of mottled seasons, and the eyes shut fast with tears now, too
In this room where such things are no longer visible
I sit in front of three lemons, cigarette butts,
and a gas lamp I picked from the summer sea, and I dream:
I am writing a beautiful poem. (*NKZ* 14: 46–47)

Nakagami echoes Rimbaud's florid language, but he clearly distinguishes his poem from Rimbaud's visions on the water. Nakagami's proposal does not sketch out the contours of an allegoric mental landscape but of a view of the Kumano River pouring into the sea. Rather than serving as a medium for utopian dreaming, the sea shivers with malice and temptation. It betrays the presence of an angry god who curses the young men because they follow speculators and clowns. The god's curse, a never-ending whisper of the silver sea, will draw the young men to the water, perhaps even to their deaths.[23] In contrast to Rimbaud's vision of the sea as a private mental landscape, Nakagami's sea "breathes blue," exerting the forces of an ancient and communal fate.

By the ancient and sacred sea, the town itself is rotting, breathing smoke, a denigration of the provincial backwater that is Shingū. The mention of "speculators and clowns" refers to the practice of land speculators who came and bought land for timber from the locals at low prices and to agents of the draft who lured the young men of the alleyway with talk of the "victory of our race." In both cases, the targets of deception are the dispossessed people of the rural town itself. The speaker warns that the price of following speculators and clowns is high: the young men will die in agony, tongues protruding from their mouths—an image of death in war that is eerily reminiscent of a hanging victim.

The dilemma of the young men, pinned between an angry sea and unscrupulous outsiders, illuminates the first part of the poem's title. In the "proposal," Nakagami speaks directly to Rimbaud, showing him what the sea looks like from the other side of the world; not as a medium for movement and dreaming, but as a reminder of the fixed coordinates of the speaker's position and the possibility of death. The coda to the poem, the "lament," expresses the poet's desire to do what Rimbaud has done: to invent new tongues, new stars, to sit down in the dawn with lemons and cigarettes, and "write a beautiful poem."

Nakagami surrenders to a mimetic urge in his poetry, and as we move forward through the poems, the speaker begins to crystallize into a single character—the young man of Shingū. No poem reflects this more obviously than a poem entitled, "Kisetsu no tame no shigaku" (A Poetics for the Season), which was published in 1968 in the Shingū *Sunday Journal*. In this poem, Nakagami uses the term Nagayama, a name for the *buraku* that was common parlance at the time, a literal representation of bounded space. In its depiction of a sexual act between brothers—a scene that reads like a murder, "Poetics" may be Nakagami's most disturbing poem, one that threatens to unravel under the weight of trauma:

> Tonight the dream of shaving whiskers, now objectified,
> My fingers moving,
> as blackly beating passions numb my tongue

That spring
Where did I put my poetics
that sustained my dedication to a stuttering, tremulous love?
Kumano River, in its aging, sickly form,
flows on and on bearing my curse
to the town thick with silver flies,
the town shivering with ague,
where the people rot as they stand.
The alarm at the railroad crossing in Kasuga-chō keeps on clicking
and I drown in the toilet of the apartment.
I laugh at a man who enjoys the end of a love affair
—he jokes about it like some cockroach
Rainbow azaleas shed their petals copiously,
Shall I tell you a tale of the night they fell to the floor?
Or reveal how a flag, fluttering over the bottom of the ground,
enfolded our starved and cursed heads?
Or recount the story of how my strangled brother and I fucked
my fingers scattering blood, frozen
brushing away thick tears like the sperm of one who enters from behind,
my throat crushed, too, I roll into the street,
drenched by the same rain that struck the swollen penis of my half-naked, headless, earless brother
The town burns, flashing a pistol, singing the song of the betrayer
The April night that threatened us and yelped at us
and tore us to pieces
my eyeball falls down into the room
Waiting for the soft thud of tidings from the season
I hear a grass flute playing inside my ear,
my hips stained with bad intentions (like Bachelard's) flies through the sky.
Kumano River floods every spring
Giving off the smell of a dead boy,
it swallows up the man who exalts over the flowers of Monaco
and gently melts a chocolate-colored love affair.
It's too late to slip into the ditch of vulgarity
but, as before, the people rot where they stand
completely rotten, they're still standing.

In room 306 of an apartment building in Nagayama
a wife and husband have sex in the missionary position
over and over again—
not tiring, still rotting, they wait for the dissolution of night.
(*NKZ* 14: 40–41)

"Poetics" unfolds from many points of view, sketching a vision of disintegration and despair in which the speaker testifies to the failure of poetry to transcend the specifics of geography and family history. The first lines of the poem remember a golden time, a lost spring when a poetics could sustain the speaker's love. In contrast, now "blackly beating" passions numb his tongue, an image that conjures up dark thoughts (even drugs) that render him silent. In the place of love and poetics, the speaker must confront the concrete coordinates of Kasuga-chō, the outcaste enclave behind Shingū Station near where Nakagami himself grew up. The people of Kasuga-chō "rot as they stand," a suggestion of their passivity and captivity and of the speaker's own horror at beholding them. We descend further into the toilet of an apartment where the speaker drowns, an image reminiscent of a line by Rimbaud, "the fly drunken in the inn's privy," but also perhaps of the rented room where the brother's disintegration took place.[24]

In the central section of the poem, we are drawn back into the family drama, the death of the brother and the speaker's uncertainty about how to even describe it. The blending of blood and tears during the sexual encounter between brothers suggests not only a strange incestuous encounter but also the heavy weight of a survivor's guilt. As the speaker has sex with the dead brother, he becomes the dead brother through a long series of possessive particles (*no*) that blurs identities. In the lines that begin "my throat crushed, too," the speaker overlaps with the brother through the rain that strikes their bodies (*ore no kono nodo mo mata tsubure atama mo mimi mo nai hanratai no ani no bōdai shita seishokuki ni furu ame ni utareta mama kono machi no rojō ni korogaru*). In this strangely ungrammatical line, the speaker acts both as the recorder of trauma and as the figure of the suicide rolling in the street. In a blur of body parts and fluids, identities merge and the speaker can no longer mark himself apart.

After the final violent spectacle of brother/self rolling out into the street, the speaker becomes lost in a spiraling sense of dislocation where he cannot find the poetics that once sustained his ardor. To underscore this point, even spring has been corrupted. The Kumano River floods yearly, giving off the smell of a dead boy floating in its waters, another echo of the inexhaustible spectacle of male death. The boy's demise is cyclical, mythic even, as if it sprang from the coordinates of the place itself and the river sucks life away—the man exalting over flowers, even a chocolate-colored love affair. As if to emphasize the dank atmosphere of Nagayama suffused with flooding water, Nakagami again describes the people of Kasuga-chō as if they were rotting: "the people rot where they stand, completely rotten, they're still standing." Seemingly unaware of their precarious state, a couple in Nagayama has sex repeatedly as they wait for dawn. The poem ends on a strangely upbeat note—the oblivious, hopeful couple, still active, as they wait for the end of night.

In this bizarre poem, Nakagami gives us his most violent version of Rimbaud. The language of the poem rises in an uncontrollable wave. In spite of Nakagami's attempts at abstract symbolism, the outlines of his own particular story assert themselves: the flooded, rotting hometown, the specter of prohibited desire, the guilt over the brother's death. The parameters of Nakagami's hell, unlike Rimbaud's, begin to take the familiar shape of the confessional family drama that unfolds behind the railroad barrier of Kasuga-chō. In the end, Nakagami discovers, one need not travel far. Hell begins at home.

Within the confines of Kasuga-chō, one image appears repeatedly: young men dying or dead. Recurring images of young male death reinforce the expendable nature of masculinity itself. Furthermore, male bodies are made even more fragile because they are either submerged in water, drawn as fragments, or represented in the process of being breached. Icarus plunges into the sea, a boy's body suffuses the river, the brother rolls headless into the street. In life young men serve as the fulcrum of violence, the spark and tinder that set the community alight. But in death, to borrow from René Girard, the boy who floats in water represents the sacrificial victim; in the river he floats, absorbing the ravages of violence into his own body, which if unleashed, would destroy the community.[25] Not only is young male death prevalent, but it is tinged with eroticism. To what can we attribute the frequency of these images?

In order to explore the prevalence of male death, we might take a conveniently marked route, searching the writer's life. In Nakagami's own life, boys and men died with alarming frequency. In 1956, for example, Nakagami lost a boyhood friend named Taryū Akihiro to a drowning accident in Kumano River.[26] Male death also plagued Nakagami's nuclear family. Chisato's father had died when she was born; she lost her first husband to illness; her second son to illness at age three; and Ikuhei, her oldest son, to suicide at age 24. Nakagami's own birth corresponded with the aftermath of a damaging and prolonged war from which many men did not return. And finally Nakagami himself provided a riveting explanation for male expendability in the story that he often told about himself: his *burakumin* origins, and what he himself described as his experience of "matriarchy."

Through his images of expendable males, Nakagami offers up his own vision of the position of men in the Shingū *buraku*. In 1977, Nakagami "came out" in a discussion with Noma Hiroshi and Yasuoka Shōtarō on the origins of discrimination, as discussed in the first chapter of this book. He described the *burakumin* community as matriarchal, but not because the women were strong; rather, it was due to a dearth of men. As he expressed: "It's almost all matrilineal households (*bokei*). Of course there's a system of monogamous relationships, but [the men] will die suddenly, or become gigolos, or go off with another woman, they just disappear like that. Everybody has to make the best of a bad situation. . . . [I]n the *buraku* nobody owns land, so people move around a lot more easily. . . ."[27]

Marriage without property to pass on, Nakagami suggests, was a more fluid affair. Perhaps even more interesting is Nakagami's tendency to link his perceptions of the Shingū *buraku* with his own writing project. Because Nakagami believed that the *buraku* lies outside the family or *ie* system in which the father passes on property and legitimacy down to the son, he subsequently viewed his own literary project as unfolding beyond the parameters of twentieth-century modern Japanese narratives. As he himself stated: "Even Uno Chiyo writes about the trouble in the family. The *ie* is trouble. This is how people are represented. But I differ, I write about human beings stripped bare who collide with each other. What lies behind this is the fact that in the alleyway nobody looks for their identity in the *ie* system."[28]

Typically, Nakagami contrasts the whole enterprise of modern Japanese literature with his own particular set of circumstances; however, if the trouble lies outside the *ie* system as Nakagami suggests, it must appear elsewhere. In fact, the "trouble" lies along fraternal lines, in those groups of young men who collide with one another, jostling for position in the absence of the father's law (in Nakagami's terms, "human beings stripped bare"). In the absence of the father, Nakagami expresses a desire for a brother, a group of brothers, who will somehow transcend the circumstances of geography and position. The fraternal longing in the poetry emerges in the figure of the boy's body floating downriver to the sea. But Nakagami's claim of freedom from the metanarratives of modern Japanese literature (in particular the problem of father and son) contains a startling tension. On the one hand, the figure of the boy in the river liberates; a liminal symbol that stirs desire, he floats free of the restrictions of conventionally determined patriarchy. On the other hand, the boy, forever the beautiful young Icarus, arrested in death, represents death for the speaker himself, and as such he is taboo. No matter how confidently Nakagami explained the concept of the "matriarchy" in interviews and discussions, his poetry addresses this contradiction. It poses a pressing question: if poetry, with its lyricism and abstraction, represents a realm of merging and transcendence, a whisper that calls one to death, how does one mark oneself off from one's brothers? How does one embrace difference and survive? In the end, the speaker must retrace the steps of the brother by traveling into the water himself.

A Walk to the Sea

Before Nakagami turned to prose, he made one last gesture to poetry: "Umi e" (To the Sea, 1967), a densely layered poetic narrative that moves back and forth through points in time, geographical locations and speaking subjects: *boku* ("I"), lover, sister, and brother. In this work Nakagami embeds poetic passages in prose so that prose and poetry are juxtaposed even as they speak to one another. In the critical literature, "Umi e" has received attention for its depiction of the sea, which is viewed as a forerunner to Nakagami's later fictional topos, the *burakumin* alleyway (*roji*). Watanabe Naomi, for example, reads the sea in "Umi e," as a purely textual space that gives birth to the character of a laborer named Akiyuki: "a never-fixed shape that transcends the borders of metaphors of the womb and female sexuality, . . . a realm of purity which dreams the dead brother, the wailing sister, the stinking hometown. . . ."[29] In true poststructuralist fashion, Watanabe reads Nakagami's mature work through the prism of "Umi e." A work written in 1967 turns out to be, as it were, Nakagami's "last word."

Creative as it may be to read "Umi e" through the lens of the later fiction, however, such a generalized reading flattens out the peaks and valleys of what this work meant in its own time. Nestling chronologically with the poems, "Umi e" not only echoes and refines the concerns of Nakagami's early work but also reverberates with Nakagami's struggle over masculine expendability. The sea of 1967 overflows with the flotsam and jetsam of memory and unmitigated family trauma, if not actual human bodies. In twelve sections, the first person narrator (*boku*) practices a variation on a single extended theme—the layers of his own consciousness as they relate to history and to place of origin, or, as he puts it more than once in the text, the "me inside of me." Rather than envision a body floating on the water as in the poems, "Umi e" internalizes water and landscape itself and projects body fluids outwards. Nonetheless, the sea itself is the site of masculine death, the final destination of the body of the boy floating in the river. The "me inside of me" is born in water, made of water, returns to water.

"Umi e" takes place in a small provincial southern town to which the speaker returns after a considerable hiatus. The title suggests not only an ode to the ocean, but also a physical destination in its use of the directional particle "e" (to). "Umi e" literally traces the speaker's journey step by step from a bus stop through the town to the beach and the sea beyond.[30] Gazing out of the bus window on his way into town, *boku* sees "the skinny, feeble river," and then describes his mental state: "I'm going limp. It's always the same when I get to this town—my nerves go completely slack, and I feel so limp that I react dully to everything around me" (*NKZ* 1: 55–56). Depicting graphic sensations of nausea and listlessness, the speaker ensures that the reader will not mistake his account of the journey home with those in other Japanese *shōsetsu*—as a means to spiritual healing and deeper self-knowledge.[31] As in the poems, the contours of the town smother him.

While conveying the speaker's dismay at arriving home, "Umi e" also moves back and forth in time, sketching out two other narrative lines: *boku*'s memories of an old relationship that he has outgrown and the suicide of his brother, which he dates in the text as having occurred in March 1959. In the first part of "Umi e" these sections are clearly marked: Sections 1 and 3 describe a bus journey to town and Sections 2 and 4 unfold as memories of the speaker's past life in the town. In Section 4, for example, the speaker remembers his old relationship in a passage that is dotted with references to Rimbaud:

> You and I are walking. The season is in the veins of fallen leaves. O season, o season, I sing. At each step, leaves beneath our heels crackle on the pavement.
>
> You keep on talking, but strangely your words break apart and dissolve, never reaching my eyes. The town pulsates steadily in my

field of vision. Shrinking ever smaller, the small town by the sea enters my body and heats my blood.

Dusk, a cheap box painted with bright colors. The town goes completely silent and the night, a hard, glittering jewel (like a festival for a child-like goddess in a meadow that Coltrane conjures up), sings a song that is poetry itself. "Oh, oh, oh," you and I try to melt into the town like tears.

We know that the town by the sea, pregnant with the white amoeba night, will absorb our pitiful body fluids. A breeze stirs. Then our body fluids, still not dry, turn into a sad coldness like an encounter with a dictionary of forgotten words.

You suggest merging with my body. "That's impossible," I turn to you peeling off advice filled with the bitter echo of Oedipus' script.

A dog jumps out from the shade of a telephone pole. Brown and grotesquely fat, the dog passes between you and me barking like some hypochondriac.

No doubt it saw a signal of depressive unease like sex passing between us (maybe it was love). So, beat that dog to death.

Faintly we hear the sound of the tide. Now the sea belongs to us.

(*NKZ* 1: 58–59)

The first lines of this section echo the rhythms of footsteps, two friends/lovers walking down a street in autumn. The drama between the two people plays out against the backdrop of the shrinking town, a cheap box that cannot hold them. Confident that the coastal town will absorb their pitiful body fluids, the two embark upon a physical/literary encounter only to discover that their body fluids, still wet, bring sadness and disappointment like "a dictionary of forgotten words." When the friend or lover suggests that they merge their two bodies, the speaker recoils as if this would signal the breaking of a taboo. At this point the fat dog appears, marking a grotesque, even sarcastic intrusion into the realm of poetry. The brown dog's corpulent shape immediately rescues the speaker from any romantic notions; it serves as a sarcastic reminder of who he is; and it reminds him that there are watchful eyes in the shabby confines of the town around them. Humorously, the dog "barks like a hypochondriac," suggesting that the whole endeavor has been an overblown joke from the beginning. Further, because the dog has picked up a signal between the two (depressive unease like sex or maybe love) it must be beaten to death.[32] The beating of the dog signals the firm repudiation of the shabby town and anyone who might witness relations between the two. After the beating of the dog, the speaker fixes his attention firmly on the sea beyond, or as he boldly declares, "now, the sea belongs to us."

In order to further explore this ambiguous portrayal of an encounter between two people, we might look forward to Section 8, in which *boku* speaks more directly about an old love affair. First, he indicates that his companion is a woman—he uses the word *kawaii omae* (you pretty thing)—and he then explains why he rejected her. As a member of the majority (not *burakumin*), the woman carries "vulgar blood" (*zokubutsu domo no chi; NKZ* 1: 67) in contrast to the speaker's "pure" blood of the outcastes. No matter how many times the speaker has sex with the woman, he will not accept her (*yurusu*). Nor will he "allow her into his blood that flows purely like Kumano River" or let his sperm remain in her body (*NKZ* 1: 67). Body fluids, in their liquid and unstable nature, begin to define identity—where "I" ends and "you" begins—and to define difference—what marks "me" apart from "you." Through the failed love affair with the "vulgar" woman, we begin to see that the sea refers not only to the space of masculine sexuality, if not homosexuality, but also to the speaker's own point of origin in the *buraku*. In both encounters, the speaker craves not love or connection to others but a retreat from the riddle of his own desire.

In his rejection of the lover, Nakagami suggests that the real obstacle to an understanding of the "me inside of me" lies buried in his watery past. The walk toward the sea moves back in time in order to unravel the cause of the disgust that *boku* experiences in the present. Sections 5 to 10 detail the speaker's approach to the ocean, as he moves closer to and finally enters the water himself. In fact, the sea encloses the trauma of the brother's death. Section 5, for example, opens with the speaker getting off the bus and walking toward the sea. Then, as the text indents, *boku* speaks in the voice of the brother who hanged himself in 1959: "I am walking. Beginning to walk toward that sea inside of me. The sea that ate me alive, that knocked me down, that crushed my throat. I'm walking toward that sea" (*NKZ* 1: 60).

In numerous passages, the brother's voice becomes a fragment of the narrator's own psyche. At the same time, the sea is elided with the people of the town who supposedly hastened the brother's suicide. Such passages echo scenes in "Kisetsu no tame no shigaku," where the town itself, singing the song of the betrayer, is engaged in a conspiracy against the brother, and where townspeople spin a secret murder plot in the "age 13 stanza."

Finally, in Section 7 of "Umi e," the speaker, in full view of the sea, approaches the brother's death from a different perspective, abandoning poetry to draw the contours of a story. Sitting down on the concrete embankment by the sea, he recalls the day when he first learned of his brother's death. The text indents, but the "story" is told in prose:

> That day it was the same. It had been this cold, too, the day my sister with gentle, warm eyes, faced the sea, overcome with anger.
>
> "Brother's dead," she said, stroking my child's head roughly. White tears fell on the back of my neck. My sister wept, shaking with grief.
>
> How can I ever forget my sister that day? How can I forget the sea, drinking in all that anger, and pounding the beach for us?
>
> A closed rose bud was waving in the wind as if it knew of my sister's grief.
>
> "Brother drank poison. For my sake." Sister's voice shook. I trembled fearfully, her words piercing me like an oddly shaped spear. (*NKZ* 1: 63)

The speaker immediately suspects the import of the sister's words: the stain of incest and the fear of public disgrace that drove the brother to suicide. "Umi e" does not directly address the issue of whether the sister's marriage drove the brother to suicide but Nakagami has started to write fiction in this passage. He dangles possible clues for the brother's death—the incestuous love affair, the sister's marriage—and he sketches in the details in the form of the bottle of poison, the waves pounding the beach, and finally, the tears on the child's neck.

The scene on the beach constitutes an early attempt to fictionalize the incomprehensible nature of the brother's death. But in later sections of "Umi e," Nakagami resists his own narrative impulse, and continues to explore the abstractions of poetic discourse. In a dialogue that is more reminiscent of Rimbaud's *A Season in Hell* than anything else Nakagami ever wrote, a woman and a man discuss love and death. In the first part of the "dialogue," the speaker simultaneously plays the roles of both *boku* in the present and the dead brother. The woman, whose words are presented in prose form, plays the part of *boku*'s past lover and his older sister. Drawing on classical Greek literature, the man is Narcissus, the man who loved himself too much; and the woman takes the part of Echo, the nymph who lost her voice and her life for Narcissus. The woman accuses the man of being one who practices incest, a narcissist who rejects her offer of love because of his fascination with himself. But the man rejects the woman's charges, telling her that rather than being a narcissist, his preoccupation with himself reflects his need to know how he is internally constituted in relation to the grotesque sea that killed him. (Again the word "grotesque" suggests the majority community, the *zokubutsu domo* of earlier passages.) In the last stanzas of the dialogue, the woman makes a final plea:

Woman:
I really love you, but my love is like light deflected from a tin roof. Can you hear me? I feel your penis in my hand but you're frozen like a deep-sea fish. Why is that so?

> Man:
> Sea
> Mad sea
> Sea of never-ending desire
> Wailing sea that enfolds me
> What am I?
> What is the me inside of me? (*NKZ* 1: 72)

The woman reaches out, offering love to the man, but the man, who is caught up in the conundrum of his own identity, cannot respond. She feels his sexual desire, but his body is frozen—as if he belonged to the sea depths, as if he were already drowned and dead. Once again, the speaker becomes both the suicide and the survivor at the same time. The speaker, saddled with his curses and his confusion, expresses his desire to examine himself—the "me inside of me"—as if by moving inside himself, he might at last come to understand the events that led to his (the brother's) undoing. He might begin to unravel the riddle of his own sexual desire, his detachment, and his identity in relation to the "vulgar ones." In the last two sections of "Umi e," the speaker abruptly sheds the histories of the brother, the sister, and the lover. Turning again to the riddle of "me inside of me," he feels the eyes of the "vulgar people" on him, wanting to kill him. Just at the moment when the reader anticipates that the speaker will join his brother in death, however, the speaker declares that he has rid himself of history, burned his résumé, and disavowed the past and the present. Suddenly he transforms the sea into the space of purity and he writes in prose form:

> I am made pure. The waves on my chest have lapped me clean. I'm not a fallen angel anymore. Look at the downy golden hair on my body. Sea, you're my brother, my sister, myself. Sea of the tides of my blood, I'm purity itself. The waves send me an echo of love wildly. . . . (*NKZ* 1: 76)

Within this re-envisioned sea, the speaker expresses his gratitude to the water, "its gentleness in melting my leftover anger and everything else away," and he calls the sea, "myself" (*NKZ* 1: 77–78). Rather than allow the sea to destroy him, the speaker claims the water as a familial space, the purifying tide of his own bloodline overflowing with the essences of his brother and sister. Further, by merging with the sea and finding a purified space in which to reside, he breaks with Icarus and chooses survival. Now the sea belongs to him.

The new sea, a purified and purifying body of water, allows the speaker to shut out the vulgar people and embrace his own vision of difference. But then the speaker goes further. As he claims the sea for himself, he ejaculates into the waves. "Oh, oh, oh," he cries, "sea, I'm coming, words won't kill me, it's a real ejaculation, o, o, o" (*NKZ* 1: 78). Not only does the speaker fill the waves with endless copies of himself, the expendable male floating on water, but his literal ejaculation plays with words. The phrase, "words won't kill me" suggests that words alone won't bring him to orgasm, and reveals the speaker's determination to transcend the abstractions of poetry. While the speaker recognizes the lure of the sea (blissful dissolution and death) he expresses the urge to survive: to bring the world into the text and to make things "real."

On every page of his poetry, Nakagami reveals why he would ultimately abandon poetry. The blurring of identities became too obvious and the slippage between voices too easy. He needed a more rooted context, as in the Kumasaka poem where he drew in the contours of a familiar landscape. Poetry did not offer differentiation but merging and dissolution, the endless call of the brother's voice. However tantalizing poetry may have seemed to Nakagami, his work lay in another direction. As Virginia Woolf wrote of Emily Brontë: "She was novelist as well as poet. She must take upon herself a more laborious and a more ungrateful task. She must face the fact of other existences, grapple with the mechanism of external things, build up, in recognizable shape, farms and houses and report the speeches of men and women who existed independently of herself."[33] Like Brontë, Nakagami once and for all took hold of the anchors of plot, character, even the "recognizable" forms of landscape itself. After 1969 he would never return to pure poetry.

As readers of Nakagami, we do well to remember the early poetry even as it recedes into the distant past. With its abstraction and its intertextuality, poetry gave Nakagami the tools to explore the coordinates of his origins, allowing him to experiment freely in ways that he did not do so easily in his early fiction. In the poems, all the cacophony resounds: conflicted desire, fear, hope, despair. Moreover, Nakagami never abandoned certain elements of poetry—the impatience with conventional syntax, the sudden digressions and repetitions, the rich threads of imagery, and the dense compression of language. In poetry, too, by literally turning the male body inside out, searching for the "me inside of me," Nakagami embraced difference and found the key to his own survival: an ethnic, even mythic identity, rooted in the brother-sister pair. Finally, through poetry, Nakagami mourned his own brother and found new brothers, both literary and real, who led him out of his provincial Shingū to begin his life as a writer in Tokyo.

THREE

Brother-Sister Love and the Creation of Akiyuki

It's the same as if I had never written a word about my real father.
—Nakagami Kenji, "Sakuragawa"

On July 29, 1978, Nakagami Kenji addressed a local audience at the Rinpōkan, the *buraku* community center in the Kasuga district of Shingū. His subject that day was a folksong about brother-sister love, replete with a bold confession, mistaken identities, and tragic death. During the 1970s the song was still performed (and danced) every year in August at the *obon* festival for the dead in Shingū. As if to guarantee the authenticity of his materials, Nakagami played a tape recording of the song made by a woman who lived around the corner. The old woman sang:

It happened in Nishijin, Kyoto,
the brother, Monten, was twenty-one
the sister, Okiyo but nineteen;
Monten fell in love with Okiyo
Taking to his bed
his passion consumed him
three meals a day became two
two meals a day became one

till no food could pass his lips

[. . .]

[Monten spoke:]
"I don't need a doctor; I don't need a nurse
A single night would cure me
with two pillows and three quilts
if only you would sleep with me
I beg you, Okiyo"

Greatly startled, Okiyo replied:
"What are you saying, Monten,
aren't we brother and sister
If people hear, they would damn us"

[. . .]

Withdrawing, Okiyo went to prepare
she put up her hair, made-up her face
from the heirloom chest she took
a white gown of rough silk to wear beneath
a black robe of rough silk to wear on top
Winding a fashionable *obi* with circle patterns around her waist
She tied it, patted it once with her hand
And swirled it to the back.

[. . .]

Monten saw a figure approaching
"That must be Okiyo's husband
if I kill him, she'll be mine!"
Aiming his revolver, Monten fired
Then he heard a woman's shriek
"Ah, who goes there? Forgive me!" Monten cried.
He ran to the body and raised the hat
only to see it was Okiyo who had planned this all along:
"My sister has deceived me,
but if I die here, we'll die together as one,"
so said the brother
in Nishijin, Kyoto.[1]

As Nakagami himself pointed out in his remarks that day, the melodramatic tale of love and deception takes place not in Shingū but in the Nishijin area of Kyoto. Nakagami suggested that the folksong, which originated in Kyoto, was brought home to Shingū via a "silk road" by people of the community who had roamed far and wide in search of work. He then asked why the song had retained its popularity in Kasuga, the *burakumin* neighborhood of Shingū. At three points in the discussion, however, he categorically rejected the notion that the song simply enacts the incest taboo—a nearly universal prohibition.

Nakagami instead proposed two explanations for the song's popularity. First, the brother's obsession with the sister simply expresses his burgeoning sexuality, or, in more general terms, incestuous love symbolizes the defeat of the older generation by the defiant young.[2] Second, Nakagami notes that the song parallels the myth of Izanami and Izanagi, the incestuous sibling gods who created the islands of Japan. Through the folksong Nakagami reads an ethnic identity for the people of the *buraku* of Shingū, investing folk practices with potent symbolic power:

> It seems to me that this song is an inside-out, upside-down song about the birth of a country. An inverted *Kojiki* if you will. Many kinds of myths take this shape. In other words, from a brother and sister you can make a country. And here, in the middle of the *buraku*, doesn't this birth of a country take the form of a brother-sister love suicide? In order to give birth to a country, doesn't something have to die? Or, to put it another way, the country that emerges from the brother-sister suicide is an inside-out country of darkness, an upside-down country—that's my sense of it.[3]

Through his "mythic" reading of the song, Nakagami transforms a tragic love story into a story of birth and beginnings. More importantly, Nakagami reveals his vision of the *buraku* not as a marginal subculture but as the invisible substratum that supports the "country of light"—Japan, with its imperial court culture and its official set of myths. Rather than serve as a conduit for nostalgia, folk practices upset assumptions about present-day cultural forms.

Both explanations of the incest motif—whether it depicts sexual liberation or marks a mythic founding—serve another purpose vis-à-vis Nakagami's audience. In Kasuga, at least, the topic of incest cannot be a neutral one, since discrimination against the *burakumin* usually focuses on notions of impure blood. This blood, which is said to be the result of generations of inbreeding in isolated communities, supposedly manifests itself in physical deformities, genetic illnesses, even dementia. Illnesses that might easily be traced to impoverished living conditions in the *buraku* are reflexively ascribed to heredity. The logic of discrimination is circular: if you belong to the *buraku*, you are genetically inferior; if you are genetically inferior, you belong to the *buraku*.

Moreover, discrimination did not disappear with the advent of the modern era (the official end of the outcaste system dates to the Liberation Edict of 1871); instead, it took new forms. According to Fujino Yutaka, the arrival of Social Darwinism in Japan shored up prohibitions against marriage into low status groups (*burakumin*, the mentally ill, Koreans), which in turn forged a strong sense of national identity along class and social lines. In addition, Darwinist doctrines were used to equate poverty with moral weakness, as exemplified in this account that dates to 1897:

> In the *buraku*, people frequently intermarry, and in violation of both ethics and nature, marriages within families accumulate, and as one family replicates the same genes, so they pass back and forth ugly disabilities and abnormalities. Some have sores all over their eyes, or have lost all their hair; others have mouths and noses that have rotted off, and, in the worst cases, some even lack limbs. The place truly resembles a freak circus (*kaibutsu yashiki*), and could be described as an extreme example of human misery.[4]

Without much ado, Fujino debunks the notion that incestuous marriages were more common in the *buraku* at the time. In addition, many discriminatory practices continued unchallenged after 1871; since the Tokugawa period, for example, Sōtō Zen priests designated outcaste status with special marks or characters in temple death registers. These necrologies were still being used for background checks as late as 1984.[5] In both premodern and modern eras in Japan, "genetic prejudice" has resulted quite literally in the demotion of the *burakumin* to the level of animals as can be seen in the derogatory name that is sometimes used for them, *yotsu*, or four-footed.[6]

The Nishijin folksong makes reference to such beliefs about impure blood and ethnicity when Okiyo states that if she and her brother commit incest, "people will damn us" (*chikushō to iware*), or more literally, "call us beasts."[7] Through her dramatic disguise, Okiyo tries to prevent her brother's transgression, but fate asserts its power; the story ends not in an actual act of incest but in a metaphorical one, a makeshift double love suicide, the last course of action for unlucky couples in love. In his discussion that day in Shingū, however, Nakagami avoided any mention of Okiyo's resistance, focusing instead on the brother's desire. Nor did he suggest that the song's popularity might reflect an awareness of stereotypes on the part of the *burakumin* of Shingū, or that the fatalism of the story itself might be a response to harsh discriminatory attitudes. Instead, Nakagami brushed over the darker side of his ethnographic materials, painting the folksong in the most positive light. By reading an alternate ethnic identity in folk practices, Nakagami inspired pride in his audience, the people of Shingū themselves. Having founded the Buraku Seinen Bunkakai in Shingū in February of that same year of 1978, Nakagami also revealed his intention to document and preserve *buraku* culture even as he feared that it was drifting toward extinction.

The Creation of Akiyuki

During the mid- and late 1970s, Nakagami put his ideas on incest and nation-building into practice in his fiction. Between 1975 and 1983, Nakagami created a character named Akiyuki, a young laborer whose story stretches over three books: *Misaki* (The Cape, 1975), *Karekinada* (Withered Tree Straits, 1977), and *Chi no hate shijō no toki* (The Sublime Time at the Ends of the Earth, 1983). As discussed in the first chapter of this book, the Akiyuki series catapulted Nakagami to fame. One reason for the favorable reception of the Akiyuki works lay in their accessibility. Nakagami borrowed certain rhetorical devices from the *shishōsetsu*—the quasi-autobiographical form that explores an individual's vision of the world, elevates sincere feeling to the level of moral privilege, and consciously and, at times playfully, blurs the boundaries between life and text. In the creation of Akiyuki, a protagonist who examines himself from myriad angles, who ages chronologically from work to work and whose story crisscrosses Nakagami's own, Nakagami approximates *shishōsetsu* style. Further, Nakagami works along the mimetic backbone of modern Japanese literature, recording the lilt of regional accents, listing the tools and the jobs done, and painting slices of a rural landscape.[8]

True to his *shishōsetsu* leanings at this time, Nakagami also picked up a central plot line of modern Japanese literature in the Akiyuki works: the story of the rebellious son who forges his own identity in a protracted struggle with a powerful father. A concern with paternity characterizes much twentieth-century Japanese fiction, even in works that are not commonly classified as *shishōsetsu*. In *Sorekara* (And Then, 1909) by Natsume Sōseki and *Ie* (Family, 1910–11) by Shimazaki Tōson, for example, the dislocations of "becoming modern" are played out in skirmishes between an authoritarian father who represents the old patriarchal *ie* or family system and a rebellious son who has taken up the pen. In many cases the issue of paternity is complicated by the presence of other fathers or pseudo-fathers who vie for the son's attentions. The tension between these various possible fathers becomes a touchstone for the hero's conflicts within himself. *An'ya kōro* (A Dark Night's Passing, 1921–37) by Shiga Naoya, for example, features Kensaku, a young writer who discovers that his grandfather is actually his father, the result of an illicit affair between his mother and her father-in-law. The news distresses Kensaku but it also frees him from his nominal father's rule and confirms his own sense that he has always been different. Years later, Ōe Kenzaburō works through the father-son conflict in the form of outrageous satire, in stories such as "Mizukara waga namida o nuguitamau hi" (The Day He Himself Shall Wipe Our Tears Away, 1972), and "Warera no kyōki o ikinobiru michi o oshieyo" (Teach Us to Outgrow Our Madness, 1969). In these texts, permeated with the presence of real or imagined fathers, writers touch on the "riddle that the existence of the father poses to the son," to borrow the words of Shiga Naoya.[9] In the Akiyuki series, Nakagami, too, foregrounds Akiyuki's struggle with his biological father, a man named Hamamura Ryūzō, who looms larger than life in what promises to be a proper oedipal conflagration.

Critics in both Japan and the West have noted the presence of the father-son plot in the Akiyuki series, gauging Nakagami's achievement in what Edward Fowler calls the "heartland of language and literature in Japan."[10] These critics generally concur that Nakagami's father-son conflict promises more substance than it can deliver. Yomota Inuhiko, for example, comments on Nakagami's creation of "perverse" versions of the father-son plot.[11] Karatani Kōjin states that in the story of Akiyuki and his father, Ryūzō, Nakagami has taken apart the modernist plot in which the hero depends on conflict with the father to forge a sense of self. At the end of the twentieth-century, the oedipal line runs empty.[12] Hidaka Shōji makes a similar point.[13] Mark Morris, too, has written that the oedipal plot fizzles in *Karekinada*.[14] And in a discussion of *Chi no hate shijō no toki*, Faye Kleeman writes about the "deconstruction" of the father.[15] While each critic focuses on different aspects of the father plot in the Akiyuki works, the voices accord to a remarkable degree. To what can we attribute this degree of harmony? What, in turn, do deconstructive readings reveal about the critics themselves?

First, critics focus on the father-son plot not simply to practice thematic readings but to position Nakagami vis-à-vis other modern Japanese writers. As we have seen father-son tension serves as a lynchpin in depictions of the emergence of the modern. Second, in Japan, at least, the focus on the father-son plot is best understood in the context of a sea change in reading practices in Japan in the 1980s and 1990s. By this time a younger generation of post 1960s critics had come of age. Openly rejecting biographical readings and author-centered criticism (and in very oedipal tones, their own intellectual "fathers"), they focused on certain formal aspects of the literary text: its self-contradictory workings; its intertextuality; its inherently ideological underpinnings.[16] In this context, Yomota Inuhiko, for example, reads the Akiyuki works not as a series but rather as a group of texts in which each succeeding work critiques and revises the proceeding one.[17] Karatani Kōjin makes a similar judgement in relation to *Chi no hate shijō no toki*, the final work in the series: it is "a critical reading that surpasses the previous work."[18] Moreover, Karatani states that the achievement of *Karekinada* lay not in adding anything new to modern literature, but in highlighting Nakagami's ability to repeat and revise his work over time.[19] In the heady atmosphere of postmodern theory of the 1980s and early 1990s, Nakagami satisfied a certain critical agenda, proving that fiction could only offer "revision," not resolution.

Before we fold Nakagami's fiction back into its time and its place, however, we might consider other approaches to the work. My question is not whether Nakagami consciously turned modern plots inside out but whether in fact he bypassed them altogether, traveling to terrain rarely visited by other writers. In order to account for the strange father, Hamamura Ryūzō, for example, we need to cast our nets beyond the father-son story for other plot lines that might prove binding. We might also read the Akiyuki works chronologically, not to erase the dissonance among them, but to gauge how certain threads wind back and forth, how some dwindle and fade while others come to the fore. Finally, we might consider the tension between Nakagami's ethnographic work and his fiction. The Akiyuki works present a notably darker picture of origins than Nakagami's positive reading of the Nishijin folksong suggests. This picture lies buried within the texts themselves, forming a riddle of words, a knot to be traced and carefully unraveled. There in a jumble of loose threads, we might discover not only what Nakagami tore apart but also what he made anew.[20]

Misaki

Misaki tells the story of Akiyuki, a young laborer aged 24, who works in his family's contracting business. The bastard son of a local speculator, Akiyuki grew up with a single mother surrounded by half-siblings from her first marriage. Ikuo, an elder half-brother, committed suicide when Akiyuki was twelve. Mie, a half-sister, stands at the center of the action, succumbing to madness after a murder among her in-laws. Gradually forsaking the present, Mie retreats into her storehouse of memories about her beloved older brother. In addition to Mie, Akiyuki learns that he has another half-sister, a prostitute in the red-light district. According to rumors, she is the daughter of Akiyuki's biological father and she may also be her own father's lover. At the end of *Misaki,* Akiyuki sleeps with this half-sister, whom we shall call Satoko (her name in *Karekinada)* for the sake of convenience, since Nakagami dispenses with proper names for some characters in this work.

Enmeshed in complex family relations, Akiyuki reads like a character in the negative, made up of others' features, names, and body parts. Most importantly, Akiyuki simply appears as *kare* (he) in *Misaki,* his proper name being used only when others address him by it. The use of *kare* to refer to Akiyuki but not to other males (who are given proper names) suggests a special role for the character.[21] In the absence of a proper name, the use of *kare* reinforces Akiyuki's own lack of a fixed position in his family and his staunch rejection of the prerogatives of adult life: name, social position, and social contracts (sexual and otherwise). Periodically, Akiyuki indulges in introspective moments that echo the early poetry:

> The alley in front of the boss's house was bathed in sunshine. He could smell the ditches. There were no signs of life anywhere but here. Next to the railroad crossing, where the alleyway curved off to the left, a single tree was gently shaking its leaves. The tree reminded him of himself. He didn't know what kind of tree it was and he didn't care. The tree had no flowers or fruit. It spread its branches to the sun, it trembled in the wind. The tree doesn't need flowers or fruit. It doesn't need a name. Suddenly he felt he was dreaming.[22]

Enclosed by the alleyway itself, Akiyuki rejects names in a story that overflows with names but contains none that fits him. At first Akiyuki's contemplations link him to other *shishōsetsu* protagonists who forge an identity in moments of "withdrawal and retreat," to borrow Paul Anderer's formulation.[23] But Akiyuki, having come through a difficult birth, pressed by the forces of blood and geography, possesses a vulnerability that stands out even among a crowd of self-absorbed *shishōsetsu* heroes. Unable to comprehend his relations to others and feeling himself on the verge of dissolution, Akiyuki models himself on the dance of the nameless tree. Like the *boku* of the poetry, Akiyuki asks: "with no name and so little to anchor me in the world, where do 'I' end and others begin?"

Misaki begins in poetry but Akiyuki cannot dream indefinitely nor can he shut out the world. Toward the beginning of the story, Akiyuki stops short in front of his reflection in the mirror. Looking back at him is the wicked mask of his biological father, a man who drifted to the alleyway after World War II, impregnated three women, including Akiyuki's mother, and made a fortune on shady land deals, arson, and intimidation. At first Akiyuki refuses to identify with this larger-than-life father: he rages against his father's blood and engages in regression. He will literally remain a child by not having sex. Walking through the red-light district, Akiyuki encounters and rebuffs a prostitute:

> The alley in the red light district smelled faintly of sewage and piss. "Come here, handsome," a woman called to him. He didn't answer. "Stop in for a while," said the woman, now taking him by the arm. He could smell makeup and liquor. He had money. But he'd never had a woman and he didn't want one now. Didn't want to dirty himself in something pointless and messy. No, no, he worried that if he did it just once, he'd become obsessed with it and end up with his mind in the sewer just like that man, who couldn't keep his hands to himself.
>
> "Come in, I'll give you a deal," said the woman pulling at his hand. The tree at the corner of the alleyway was shaking. Akiyuki's breath was ragged. C'mon, pull my arm one more time, he thought, then I'll get drunk and hold a woman for the first time, for real not in

my dreams. Really know a woman for the first time. Overflow. But the woman let go of his arm.

"I'm broke," Akiyuki said.

The woman looked away. (36)

In his dejected rejection of the prostitute, Akiyuki banishes his father with his dirty hands and consuming lust. Dreading the possibility that he resembles his father but unable to ignore what his reflection in the mirror tells him, Akiyuki strikes a bargain with himself. Repeatedly he wends his way to the red-light district in search of Satoko, the prostitute half-sister on his father's side. At the end of *Misaki,* in a cheap room above a bar, Akiyuki has sex for the first time with his sister:

This woman was definitely his younger sister, he thought. Their hearts were beating hard. How I've longed for you, their hearts were saying to each other. With his ass in the air like an animal, he didn't know what to do even though she meant so very much to him. He wanted to pluck out his beating heart and press it into her breast, merge their two hearts, rub them one against the other. The woman moaned. Their sweat flowed. I'm your brother. We two are the pure children of that man, the one I can now call "Father" for the first time. If only we had hearts for sex organs. Akiyuki wanted to rip open his chest, and show his sister, her eyes closing as she strained and moaned, the blood of that man running through his veins. (104)

The final scene of *Misaki* startles not for its eroticism or its overt violence (there is more violence in later work) but for its emotional tenor—as a desperate plea for the distant father. What Akiyuki wants from his sister is not simply sex but a witness to his own particular trauma, the overwhelming alienation and dislocation that attends his position as the abandoned son.[24] Moreover, the use of the words "pure children" suggests that Akiyuki will only come into his birthright through breaking the incest taboo. He needs the sister in order to make the father's blood literally "overflow" or "spill over" (*afureru*), to make the connection between father and son apparent in the world. Even as he becomes a "man," however, Akiyuki expresses such childish longing, not for an autonomous existence but for connection, the melding of body fluids, for a heart that literally "beats as one." In *Misaki* Nakagami has come of age as a writer; it seems that he has tackled the oedipal plot.[25]

The last scene of *Misaki* caused members of the Akutagawa Prize committee to stumble when they awarded Nakagami the prize in early 1976. In the blunt style that seems to characterize the committee, the writers Yoshiyuki Junnosuke and Yasuoka Shōtarō engaged in a short argument over the final scene. Yasuoka Shōtarō disliked the scene, stating that the language "drifted" and that it cheapened the work. Yoshiyuki Junnosuke countered that the young man was simply bolstering his courage to have sex for the first time: "In order to use his penis, this character has to wonder whether it's his half-sister or not. What I mean is there's no incest in this work. It has some glaring weak points, but it's incredibly compelling and filled with energy, and is suitable (*fusawashii*) for the Akutagawa Prize."[26]

Yoshiyuki states that there is no incest in *Misaki*. But he makes the remarkable suggestion that all young men tend to think of their sisters before they lose their virginity! He makes this dramatic statement even though Akiyuki is quite clear that the prostitute is his half-sister by his biological father. The word "suitable," too, strikes an odd note. Is the work suitable because it has energy, or because it does not depict incest? In fact, Yoshiyuki hints that the presence of incest might suggest something amiss with this candidate. Yasuoka's comments are more complex. He identifies incest in *Misaki*, but he also criticizes Nakagami for giving in to the familiar modern plot lines—the son who engages in open conflict with the father. Further, Yasuoka implies that he finds fault with Nakagami for falling back on stereotypes about the *buraku*, a community in which men, isolated and wary of strangers, supposedly sleep with their sisters.

Yasuoka raises an important question as to whether incest between Akiyuki and Satoko solves Akiyuki's dilemma. Does Akiyuki, in bed with Satoko, forge his own sense of self in defiance of the father? In fact, incest with Satoko, a frail character, seems too easy; neither Akiyuki, nor Ryūzō (who eventually discovers it in *Karekinada*, the next work), nor Satoko feel the "horror of incest," to use Freud's terms. In fact, however, there is plenty of "horror" in *Misaki* and *Karekinada*; it simply does not lie where Nakagami would have us look. We need instead to peruse the margins.

According to Freud, the desire for incest springs up as a primary human instinct that is gradually and systematically repressed as the child becomes socialized. In Freud's scheme, surrendering to incestuous desire signals regression to an earlier undifferentiated state of being.[27] Given the seemingly universal nature of the incest taboo, it would be odd for Akiyuki to feel nonchalant about sleeping with his sister. In fact, he does not. Turning back to *Misaki*, we find another tale of incest, one that is repressed, barely intuited, a secret that lies shimmering below the surface. Barely spoken of, this incest, which lies along the mother's line, proves to be the true transgression. In fact, sex with Satoko serves as an elaborate defense to cover what is truly at issue in *Misaki*—the fact that Akiyuki feels a dangerous temptation to submerge himself back into the mother's line.

Incestuous desire, both in the past and the present, threads through the story of Mie, Akiyuki's elder mad half-sister. Lying in her sickbed, Mie calls out to Akiyuki, "as if he were her lover" (83). Periodically, Mie's mind slips back into childhood when she spent her days with Ikuo, her beloved older brother who committed suicide at the age of 24. We are never told explicitly that Mie and Ikuo were lovers, but their relationship conforms to the pattern of brother-sister love, and Ikuo's death fuels Mie's madness.[28] Mie subsequently reads her obsession with Ikuo into Akiyuki's features: Mie tells Akiyuki that he looks like Ikuo; he is the same age as Ikuo was when he died. She walks home with Akiyuki, saying, "hold my hand like brother used to" (17). Mie proves doubly dangerous for Akiyuki: in the present, she tempts him with love, and by collapsing time, she wills him to identify with the dead brother, to become Ikuo for her sake.

Akiyuki, too, desires Mie, but at the same time, he recognizes her true form. Appointed as her guardian, Akiyuki watches

Mie attempt suicide, and recognizes that she no longer looks human but resembles "another sort of creature altogether" (96). She passes freely through the membrane that separates the dead and the living, and she represents the bloodline purifying and turning inward on itself. It is this figure of poetry and beauty whom Akiyuki must resist. In contrast, Satoko, the patrilineal half-sister, liberates. Because she "doesn't resemble anyone" (81), she promises to free Akiyuki from the incestuous tangles that define his life. Just before they go to bed, however, Akiyuki checks one last time. He asks Satoko, "do you ever think of dying?" (103) But Satoko, a flesh-and-blood creature of this world, mocks him; she doesn't have time to worry about death. She plans to catch herself a rich man and get out of the sex business. At this moment, Akiyuki realizes that sleeping with Satoko will not cost him psychic capital.

Not surprisingly, the secret of Akiyuki's incestuous and deadly longing for Mie is hidden throughout the two novels, except for one point in *Karekinada* when Akiyuki admits that the case with Satoko was not as simple as it seemed. He states: "The real secret wasn't that he slept with Satoko, but that she was so like Mie, that was the real secret."[29] Here Akiyuki marks the difference between incest along the father's line (playful self-creation) and incest along the mother's line (abhorrent repetition). By sleeping with Satoko (who looks like Mie but is not identical to her), Akiyuki satiates his desire in the realm of the father. If he sleeps with Mie, however, Akiyuki risks sinking further into what is referred to repeatedly as the "mother's nest."[30] Narrative itself would be suspended, losing forward movement and looping around itself in the service of repeating what has already transpired or telling what is already known. In its self-referentiality, incest along the mother's line is backward looking, narcissistic, conforming to fixed patterns. Because Akiyuki has no certain knowledge of his father, he cannot measure himself in masculine terms; in fact, his mother has told him repeatedly that she would like to squeeze his father's blood from his body. For Akiyuki, incest along the mother's line thus represents submission, or to quote Richard King, "incest represents, on one level, the desire to be done with the whole thing."[31]

Akiyuki desires to succumb to Mie—to a poetic merging of identities; but he chooses survival by pursuing Satoko. Carrying him closer to the father, Satoko gives Akiyuki the will to live within the constraints of time and the chance to roam and differentiate himself. The hidden story of Mie nevertheless complicates reading *Misaki* as a proper *shishōsetsu* story of a young man attaining adulthood against the foil of the father. The story of Mie tugs at Akiyuki, pulling him out of the world. Her pain and her madness are emblematic of her clan and represent the tangle of outcaste origins. In fact, rather than feature a son who measures himself in terms of difference, *Misaki* reads like an anti-*shishōsetsu* because it reveals the dangerous possibility of stepping out of the world altogether. *Misaki* records the tyranny of the blood, the past that still binds, not the birth (no matter how difficult or conflicted) of an authentic self. Interestingly, in a 1985 discussion with Murakami Haruki, Nakagami aligned himself with the *shishōsetsu* writers but then sketched out the differences:

> *Nakagami*: I can feel another difference between you and me. There's a stickiness, an absolute quality to the ties between parent and child. In other words, blood. I think that the difference is whether you keep these absolute ties in mind or cut yourself off from them completely.
> *Murakami*: You're right. First of all, I never write about the parent-child tie.
> *Nakagami*: This also leads to what you were saying earlier about whether one writes *shishōsetu*-like material or not. My work resembles the *shishōsetsu*, but it is different from any other *shishōsetsu* ever written. Most *shishōsetsu* wash away the absolute ties of blood. . . .[32]

To Nakagami, the "absolute ties of blood" are indispensable to writing; and in *Misaki* he records the dangers of reading oneself inwardly in relation to the maternal realm. The title of the work itself refers to the original community of outcastes who lived on the cape cut off from the town and denied easy access to the sea. Harsh and unforgiving, the land itself serves as a geographical marker of the *buraku*, literally a physical representation of what it means to be a dweller in a land apart. Given these associations, it is no surprise that Mie, during a picnic to the cape, regresses to a childlike state, grasping a small plastic basket and repeating, "if only brother were here" (83).

Unlike many realist writers who reduce landscape to a projection of individual consciousness, Nakagami works the other way, showing how Akiyuki's preoccupations are both a function of landscape and an accident of birth. Nakagami begins with the problem of anxiety over one's origins, like many *shishōsetsu* writers, but he then widens the scope of his work to illuminate the problem of outcaste identity, an issue that has normally remained outside the purview of both the *shōsetsu* and the *shishōsetsu*. Moreover, with its family romances, its tragedies, and its madness, *Misaki* paints a far darker and more complex picture of origins than Nakagami's ethnographic work suggests. Specifically, Nakagami depicts the oppressive functions of community, rejecting literary visions that privilege rural loci over the corruptions of modern urban space. At this point in time, however, Nakagami has not yet fully realized the implications of his vision; his gaze rests squarely within the parameters of the "land hemmed in by mountains, rivers and the sea." It is only in 1977, with the writing of *Karekinada* that Nakagami looks up and out, his gaze moving from the cape down the Kishū coast to the bleak and barren straits of *Karekinada* where waves pound the rocky shore.

Karekinada

Karekinada fills in the portrait of Akiyuki, now aged 26, in addition to telling the story of his mother and his father. The central event of *Karekinada* is a fratricide, another blood-linked pseudo-incestuous act that mirrors Akiyuki's search for Satoko in *Misaki*. In *Karekinada*, we learn that Akiyuki's father, Hamamura Ryūzō, had settled in the town and had three children by another women, two of whom are boys. Akiyuki has a tense relationship with Hideo, the middle son. During the August festival for the dead, the old women of the alleyway sing and dance the brother-sister love suicide song. (The Nishijin folksong appears in its entirety in the text with only slight variations from the actual recording in certain lines and phrasings.) After the dance, Akiyuki encounters his father by the riverbank and challenges him to deny rumors that he destroyed the homes of the poor people in the alleyway in his thirst for profits. Lurking in the shadows, Hideo, the legitimate middle son, listens to Akiyuki's tirade and later stalks him by the river. When Hideo first attacks, Akiyuki struggles to control himself, but when Akiyuki feels the impact of his fist on Hideo's face, something within him snaps: Akiyuki bashes Hideo's skull in with a rock. In one of the most violent scenes in modern Japanese literature, Akiyuki leaves his younger half-brother's body convulsing in the water.

It happened in an instant.

"Watch out!" Tōru gave a strangled cry.

Out of the corner of his eye Akiyuki could see Hideo behind him poised with a stone in his hand ready to strike. The stone whacked Akiyuki on the shoulder. Lunging at Hideo, Akiyuki pushed him to the ground. Hideo had the body of a grown man, but he was delicate in build.

"Damn," protested Hideo lying pinned on his back.

"What's your fucking problem," Akiyuki slapped Hideo hard across the face. When Akiyuki let go a little, Hideo jumped up quickly.

"Fuck you!" Hideo struck out at Akiyuki again. Unable to summon the urge to hit him back, Akiyuki pinned Hideo down flat. It was just like holding down a struggling girl. Hideo fought to get free. At the moment when Akiyuki looked up and said to Tōru, "Lend me a hand, will you," Hideo's fist hit him squarely in the nose. Warm blood gushed down. Akiyuki looked straight into Hideo's face. Hideo's eyes were watching him. They had a crazy look in them. Aiming at the eyes, Akiyuki curled up his fist and putting all his strength into his arm, he punched Hideo full in the face. Along with the pain of the impact of his fist on Hideo's face, something inside Akiyuki tore open.

His body was burning. A flame coursed through him. Hideo struggled to push Akiyuki off. But Akiyuki held him down, picked up a wet rock from the riverbank, and bashed in his head. He was going to kill the son of a bitch. Blood dripped from his nose. Hideo's shirt was stained black with it. Letting out a scream, Hideo covered his face with his hands, trying to ward off the blows. This Hideo was different from the one he met in town; different from the one who not ten minutes ago had stared at Akiyuki with empty eyes and then suddenly come at him with his fists, shouting, "you mother fucker, how dare you talk to my father that way!" He looked like he was moaning in pain or lying prostrate with grief. Aiming at Hideo's forehead, Akiyuki struck again.

There was blood everywhere. But in the darkness Akiyuki couldn't distinguish between the black water of the river and Hideo's blood. A flower floating in the swollen waters of the river appeared in Akiyuki's field of vision.

Tōru pinned Akiyuki's arms from behind. It had all happened in an instant. "That fucker, that fucker," said Akiyuki rising. He could see people running toward him. The riverbank lay in gloom. The air was still. Hideo lay with his face toward the shallows, his hands covering his face, his body trembling.

The Takehara family with Fusa stood on the riverbank. Hamamura Ryūzō stood there, too. Akiyuki's breath was ragged, his body empty. I killed him, Akiyuki thought.

"Oh my god, it's bad!" a voice sounded and Tōru shoved Akiyuki, shouting, "Run." Akiyuki's legs felt as if they would fall off and he couldn't move.

"I bashed in your son's head," Akiyuki spoke into the gloom.

Something that could have either been Hideo's blood or the water of the river made little waves as it lapped between the rocks. It flowed black all the way to the sea. To the sea that stretched endlessly around Arima, this region and even through the straits of Kareki. "Run!" yelled Tōru.

"Where to?" said Akiyuki.

Akiyuki looked down at Hideo. Lying there with blood streaming down and his body convulsing, he didn't look like Hideo. He was somebody without a name. (*NKZ* 3: 452–54)

At the moment of his death, Hideo loses his name and comes to represent all embattled victim brothers. Like the expendable males of the poetry, Hideo's blood merges with the water, floating down river toward the sea. And, as in the poems, there is the suggestion of homoerotic tension; delicately built, Hideo resists Akiyuki "like a struggling girl." The murder of Hideo also follows the pattern of reciprocal acts of violence between other brother pairs: Yasuo murders his brother-in-law, Furuichi, and Hideo beats up Gorō, the lover of Mie's daughter. Such violence testifies to the trouble that runs along fraternal lines in the alleyways. In the absence of fathers, the sons make each other into victims. As Akiyuki states, violence had nothing to do with other people; it was one bloodline in his body colliding with another (*NKZ* 3: 291).

The most obvious way to read Hideo's murder is that it reduces Akiyuki's rivals for the attentions of the father, despite the presence of Ryūzō's legitimate eldest son. Over the course of the novel, tension has been growing between Akiyuki and Hideo over Akiyuki's relationship to Ryūzō. Nevertheless, the violence that Akiyuki unleashes on his younger brother seems excessive even under the circumstances. Read within the context of the history of Akiyuki's mother's side, however, the murder of Hideo cloaks another story of violence and despair that fuels Akiyuki's rage (much as sex with Satoko masked Akiyuki's desire for Mie). Beneath the present fraternal conflict lies the unresolved conflict between Akiyuki and Ikuo, the matrilineal half-brother who committed suicide at the age of 24. When Akiyuki's mother, Fusa, remarried, she moved to her new husband's house, taking only Akiyuki with her and leaving her grown children behind. Mentally unstable and alcoholic, Ikuo grew enraged, storming into the new house and threatening its members with a knife. In despair, Ikuo later hanged himself from a tree in the garden of the old family house. His death still haunts the living:

> Akiyuki remembered. . . . In a drunken blur Ikuo had walked alone down this street planning to murder his mother and his younger brother, Akiyuki. Plunging the knife into the tatami, he'd screamed, "I'm going to kill you."
>
> Akiyuki played the scene over and over again in his mind. At 20, at 24, and now at 26, he kept thinking that the only reason he was still on this earth was that he had gotten Ikuo's life because there was only room for one of them. (*NKZ* 3: 289)

The recitations of Ikuo's story that dot the narrative, however distracting and superfluous they may seem, link past and present violence. Put simply, Hideo serves as a substitute for Ikuo, the brother who truly tormented Akiyuki as a child. More accurately, however, the murder of Hideo accomplishes a substitution whereby Akiyuki steps into Ikuo's shoes and fulfills Ikuo's thwarted desire to spill his younger brother's blood. After the murder, Akiyuki experiences a shocking realization: "He was exactly like Ikuo, who had died at the age of 24 when Akiyuki was only 12. In place of Ikuo, Akiyuki had killed Akiyuki" (*NKZ* 3: 457). Through substitution, Akiyuki appeases the ghost of his dead older brother. But his substitution of Hideo for Ikuo draws one small but crucial difference: Akiyuki chooses a victim who resembles himself and Ikuo, but not too closely. As with Satoko, Akiyuki picks someone from his father's line, thus narrowly averting what would have been a truly self-defeating act of "incest," a murder along the maternal line. By choosing Hideo, Akiyuki avoids further repetitions of Ikuo's violence in the mother's family, and ensures his own survival; he finally gives himself a name. Moreover, the father, who was present only in Akiyuki's thoughts when he had sex with Satoko, now stands on the riverbank in the flesh, as witness to the crime.

Nakagami clearly distinguishes between the maternal and paternal bloodlines, separating out the two in terms of narrative function. In a discussion of incest and miscegenation in the fiction of William Faulkner, J. Hillis Miller writes that incest corresponds to constantive narration—the telling and retelling of past events, the inability to live in the present, the obsession with repeating a single pattern. Miscegenation, or the embrace of difference, on the other hand, signals performative narration, storytelling that attempts to mold the future.[33] Akiyuki enacts a ritual of miscegenation in narrative terms because Hideo has the father's blood; thus, Akiyuki can accomplish the death of the brother without stepping into the dangerous pool of past-directed repetition. In contrast, the internal replay of Ikuo's intimidation raises the specter of constantive narration repeatedly in the text. Through Hideo's body, however, Akiyuki finally grasps the future, breaking Ikuo's hold and paying for the guilt he felt over Ikuo's suicide.

In his substitution of siblings and his focus on gradations in the bloodline, Nakagami's fiction evinces a tension between incest (too much sameness) and miscegenation (too much difference) that has striking parallels with the fiction of the American South. Werner Sollors suggests that incest and miscegenation, while at opposing ends of the spectrum, often go hand-in-hand in fictional representations of slave-owning society. In Sollor's account, the violation of the two taboos (not to marry too far inward nor too far outward) occurs in a society where fathers sell their own racially mixed biological children; and brothers and sisters, unaware of secret blood ties, fall in love across racial divides. The pairing of incest and miscegenation exposes all the evils of a system of human commerce, with miscegenation inspiring the greater horror. At the same time, both strike a direct blow against the figure at the center of the institution of slavery—the white patriarch.[34]

In Nakagami's case, too, incest masks secrets and dislocations within the family line—names that do not fit and blood ties that go unrecognized. But unlike the literature of the American South, the target of incest has no single face. The problem takes more systemic dimensions—a critique of an encoded system of discrimination, a carefully organized hierarchy in which inside and outside the alleyway blood is read as destiny. We see the power of discrimination (*sabetsu*) in the characters' sharp consciousness of the smallest gradations of the blood in their parental lineage. We see it further in the look that passes between half-brothers. Moreover, the father rises out of this blood-bound system, an apparition who answers the longing for a fixed term that will smooth over eruptions of brother-sister turmoil. The question is how Hamamura Ryūzō fills this role—whether or not he follows in the footsteps of the many authoritative patriarchs of twentieth-century Japanese fiction who came before him. And if Ryūzō does not fulfill his authoritarian promise, providing the ballast in Akiyuki's struggle to define himself, we might explore what other possibilities Nakagami had in mind for a character to whom he gave the nicknames, "king of fly shit" and "rattling horse's bone" (*NKZ* 3: 252).

In the Land of the Father

Hamamura Ryūzō, Akiyuki's biological father, moves closer to Akiyuki throughout *Misaki, Karekinada,* and *Chi no hate shijō no toki.* In *Misaki,* Ryūzō is a shadowy presence, a pair of eyes that follows Akiyuki. His name is simply "that man" (*ano otoko*). In *Karekinada,* however, Akiyuki emerges from his mother's house: father and son meet in town, drink coffee together, and even discuss a job for Akiyuki. By *Chi no hate shijō no toki,* Akiyuki enters the employ of Ryūzō and even lives for a time in his father's old family home in Arima. As we move toward the ending of *Chi no hate shijō no toki,* the stage seems set for a decisive oedipal battle. Akiyuki declares his deep hatred for Ryūzō and even mulls over the possibility of murdering him. With the development of father-son conflict, it seems that Nakagami has finally entered what Fowler calls the "heartland of Japanese literature."

The first hint that Hamamura Ryūzō will not play the typical patriarch, however, is his reaction to Satoko and Akiyuki's tryst. When Akiyuki and Satoko reveal their secret encounter, Ryūzō merely laughs, offering them land where they may raise offspring of their incestuous union. Akiyuki brings Satoko out at key moments in the narrative as if to remind his father of their transgression, but Ryūzō remains impassive, refusing to take the bait.

> No matter what Akiyuki did, that man's low laugh reached his ears. As he worked at a construction site, even the buzzing of the cicadas sounded like that laugh. It gave him the creeps. . . . That man had never gotten angry at Akiyuki. Never suffered or moaned, just laughed. If you and Satoko produce an idiot child, what does it matter, he'd said. The cicadas were crying inside Akiyuki, they were crying outside, too. (*NKZ* 3: 363)

Rather than topple the oedipal plot, Akiyuki laments its absence. Not only does Ryūzō refuse to get angry with Akiyuki and Satoko, but he actively encourages them. The father's refusal to react subsequently throws Akiyuki back on his own inability to read boundaries; the cicadas cry inside, they cry outside, too, as if he existed simultaneously in two places at once. Ryūzō's reaction to Hideo's murder bespeaks a similar aloofness. Rather than rage at Akiyuki, Ryūzō simply retreats into a dark, soundproofed study and waits for Akiyuki's release from prison.

In the absence of a show of authority, however, Ryūzō does provide one advantage to his son: he offers him room to move. Out of brother-sister love and death, Ryūzō wills the birth of a country. He promises Akiyuki and Satoko a piece of land in Arima, and he provides them with an illustrious patrilineal ancestor whom Ryūzō has claimed for himself—Hamamura Magoichi, a legendary warrior of the sixteenth century. Loosely following historical lines, the story tells that Magoichi was a member of the Saiga fighters (*Saiga monto*), an armed unit of believers in the Pure Land sect (Jōdo Shinshū) who turned against Oda Nobunaga in the struggle to control the country in the 1570s. Roundly defeated after a number of uprisings, the Saiga fighters capitulated and swore an oath of allegiance to Nobunaga. According to legend, however, Magoichi fled into the mountains of Kumano with a wounded foot and one missing eye, eventually descending to Arima where he built the "last paradise" (*saigo no rakuen*; *NKZ* 3: 372).[35]

In his enthusiasm for his own invented genealogy—Akiyuki doubts the link—Ryūzō builds a monument to Magoichi in the mountains. Akiyuki reads the monument as a lingam, an ever-erect phallus, towering over the landscape. It stands as a sign of eternal life and his father's dirty blood.[36] Ryūzō's delusions make Akiyuki queasy, but he grasps onto them nevertheless. Most importantly, the story of Magoichi frees Akiyuki from the constricted space of the alleyway. In *Misaki* the people live hemmed in like "insects or dogs," but with the story of Magoichi, Akiyuki's horizons broaden. Climbing up into the mountains and gazing down over the landscape, Akiyuki picks out the trail down which Magoichi might have come. Not only does the story of Magoichi enlarge the cramped domains of Akiyuki's world, but it also inspires Akiyuki to flesh out the historical context of the alleyway. Through Magoichi and Arima, Akiyuki views the alleyway through different eyes.

Reading Magoichi's story backward in time, Akiyuki concludes that Magoichi's path resembles the path of other *buraku* families, including his own, who crossed over the mountains and followed the river down to the sea.[37] Rather than simply submit to the endless repetition of the mother's house with its past-directed stories, Akiyuki experiments with different roots for himself. Like Ryūzō, Akiyuki wills a patriarchal line into being. After Hideo's murder, for example, Akiyuki climbs into the mountains of Kumano, his foot wounded, in a backward recreation of Magoichi's descent into Hongū. Increasingly aware that his father is deluded and that Magoichi is a product of Ryūzō's mad brain, Akiyuki nevertheless practices the suspension of disbelief. Through the stories of his father, Akiyuki builds castles in the air:

> Akiyuki suddenly realized that the one-eyed, one-legged man was a fiction. A product of the feverish obsession of that strange man whose birthplace was a riddle, whose actions for the past twenty years before he'd appeared at Fusa's house were a mystery. History stated that Magoichi had perished in Oda Nobunaga's division along with other *monto* fighters. So wasn't that man claiming that a dead man had walked down through the mountains of Kumano, settled in the country of the dead where they honored the goddess Izanami at the rock shrine Hana no Iwaya, and then spawned his own descendants? Akiyuki brooded. Here he stood, Ryūzō's son and the descendant of a dead man, looking out at the sun-drenched landscape where the wind gently stirred the leaves. Maybe he, too, was a dead man. Maybe Kumano really was the land of the dead. . . . (*NKZ* 3: 439)

His evaluation of his father shifting, Akiyuki stands at the end of *Karekinada* looking down, balanced between the poles of history and myth. But when he tries out the proposition that he is the descendant of a dead man, Akiyuki discovers that myth and history, though not identical, are enfolded on each other, and he cannot easily separate out the layers. Through Akiyuki's ruminations, Nakagami plays variations on a theme.

He turns the father-son story into a parable for lost *buraku* origins and, at the same time, he creates a parable of the nation. Like Ōe Kenzaburō, who created a mad father in "Mizukara waga namida o nuguitamau hi" (The Day He Himself Shall Wipe Our Tears Away, 1972), Nakagami parodies the grotesque fictions of Hamamura Ryūzō and suggests parallels to the modern Japanese emperor, another patriarch who accepted but later rejected the myth of his own divine genealogy when it served him.[38] Furthermore, the country of Magoichi, ruled by a defeated, maimed warrior, serves as a metaphor for postwar Japan—half-blind and limping but still locked in a struggle with the ghosts of its past. In the postwar period Japan, too, reaches the "ends of the earth."

Nakagami parodies the figure of Ryūzō but he does not dismiss him. No matter how secure Akiyuki feels in his knowledge of his father's delusions, the son desperately longs for the father's mad embrace. By pasting the story of the son's quest for the father on to a story of the ethnic group/nation, Nakagami reveals the power that such myths hold when the nation is read as family and vice versa. Finally, through contradictory revelations (Magoichi is ghost/Magoichi is patriarch), Nakagami's vision in *Misaki* bears fruit. Like Akiyuki whose assessment of Magoichi springs from his own outsider status, so too must Japan draw on alternate accounts of its history to paint an accurate picture. From his vantage point of the Shingū *buraku* (both inside and outside the myths that shape the ideology of the nation), Nakagami also poses questions to his readers: once we have confronted the illusory nature of the father and the reality of our own defeat, how do we shed the fictions through which we dream ourselves? What is our country that still feeds on its beliefs in imaginary and ghostly ancestors?[39]

Nakagami poses such questions not simply to mount a critique of Japan but also because he took his own writing to task. The strength of his fictional voice depended on maintaining distance from both the Tokyo literary center and from a nostalgic vision of community. Periodically, for example, Nakagami expresses weariness with the tendency of Japanese fiction (including his own) to settle back into the familiar groove of charting the self. Not only does Nakagami wax impatient with the familiar plots of twentieth-century fiction, but at times he abruptly cuts through his own central character's obsession with himself and his family lines. In a number of striking passages in *Karekinada,* Akiyuki experiences moments "out of time" that float like small islands through the currents of his life. Once we rise above the stories through which we create ourselves, Nakagami suggests, we transcend "knowing" altogether. Antithetical to the progression of plot, such moments reveal a writer's fascination with what words themselves can do and suggest why Nakagami would abandon the realistic style of *shishōsetsu* narratives in the years to come. Climbing into the mountains of Kumano, Akiyuki leaves the bloodlines behind:

> The sun penetrated Akiyuki as if he were a tree moving in the landscape. The wind played with him as it did with blades of grass. Working away, Akiyuki understood that he became an object that couldn't think about or know itself, couldn't see or speak, couldn't listen to music. At this moment he was no more than his shovel, its hard edge digging deep into the flesh of the earth, rising up, digging back down. Everything filled him with longing. No longer himself, Akiyuki was rather the longing that he felt towards the sky, the sun in the sky, the mountains warmed by the sun, the houses dotted about, the leaves lit by the sun, the earth, the stones . . . this longing for every aspect of the land was him. Each and every thing. To Akiyuki, toiling hard, the sun-soaked landscape was like music. Even the voices of the cicadas that until just a moment ago had sounded like the Buddhist chants *Namu amida butsu* or *Namu myōhō rengekyō,* now became the mountain's breath.
>
> Akiyuki was breath. . . .
>
> "Akiyuki!" Tōru called to Akiyuki who was panting roughly.
>
> "What?" he replied in a deliberately gruff voice. He felt strangely embarrassed as if he had been caught masturbating. (*NKZ* 3: 341)

At such moments, Akiyuki is attaining equal weight with the things of the physical world rather than using nature as a map that illuminates the self. Akiyuki empties out quite literally in moments of contemplation that are akin to masturbatory release. During these "out of time" moments in the mountains, Akiyuki jettisons his past and his family history. He knows himself simply as an object in nature.[40] Hidaka Shōji has written, "the novelistic language of *Karekinada* makes the landscape into a metaphor for Akiyuki's internal life."[41] But in fact Nakagami attempts the reverse: to place Akiyuki into a metonymical relationship with the land itself, an open entity through which the world flows and recedes, thus freeing him from introspection. Indeed, Nakagami's goal seems to be to rid his main character of an internal life altogether.

The texture of Nakagami's writing at points in *Karekinada* reveals his interest in pushing at the boundaries of realistic prose. No wonder that critics (including myself) grasp for other modes of analysis as seen in the introduction to this book; they turn to poetry, to music, to oral forms, to visual motifs.[42] Perhaps Etō Jun, too, had these passages in mind when he stated that Nakagami Kenji had finally achieved the promise of naturalism. No matter how heavily the family plot lines weigh, Akiyuki can rise above them briefly, transforming words into beautifully fashioned objects and attaining "lightness of being." Such passages also unlock the key to the father who, instead of encouraging Akiyuki toward introspection and rebellion, seems more of an imaginary figure than Magoichi himself: a cipher who leads up and out of the alleyway into the mountains. In *Karekinada,* at least, Ryūzō remains unbound; the father simply *is* space. Unfortunately, Nakagami could not sustain "lightness of being" in *Chi no hate shijō no toki,* the final work in the Akiyuki series. At the "ends of the earth," Akiyuki's meditations become more tangled, his musings less playful. The father, the mother, and the alleyway weigh him down. In this massive work that runs to 486 pages in the hardcover edition, Nakagami topples the country of Magoichi; he destroys the alleyway; and finally, he erases Akiyuki himself.

Chi no hate shijō no toki

Chi no hate shijō no toki opens with Akiyuki's release from jail after serving three years for the murder of Hideo. Akiyuki returns to find that the alleyway has been destroyed; in its place lies a grassy field that awaits the machinery of the developer. Akiyuki is stunned by his first sight of what were once the twisting streets of his old neighborhood:

When Akiyuki turned the corner, he stopped in his tracks and gasped involuntarily.

"Is this your first time?" Ryōichi asked.

"Yeah, you bet it is," Akiyuki grunted taking offense at Ryōichi's tone.

Akiyuki gazed out to what lay shining beyond the layers of barbed wire that served as a fence. More vivid than a photo, the old site of the alleyway was raw and gaping, and the weeds that had sprung up almost overnight gave the place a certain beauty, bending in the wind and sending out ripples of light. It wasn't just the alleyway, the hill was gone, too. Gazing further, he looked in the direction of what had been the Shinchi district, one street beyond the alleyway, where Mon had had her bar and Satoko, Akiyuki's half-sister, had worked. But all that was gone now along with the factory and the bus yard. The wind blew, and the weeds that grew on the site of the old *roji* began to stir and rustle, whispering that the alleyway—built by drifters who had camped on the mountainside and filled in the lotus pond to make a place where other drifters had settled—was nothing more than a dream. (*NKZ* 6: 32)

In the aftermath of the destruction of the alleyway, squatters, driven out of their homes, have set up tents and cooking fires on the empty site. Whenever the developers attempt to prepare the site for construction, the squatters set fires and the grassy field remains untouched for a time. Among the raggle-taggle band, Akiyuki makes the acquaintance of Yoshi, an old speed addict and a friend of his father. In a drug-induced haze, Yoshi insists that he and the others are descendants of Genghis Khan who have swept across Asia on horseback, gathering land and subjects to build an empire. Haunted by images of Genghis Khan, Akiyuki regularly visits the squatters.

The plot of *Chi no hate* twists and turns on geographic, economic, and social dislocations as it sketches a community in decline. The novel portrays the war that Yoshi and his squatters wage on the forces that have destroyed the alleyway—the shady men who set fire to the alleyway and who now stand to profit from the development of the site. The squatters fight back with fire, repeatedly setting small blazes, but the women of the community form their own ring of defense using water. Yuki, an old prostitute; Mon, the owner of the local bar; and even Satoko, Akiyuki's half-sister, join a water cult led by a man named Saitō who preaches the restorative powers of water to reverse the effects of illness and aging. To draw converts, Saitō has even placed the body of his dead mother in an air-conditioned room in the house as he awaits her resuscitation. The spread of the water cult, with its fixation on the processes of bodily decay and emphasis on purification through drinking large amounts of water each day, is directly related to the destruction of the alleyway that was originally built on marshy ground near the mouth of a river. When the bulldozers razed the houses and the twisted streets, water bubbled up from the sewage canals and the people worried about disease even as the site itself turned a verdant green. The apocalyptic cult also paradoxically reminds Akiyuki of the origins of the alleyway, the myth being that the neighborhood was built on top of a lotus pond, a replica of the lotus pond of paradise in which souls, after death, are newly born on the petals of the lotus flowers. With the disappearance of the alleyways, history comes full circle.[43]

Mark Morris describes *Chi no hate* as "Nakagami's most eloquent failure of a novel."[44] Certainly, it is a novel that never comes into focus entirely, unsure of whether it is a story of a community in crisis, a critique of modern Japanese capitalism, or simply a continuation of Akiyuki's struggles to carve out room for himself outside the mother's line. At the same time, the story attains moments of great tension, particularly during Akiyuki's confrontation with Hamamura Ryūzō. At last it appears that the father-son story has moved to center stage.

Like the other works in the series, *Chi no hate* dangles the possibility of an oedipal cataclysm. Always rather ineffectual in challenging his father previously, Akiyuki turns detective in *Chi no hate*, actively digging up his father's secrets and musing,

"Hamamura Ryūzō is my prey" (*NKZ* 6: 395). According to rumor, Ryūzō arrived in the alleyway after World War II and entered the employ of a landowner and speculator named Sakura who had ripped off the people through high interest rates and had taken possession of their land. Following Sakura's directions, Ryūzō had set fires in the alleyway to drive the people out. In an even more complicated twist, Ryūzō admits that he was working for Sakura and he sends Akiyuki to see him, stating, "there is none as bad as Sakura" (*NKZ* 6: 161). Following his father's suggestion, Akiyuki visits Sakura, who lives in solitude in a white house on the outskirts of town. A senile old man, Sakura tells Akiyuki a different version of events. According to him, Ryūzō turned on his employer by setting fires, killing one of Sakura's men and raping his deaf servant, Moyo no Oba. Ryūzō forced Sakura out, retaining a deed to the alleyway under Sakura's name.

Akiyuki confronts his father with the rumors and asks him for the truth about the past. Ryūzō admits that he set fires to houses in the alleyway to clear space for development, but he insists that this act benefited all.[45] Later, Akiyuki turns to the squatter Yoshi and discovers that Ryūzō was the one who urged the squatters to organize. In addition, Akiyuki discovers that his father brought a development plan to the people of the alleyway, promising them that they would all become rich if they cooperated. Why, Akiyuki asks, would his father create a plan for development and then plant squatters who oppose it? Gradually Akiyuki comes to understand that the alleyway, an inward-looking and protective community, had never accepted the brash outsider Ryūzō but had made him the focus of vicious rumors. Intent on vengeance, Ryūzō now plays both ends against the middle. For the first time, Akiyuki sees the alleyway through his father's eyes:

> Thinking that Ryūzō had deceived even him, Akiyuki whispered to himself: if I could, I'd ask Ryūzō why he is so obsessed with the alleyway that he would hide his own handiwork and pretend everything was the doing of Sakura, the original owner? Akiyuki speculated that Ryūzō saw the alleyways with very different eyes from

> Akiyuki, who had been born there as Fusa's illegitimate son. Many who lived in the alleyway couldn't read or write; throwing caution to the winds, the women slept around and casually had babies out of wedlock. Akiyuki was one of those babies. The men drifted like ghosts, lacking even the basic pride and confidence necessary to sustain life. But these people who had been barred from town life had raised Akiyuki in a warmth that oozed out like secretions from human skin. The alleyway people were pleasant and kind to any stranger as long as they weren't afraid or made to feel inferior. But if the stranger had brains and guts, the alleyway rejected and isolated him, they made him the butt of rumors. (*NKZ* 6: 313)

Akiyuki contrasts his own experience of the alleyway, the site of home, with the experiences of Ryūzō who came from outside. Despite his father's birth in a *buraku* enclave in Arima, the ties of the alleyway, with its viscous qualities that bind human beings together, outweigh lateral ethnic bonds.

When Akiyuki views the alleyway through his father's eyes, it seems that he is well on the way to finally leaving the alleyway and the mother's line altogether. A lumber worker, for example, describes Akiyuki as a reincarnation of the young Ryūzō, and Akiyuki concurs—he is the young Ryūzō come back to life (*NKZ* 6: 216). As the distance between father and son shrinks, their mutual distrust and hatred grow by leaps and bounds. Akiyuki entertains murderous thoughts: "The thing he wanted to do was kill Hamamura Ryūzō" (*NKZ* 6: 222). Ryūzō, too, hates his son because "the closer he got, the more he thought Akiyuki was trying to topple him, trying to break the law" (*NKZ* 6: 230). Given the chance, however, Akiyuki cannot act on his oedipal hatred. He holds a gun out toward his father, imagining with one shot that he could "turn the world upside down" and "create a world without gravity," but he cannot kill his father (*NKZ* 6: 409). Because Ryūzō changes shape with Akiyuki's imaginings and refuses to resist his son, patricide rings hollow. In a dramatic and rather bizarre passage, Akiyuki literally borrows the identity of his father, replicating his return from jail and speaking in Ryūzō's voice:

"Yeah, that man was definitely me," Akiyuki spoke excitedly. Then he deliberately lowered his voice and spoke in a voice that was identical to Ryūzō's, whether he realized it or not.

"When I got back from jail, I walked on the dirt of the alleyway on these two feet and I cried. I thought I could become anything in those days, walking and crying. A man called *eta* or beast who works leather with water from the lotus pond; a beggar beaten up for taking a rice cake put out for pilgrims by the lumber company at Hayatama Shrine on New Year's Day. . . . even Hamamura Magoichi."

"Sounds like me talking," said Ryūzō.

"Yeah, I could become anything. No sweat. Walking around the old site of the alleyway like it was some kind of joke, I knew that Takehara Akiyuki was dead."

With these words, Akiyuki sighed, and tried to laugh the way Ryūzō had done the time that Akiyuki had told him about his affair with Satoko and Ryūzō had said, "what does it matter." But the laugh wouldn't come. (*NKZ* 6: 176–77)

By mimicking the voice of the father, Akiyuki repudiates his identification with the mother's line (Takehara). But rather than identify with his individual father, Akiyuki uses this strange man to explore various *buraku* roles—the pilgrim beaten for defiling the pure precincts of the shrine, a leather worker, even Hamamura Magoichi. The latitude with which Akiyuki reads his father dampens the sparks of an oedipal fight; over the course of many encounters, the son's mimicry waxes parodic. To further compound this effect, at the end of the novel Ryūzō turns and runs rather than confront his son. In what proves to be Nakagami's final twist of the oedipal plot, Ryūzō hangs himself in front of Akiyuki. A moment before Ryūzō knocks the chair out from under his own feet, Akiyuki rushes into the room and shouts "*chigau*!" Akiyuki means the word in both senses as "don't do it" because he isn't finished with his father and "it's wrong!" because in what might have been an oedipal novel, Ryūzō has subverted his own son's aggression and deprived him of the thrill of further pursuit. Ryūzō's willful move into death also elaborates upon the thread of Nakagami's early work: that male-male relations are predicated on loss, on abandonment, on unfulfilled desire. It is no coincidence that

Ryūzō, like Ikuo, dies by hanging. Oddly enough, we find ourselves marooned again in the tributary of the brother plot.

With the mysterious end of Ryūzō's life, Akiyuki is thrown back on his father's legacy—secrets emerging in "incomplete form." True to his nature, Ryūzō leaves cartoon cutouts and a series of letters addressed to the Pope in lieu of a will. Ryūzō's motives for courting Akiyuki remain obscure: the father's legacy adds up to odd pieces of a puzzle. At first, through the character of Ryūzō, Nakagami comments on the random forces of economic progress that precipitate the destruction of local alleyway culture. In contrast, the *roji* women, particularly Mon, the bar owner and Akiyuki's confidante, represent the guardians of local culture. But over the course of *Chi no hate* even the maternal guardians of the alleyway betray their roots. Akiyuki realizes that while his father destroyed the alleyway with fire, his mother's family picked up the construction contracts that would eventually make the family rich. Not only has the alleyway disappeared, but with it Akiyuki's refuge in the upside-down country of darkness. The last remnants of the alleyway are likened to the withered corpse of Saitō's mother, a grotesque and decaying body that once served a maternal function. Images of destruction reflect most devastatingly on Akiyuki himself: "The alleyway was Akiyuki. It was the sum of his past. Like roots exposed in earth after a day of rain, like the half-mummified decaying body viewed by the old women who suffered aging pains and who shuffled to Saitō's place, the alleyway was now just an empty hole in the earth" (*NKZ* 6: 347).

Akiyuki recognizes himself here as the product of the womb, the hole in the earth that gave him life but that now produces only death. When Akiyuki emerges from the empty hole in the earth, shaking himself free, he discovers the abyss where his father dangles before him in space. No wonder the father, who made a fortune out of his exploitation of the alleyway, perishes after he has played his role in its destruction. Without the fixed coordinates of the alleyway, the father and his dreams evaporate like mist.

In the destruction of a community, Nakagami shows his hand: for all the fury and grandiosity of the father plot, it, too, branches out from the mother's realm. The true cataclysm of *Chi no hate* is not Ryūzō's suicide but the moment when the flames engulf the alleyways before the opening of the novel and later when the mother's family signs a contract with Ryūzō's side. Not surprisingly, Akiyuki disappears in *Chi no hate,* because he is so much a product of his mother's blood and because the final betrayal cannot be reversed. The work ends on a note of exhaustion, as if the task of dreaming the father and tracing the decline of the mother's realm has taken every last bit of a writer's strength. In *Karekinada,* the high point of the project, however, Akiyuki could still dream of a mythic past, a glorious future. He could still invent a way out: "I wish he'd yell at me, knock me down, he thought. Then he'd be Ryūzō's child, he would suffer from the same madness as his father, and believe in the false story that he had a grandfather, a great-grandfather and a distant ancestor named Magoichi. It would solve the riddle that was half of himself. He would be free" (*NKZ* 3: 394).

Notwithstanding Akiyuki's desire for attention from his father, however, the riddle that is half of Akiyuki lies tangled not along the paternal line but along the maternal line—in Akiyuki's longing for his sister, in his identification with and hatred for his dead brother, and in the seeds of his own self-hatred. If he could have a paternal line, he dreams, he would be free, he could define himself on his own terms. But by *Chi no hate,* these dreams have faded and Akiyuki, aged 29, is forced to admit defeat to himself:

The cryptomeria trees had been growing here since long before the time that Akiyuki was a seed in Fusa's belly, from the time he'd been drifting in a breeze of nothingness. He felt strangely ill at ease and longed to believe with all his heart in Yoshi's Genghis Khan and Hamamura Magoichi. Both his grandfather, who had lived in the hut at Arima, and his father believed in the one-eyed, crippled Magoichi who, defeated in battle, had fled into the mountains of Kumano in search of the Buddha's country—not as one would believe in a legend but as one would revere the truth. The cryptomeria trees hadn't been here before the time Akiyuki came into being; they'd been seen by the one eye of Magoichi who lurked in the heart of the seed that was Akiyuki. That was how Ryūzō had viewed Akiyuki as he grew up, Akiyuki thought. He groaned. He'd been sheltered by his four half-siblings, children of Nishimura Katsuichirō, and his mother Fusa who had married Shigezō, and Shigezō had never done anything to make Akiyuki feel ill at ease, but the truth was that Akiyuki had been born as Fusa's bastard. He had nothing else to prove who he was. Akiyuki grew uneasy whenever he walked in the mountains. (*NKZ* 6: 218)

In one last burst, Akiyuki longs to belong to the realm of nomads (Genghis Khan and Magoichi) but he cannot shake off his apprehension. By *Chi no hate,* Akiyuki knows too much: legend and fact diverge before him. Like an angry lament, *Chi no hate* mourns the mother-*roji,* ironically the very thing that repudiates Akiyuki himself. The title of *Chi no hate shijō no toki* reveals Akiyuki's dilemma; only when one reaches "the ends of the earth," when one approaches the abyss, does one attain a fullness of being (*shijō no toki*). Only at the moment of extinction does Akiyuki grasp the contradictions of his own existence. In fact, Nakagami has written a *shishōsetsu* to end a genre. Like a black hole, *Chi no hate* folds in upon itself, the character of Akiyuki never to emerge again in Nakagami's fiction.

Nakagami energetically performs the father-son story in the Akiyuki series, yet from the beginning, the father was never Nakagami's destination. In fact, Nakagami's freedom from the trope of father and son allowed him to experiment in dramatic and startling ways with the materials of fiction. Through the story of Akiyuki, Ryūzō, and Magoichi, Nakagami transformed father-son turmoil into a dramatic questioning of ethnic and even national identity. On the one hand, he created a mythic vision: an "upside-down country," a land at the ends of the earth where the children born of brother-sister pairs live peacefully in Magoichi's land by the sea. On the other hand, Nakagami withered this mythic vision at its very roots through his permutations of father-son strife. He could experiment so freely with patriarchy because it lay some distance from him, and like Akiyuki's affair with Satoko, it didn't cost him much in the end.

But the mother plot was different. Writing from the pain of his own beginnings, Nakagami spins a story of lamentation and loss, of turning inward, of exhaustion setting in. There, along that thread, we glimpse the writer thinking aloud about the process of language itself—how writing itself rises from a condition of absence, drawing on a longing for a point of origin that while ever-present is always shifting further out of view. The space called "home" or "mother's nest" disappears, but that is not the point that Nakagami intends to make. Rather, the destruction of the alleyways in the mid-1970s gave Nakagami his opportunity to take *what had once been* and transform it into a marker for his own position, a writer perched on the edge of a national literature taking a critical stance but nevertheless gazing in. Rather than asserting a single point of view, however, Nakagami strove for multiple and simultaneous points of view. In *Chi no hate* Akiyuki muses about the alleyway, a place where "if you said something was one way it was; if you said it wasn't, it wasn't" (*NKZ* 6: 319). In the Akiyuki works, we stand inside the heartland of Japanese literature but we are outside, too.

Each work in the Akiyuki series stands alone, complete unto itself, a lifetime of writing pressed into seven years. Read together, however, the Akiyuki works constitute Nakagami's greatest fictional achievement in thoroughly sketching out the transformations in Akiyuki's psyche and the contours of his world, from the womb of the alleyway to the horizons of Magoichi's country. With their huge scope, their lyrical flights, and their mimetic obsessions, the Akiyuki works navigate between periphery and center, creating a unique vantage point—an empty field of grass, the old ring of a communal well, a lotus pond that dissolves into a dream. Through his story of Akiyuki, Nakagami also tells the reader: this is what fiction can do, and this is what fiction ultimately fails to do. Nakagami strode through the field of a national literature, giving testimony to the unique power and the figurative possibilities of "original" despair.

FOUR

Knowing Pleasures: Sennen no yuraku, *a Tale for Our Times*

In March 1978, Matsune Hisao, a shoe salesman and self-published haiku poet, took Nakagami Kenji into the neighborhood to meet an elderly woman named Tabata Ryū. Eighty-eight years old and ill in bed, Tabata Ryū (nicknamed Oryū no Oba, or "Old Lady Ryū") told Nakagami stories about the old neighborhood and about her deceased husband Reijo, a special *roji* priest.[1] Like others in her community, Oryū no Oba had never learned to read or write, but according to Matsune, she had a "mind like a computer," and she held the birth and death dates of everyone in the neighborhood in her head. Walking back from Tabata's house, Nakagami reported to Matsune that this "discovery" was worthy of the ethnologist Yanagita Kunio.[2]

In July 1980, Nakagami began to publish a series of tales about the alleyway that were later published in book form with the title *Sennen no yuraku* (A Thousand Years of Pleasure, 1982). The narrator of each tale is none other than the fictional character Oryū no Oba, an old midwife who is married to the alleyway priest. Oryū no Oba's "tales" consist of six stories about the Nakamoto clan, young men who were born with marks of extraordinary beauty, and who die young and violent deaths. Conceived at some distance from the realism of the early work, *Sennen no yuraku* lacks a stable male protagonist, an Akiyuki or a younger brother who contemplates but then resists the older brother's fate. The Nakamotos have no choice but to yield to the violence they face, and *Sennen no yuraku* intensifies the pattern of young male death: six faces, not one, are reflected in the mirror. In six stories, each with the same ending, Nakagami explores the relentless flow of special blood that dissolves names and histories in a pool of sameness and repetition.

Ironic as it may seem, Nakagami's "discovery" of Oryū no Oba reveals the distance that he had traveled from his Shingū roots. It was only from Tokyo that Nakagami could abstract and refine the fictional possibilities of the Kumano region.[3] The discovery of Oryū also solved a dilemma for Nakagami. By the late 1970s and early 1980s, Nakagami had reached a crossroads. Would he continue to chronicle life in the alleyway as he had done in the Akiyuki series, or would he use the alleyway to make something new? The creation of Oryū signaled that he had chosen the latter. In fact, *Sennen no yuraku* marked a new phase in Nakagami's writing life—his conscious and ambitious attempt to (re)create the *monogatari* (tale) form within his own fiction.

In this chapter we will consider Nakagami's experiments with the *monogatari*, first exploring the term itself, then examining the various uses to which the term was put, and finally putting one work to the test to examine what the *monogatari* form has contributed to modern Japanese literature. Strictly speaking, we can trace Nakagami's interest in local tales and legends back to the early short story collections of the 1970s. But his conception of the value of the *monogatari* as a distinct mode of representation dates to the late 1970s, particularly to his 1979 "Monogatari no keifu: danshō" (A Genealogy of the Tale: Fragments), the essay that was published in the volume *Kobayashi Hideo o koete* (Beyond Kobayashi Hideo). With a like-minded circle of young critics and writers, Nakagami re-evaluated modern Japanese literature, questioning deeply engrained habits of reading and analysis. Turning away from realism, he forged a vision of the Kumano region as a site of impenetrable darkness, strange marvels (*ryōi*), inversion, and difference. His ventures into the *monogatari* form would produce his most daring and experimental fiction to date.

Before we begin to explore the *monogatari*, however, a note of caution is due. In the work of the 1980s writers and critics, the word *monogatari* works like a catch-all term, its definition shifting according to context. Moreover, behind the rubric of the *monogatari*, we often catch a glimpse of the true target of the critics' ire—the *shōsetsu*, with its reliance on "personal" experience, its naïve assumption of selfhood, its humanist underpinnings, and its thoroughly middle-class sensibilities. Finally, certain discussions of *monogatari* in the 1980s sound a note of anxiety as if the central point were not literature but rather the chance to engage in thinly veiled ruminations on national identity. Who are we as Japanese nearing the end of the Shōwa era; and how do we reconcile our rich past with the rapidly changing world we live in?

Notes on the Monogatari

Nakagami and others gathered around the rubric of the *monogatari* in the 1970s and 1980s, which in its most universal form can be translated as "narrative," or a transmitted body of information. In the context of premodern Japanese literature, the term carries the specific meaning of "tale" (as in *Genji monogatari* or *Heike monogatari*), although Haruo Shirane points out that *monogatari* was used widely during the Heian period to connote "gibberish, idle talk or a work of prose fiction in the vernacular."[4] Using linguistic tools, the literary historian Konishi Jin'ichi gives a broad definition of *monogatari*, distinguishing it from other genres, such as the court diary (*nikki*). Konishi defines *monogatari* as: "a prose composition, that is concerned with events involving either fictional or historical characters. . . . The keynote of the *monogatari* is the past tense exemplified by the suffix *keri* with its connotations of transmitted recollection."[5] To Konishi, *keri* functions as a distancing marker, a means of setting a story back in time and place, similar to the fairytale opening "once upon a time." Furthermore, the use of *keri* suggests that the teller of the tale is not the inventor but the guardian of widely shared cultural stories and myths.

The concept of "transmitted recollection" removes the *monogatari* from the romantic domain of single authorship and gives it the patina of shared cultural memories. Not surprisingly, given this cultural context, many discussions about the *monogatari* focus on its relation to myth and the presence of mythic archetypes as the distinguishing characteristic of the genre. Norma Field argues that the tension between the mythic and the fictional brings the *monogatari* to life. In *The Splendor of Longing in the Tale of Genji*, Field analyzes the differing mechanisms of myth and fiction in the *Genji monogatari*, stating that the former works with a "logic of identity" while the latter turns on a "logic of resemblance." The "logic of identity" refers to an unchanging essence (i.e. a deity), impervious to change, while the logic of resemblance refers to the workings of the profane world. To illustrate the mythic mode, Field mentions the sanctity of blood ties along imperial lines (an unchanging element that belongs to the "logic of identity"). Ultimately, when the characters experience disappointment because the seemingly identical substitute does not fulfill the promise of the original, the logic of resemblance comes into play. Field elaborates:

> Now it is true that resemblance in the *Genji* is usually based on blood tie, which is purportedly natural and beyond human control and therefore a mythic element. Physical resemblance based on blood tie, however, is found not to guarantee moral similarity, let alone identity as Genji learns in the case of the Third Princess, a hoped-for Fujitsubo substitute. What the tale shows repeatedly is that the confusion, created by desire, of resemblance and identity, is a fertile one for fiction.[6]

Working along similar lines, Fujii Sadakazu also traces the strands of myth in fiction and fiction in myth. He writes that the "logic of resemblance" is not merely a relic but an active presence, "the sign of a stance the fictional narrative assumes toward myth."[7] In a 1985 discussion with Fujii Sadakazu entitled "Monogatari to wa nani ka?" (What is the *monogatari*?), Nakagami himself weighs in on the topic of myth, stating categorically that the *monogatari* must have a "mythic tail" (*shippo*) or it does not qualify for the genre.[8] He further states that the *monogatari* preserves its mythic kernel, but it derives its power from engaging in a ritual of "killing the gods," or forcing the myth into the bright light of day.[9] In sum, the word *monogatari* implies the continued survival of certain mythic tropes in fiction even as the text itself attempts to subject "myth" to the forces of what Nakagami terms "entropy," the process by which a thing moves from a state of order to one of increasing disorder.

The assertion of unchanging mythic strands within the Japanese *monogatari* raises the specter of cultural essentialism. But Fujii and Nakagami resist this strenuously, beginning with the notion of "god killing," and continuing with the origins that they assign to the *monogatari*, which springs into being not in the pristine and sanctified homeland but in contact with far away lands. Fujii suggests that to create new *monogatari* one needs to tap into some powerful destructive force (*hakairyoku*) that comes from outside.[10] The *Utsubo monogatari* (Tale of the Hollow Tree), a tale in which the hero travels to China and brings back two divine kotos to Japan, serves to illustrate Fujii's point. Karatani Kōjin, too, turns his gaze outward: he notes the influence of esoteric Buddhism and Chinese literature in the *monogatari* because it has the "power to construct."[11] Through their stress on foreign origins, critics depict the *monogatari* not as a vessel of pure Japanese culture but as a space in which tensions between the foreign and the local can be staged, dramatized, and resolved. Nakagami, too, in concert with Fujii, rejects the notion of a pristine Japanese cultural form; he states openly that the best *monogatari* are filled with rough edges:

Everyone holds up the *Genji monogatari* as a model of the form but I'm not happy with that. The *monogatari* must be more dynamic, it has to move. And it can't just be beautiful; it must be a text in which past, present and future is possible, in which every variation is possible. To me, the *Utsubo monogatari* has these qualities, not the *Genji*. It's a *monogatari* with an anti-*monogatari* built in.[12]

In his usual manner, Nakagami expresses his antagonism to high culture, arguing for a rough-edged fiction that contains the seeds of its own undoing. He further links the dynamism of the *monogatari* to the issue of oral recitation. While not confusing the *monogatari* with purely oral literature, he believes that the early *monogatari* must have been recited out loud and that the dynamism of the form depended to a large degree on the presence of the human voice: "I wonder what form the original *monogatari* took. In the age of myth, how would the human voice have functioned, I mean the actual physical voice? It's a big question. . . ."[13] Nakagami has a specific vision of *monogatari* in mind: not the high classical products of the Heian Court but *monogatari* in which the seams are visible—filled with rough mythic archetypes and intrusions of the foreign and the strange.

Given the breadth and complexity of classical *monogatari* criticism, it seems questionable to argue for the existence of true *monogatari* form in the modern period. But we might be able to use the term if we can locate loosely related techniques in the modern *shōsetsu* that mimic "*monogatari* style." Modern writers do not use a strict equivalent of *keri* but they do find other ways to distance narratives in time and space. Certain rhetorical mechanisms disrupt the illusion of a continuous narrative voice and suggest transmitted recollection. Noriko Mizuta Lippit, for example, explores the concept of "twice-told" tales, narratives that make direct or indirect reference to stories that have come before.[14] In Enchi Fumiko's "Nise no en shūi" (Love in Two Lives: The Remnant, 1958), a young woman copies down a modern translation of an Ueda Akinari tale entitled "Nise no en" (The Destiny That Spanned Two Lifetimes, c. 1802), for her dying professor. A satirical account of a priest named Jōsuke who is reborn as a common peasant in order to enjoy the love of a woman, the story sparks connections in the young woman's own life. Ruminating on the power of stories to influence reality, she asks, "Is it because Akinari based the tale on some existing ancient story that he let Jōsuke fulfill his obsessive desire to love a woman, even letting him be born as a dull countryman to do so?"[15] After a fantastic encounter with a man in a bamboo grove, who is partly Jōsuke, partly her dead husband, and partly the dying professor, the young woman receives her answer: the story does shape events in the world. Through the use of transmitted recollections, "twice-told" tales such as "Nise no en shūi" chafe against the constraints of straight realism, bend narrative time, and ruminate on the powers of storytelling. We see literature in the act of contemplating itself.

In addition to their use of common rhetorical devices, modern *monogatari* also contain certain overlapping thematic preoccupations. Like the *monogatari* of the Heian period, they revel in disruptions of the supernatural—in strange transformations and uncanny occurrences that suddenly alter the plane of everyday life. Nakagami uses the term *ryōi,* or strange marvels, to account for this side of *monogatari* writing. Karatani Kōjin, on the other hand, accounts for such predilections through an analysis of historical conditions. To Karatani, the modern *monogatari* was an "excluded space" in the early modern period; it fought an uphill battle, becoming visible only in the process of being relegated to the margins. In Karatani's own words: "Let me state that what Tanizaki called plot can be equated with the Japanese word *monogatari,* and *monogatari* can be seen as a space that was excluded, becoming visible in the process of being excluded, by what was established as a system in the third decade of Meiji and by the homogeneous space of one-point perspective."[16]

Karatani uses a visual metaphor to suggest that *monogatari,* in contrast to *shōsetsu,* represents multiple, even fluctuating, points of view. We see a desire for heterogeneity and for the recognition of previously ignored spaces. Behind the spatial metaphor of the *monogatari,* however, the target of Karatani's ire comes into view: the ideologically driven creation of a modern system with its "homogeneous space of one-point perspective." As in the works of other critics, the term *monogatari* shows endless flexibility, fitting various definitions from mythic storehouse, to self-reflexive tale, to rough and dynamic narrative. We now turn to Nakagami's own vision of the *monogatari* genre to explore what he himself found in the concept, first in his critical thinking, and then in the stories that he set down on the page.

Nakagami on the Monogatari*: How to Read a Tradition*

In 1979, Nakagami Kenji published "Monogatari no keifu: danshō." The most compelling statement of his literary credo, "Monogatari no keifu" comments on the links between discrimination, aesthetics, and literature in both ancient and modern Japan. Like others before him, Nakagami employs the concept of the *monogatari* to critique the flaws in the edifice of modern Japanese literature. In general, Nakagami views the *monogatari* as a product of an oppressive and powerful cultural system to which he assigns the name *hō/seido* (law or system).[17] More specifically, the *hō/seido* consists of a narrow set of verbal and visual associations that suppresses all expressions of heterodoxy. As Ken Ito has pointed out, the term *hō/seido* might better be translated as "code" rather than "law/system" because it serves as the basic grammar of meaning in a culture—much like a musical theme.[18] Nakagami reads the presence of the *hō/seido* everywhere: in the image of the masochist bending down before a woman's beautiful foot; in the tendency to automatically read the word "flower" (*hana*) as cherry blossom; and even in a sign for "strawberries" (*ichigo*) in *hiragana* outside his door which, oddly enough, reminds Nakagami of the arrogant claims of a unique Japanese language and culture.

"Monogatari no keifu" soon turns to a discussion of specific writers whom Nakagami links to the modern *monogatari*: Tanizaki Jun'ichirō, Ueda Akinari, Origuchi Shinobu, and Enchi Fumiko. Overall, Nakagami's hatred for *shōsetsu* writers surpasses his scorn for *monogatari* writers, but all writers come under his harsh scrutiny. One thing saves the *monogatari* writers from a vitriolic dismissal; they at least acknowledge the existence of the "code," rather than try to bury their heads in the sand. In a discussion of Tanizaki Jun'ichirō, Nakagami explains: "Tanizaki is the writer who embodies the *monogatari* form, my declared enemy, and Tanizaki makes the perfect target for attack because, whether consciously or not, he avoided the poisons of humanism [*ningenshugi*] and the *belles lettres* [*bungakushugi*] that reside within the parameters of modern Japanese literature."[19] Unlike writers who believed in the possibility of human reform, Tanizaki inadvertently at least made a more perceptive choice.

Both in his discussion of a law or system that permeates all forms and in his lack of a clear definition of the *monogatari*, Nakagami periodically slips into the role of ideologue in his "Monogatari no keifu." Yet the rough edges of this work can be smoothed if we place the essay in its original context: between the covers of the book stamped with the title *Kobayashi Hideo o koete*. Indeed, Nakagami's essay might best be read in tandem with Kobayashi's famous 1935 essay, "Watakushi shōsetsu ron" (Discourse on Fiction of the Self), which discusses the preponderance of personal fiction in Japan.[20] Beginning with the titles of the two works, Kobayashi explores the dynamics of semi-autobiographical fiction (*shishōsetsu*), while Nakagami focuses on the legacy of the *monogatari*. But both authors energetically critique the realism and the personalism of modern Japanese fiction.

Kobayashi Hideo's essay measures modern Japanese fiction against nineteenth and twentieth-century European models, in particular André Gide and Guy de Maupassant, and concludes that the Japanese did not succeed in creating fiction with the same ideological breadth as that of European writers. Kobayashi ascribes this failure to two conditions. First, a native tradition, "like too many old and outmoded kinds of cultural fertilizer," survived the advent of modernism and blocked the absorption of new ideas.[21] This ingrained tradition favored writing based on personal experience, producing texts that had little ideological content. Second, Japanese writers were not able to write in the style of European naturalism because the ideological conditions that produced such writing in the West were absent in Japan. In the end, Japanese writers simply mined Western works for style. Kobayashi explains the mechanism by which the personal dominates: "Our I-novelists felt not the least anxiety about believing in the self and in personal life because the world of the self, without mediation, assumed for them the shape of society. And so the *watakushi shōsetsu* turned decadent on a subtle mixture of the dregs of the feudal self and society."[22]

In "Monogatari no keifu," Nakagami addresses Kobayashi's ideas in a discussion of Japanese writers who cling to personal experience. In contrast to Kobayashi, who views Japanese fiction in the mirror of the West, however, Nakagami severely critiques Japanese writers for their blindness to conditions within Japan itself—in particular to the oppressive presence of the *hō/seido* that permeates all cultural forms. In particular, Nakagami openly expresses his hatred for the *shōsetsu*, a vessel of watered-down humanism that cannot confront the harsh realities of a discriminatory and elitist cultural system. Typical of its failures, according to Nakagami, is *Hakai* (Broken Commandment), Shimazaki Tōson's 1906 work, an early modern treatment of the *burakumin*. Rather than praise Tōson for his bravery in broaching a taboo subject, Nakagami seizes on the scene in which an outcaste teacher named Ushimatsu confesses to his students that he has hidden the truth of his background. Nakagami asks:

> Why does *Hakai* have to end with the confession about being an *eta* [outcaste]? Unlike scholars and critics, I believe that Ushimatsu Segawa's confession is simply a sign of Tōson's weakness, and considering that the *eta* is a product of the *hō/seido* and that discrimination against Segawa is equivalent to a *monogatari*, then Tōson has plunged the issue of the *hō/seido* and the *monogatari* into humanism and *belles lettres*. . . .[23]

Nakagami lambastes Tōson for his naïve illusion that Ushimatsu could be saved by appealing to those around him. In fact, Tōson provides a fantastic ending to Ushimatsu's story:

Ushimatsu leaves Japan to work on a Texas cattle ranch. In his condemnation of this type of humanist realism, Nakagami, like Kobayashi, suggests that modern Japanese literature lacks vigor and conviction because it is blind to conditions on its own soil. In this, he sounds a call to writers to return to literary roots, albeit ones that originate far from the center.

Nakagami next tackles words themselves in a response to Kobayashi's ideas on language. In his "Watakushi shōsetsu ron," Kobayashi states that a written tradition continued to exert its influences long after the advent of the modern period. Kobayashi refuses to judge, stating, "the issue is not one of tradition being good or bad. I would like to say that it wholly exceeds our ability as writers to analyze the power that these traditions actually exert on us."[24] In spite of this disclaimer, he then goes on to suggest the power of tradition at the level of individual words, concluding that words only become moving and powerful because they have built up connotations over time: "A neologism, no matter how clever its invention, will not possess the fascination of a word that has endured, stained with the sweat and blood of generations."[25]

Never one to accept a declarative statement at face value, Nakagami rises to the bait in "Monogatari no keifu," attacking Kobayashi's claim that the writer cannot determine the hold of tradition. On every page, Nakagami attempts to prove Kobayashi wrong by analyzing his own ambivalent relationship to Japanese tradition. Rather than accept the notion that words stained with sweat and blood are more compelling because they are grounded in tradition, Nakagami states that we must be aware of and openly resist the suggestive power of words. Even the lovely image of the cherry blossom, Nakagami states, is the product of a mechanism that ranks objects according to their weight in a prescribed tradition—to the degree to which they are stained with sweat and blood. Such words, with their tissue thin layers of connotations, merely trap the writer, strengthening the hold of the *hō/seido* and silencing other forms of speech.

Tanizaki's Birds: Working with the "Code"

In "Monogatari no keifu," Nakagami expresses particular ire for Tanizaki Jun'ichirō, as we have seen. Tanizaki's mid-career works, such as *Yoshino kuzu* (Kuzu in Yoshino, 1931) and *Shunkinshō* (A Portrait of Shunkin, 1933), respectively represent the flowering of the "code." Nakagami pays particular attention to *Shunkinshō,* a story that will have important implications for his *monogatari* writing. *Shunkinshō* tells the story of a young servant, Sasuke, who devotes his life to a cruel but possessive mistress who transforms him into a virtuoso on the *shamisen.* Sasuke begins to serve the blind Shunkin as a teenager accompanying her to her music lessons and even washing her hands in the lavatory; later the two become clandestine lovers, but Shunkin refuses to marry Sasuke even when she becomes pregnant with his child. When Shunkin is 36 years old, a tragedy befalls the couple: a mysterious interloper disfigures her beautiful face with boiling water. In response to the attack, Sasuke puts out his own eyes, rather than mar his vision of Shunkin's ideal beauty and humiliate the woman he loves. Appreciating the depth of Sasuke's sacrifice, Shunkin surrenders to Sasuke in a moment of gratitude and the two live happily together in their dark world depending on no one but a young servant.

In Tanizaki's preoccupation with what Ken Ito calls "world-building," his refusal to bend to the dictates of realism and his insistence on the primacy of masochistic pleasures, Nakagami sees pure *monogatari* form.[26] At the same time, Nakagami expresses admiration for his wayward literary father. Tanizaki at least "bumped up" against the system, revealing its powers through masochism and fetishism. And even though masochism may be an expression of devotion to the system, Nakagami also sees moments of playful subversion. By "readjusting" certain objects, Nakagami writes, "Tanizaki throws his true intentions towards the *hō/seido* into high relief."[27] As an illustration of Tanizaki's craftsmanship at manipulating the "code" of the system, Nakagami seizes on the name that

Shunkin gives to one of her bush warblers—Tenko. The bush warbler is a stock poetic marker from classical poetry, linked with the coming of spring, the scent of plum blossoms, and the awakening of sexual desire. Added to this poetic existence is the name Tenko, "drum from heaven," which refers to a *nō* play of the same name. The play tells the story of a young boy, a commoner, who receives a magical drum from heaven on which he plays beautifully. When word of the drum spreads, it is taken from the boy and given to the emperor whereupon it falls mute. The name Tenko summons up the transforming power of poetry and music and the ability to create art no matter how low one's social status.[28]

In "Monogatari no keifu," Nakagami notes the ways in which the tiny body of Tenko is made to carry the heavy weight of the traditional aesthetic of art that is born of blindness. Shunkin values Tenko above all else, spoiling the bird while bankrupting the household and letting the servants go hungry. Sasuke, too, worships Tenko, but only after Shunkin's death when the bird's voice replaces Shunkin herself. Listening to the bird sing, Sasuke relives his blissful union with his lover in the shadows. To keep his memories alive, Sasuke weeps, burns incense before Shunkin's memorial tablet, and sings his dead lover's masterpiece, "A Bush Warbler in Spring." To Sasuke, who has spent his life defying reality in favor of the world of the imagination, the bird's voice becomes simply another instrument of obfuscation.

Beneath Tanizaki's evocation of a perfect realm of art, however, Nakagami discovers a clever inversion. Tenko is first mentioned in the context of Shunkin's complicated toilette; she uses the bird's droppings to soften her skin. By linking bird droppings to the trained voice of a bush warbler to the name Tenko, Tanizaki folds scatology into the divine. Nakagami argues that through this inversion, Tanizaki further explores the dimensions of the *hō/seido*:

In truth, the name Tenko ["Drum from Heaven"] floats blindly beneath the *hō/seido* and has the power to give readers of *Shunkinshō* a sense of relief. Even if they don't recognize the *nō* play, the connotations of an unfamiliar realm—heaven—generalize the appeal of this *shōsetsu* which thoroughly exposes the power of the *hō/seido.* This is, of course, Tanizaki's intention. To get right to the point, the *hō/seido* replaces the humanism and the *belles lettres* that Tanizaki himself rejected. And what sustains Tanizaki in his worship of the system is his childish dependence on and his flirtation with what could be called a rough form of religion.[29]

When Nakagami envisions the *hō/seido,* he sees Tanizaki in a posture of supplication, a child still dependent on its mother, a telling interpretation of one writer's view of the powers of narrative. Not content to merely theorize about Tanizaki, however, Nakagami takes more direct action in his own fiction writing. One year later, Nakagami puts his own critical theories to the test, incorporating the name Tenko into his fiction but with a significant departure from Tanizaki's subtle inversions.

The name Tenko appears in *Sennen no yuraku,* given to a bush warbler with a beautiful singing voice, in the aptly titled first chapter, "Hanzō no tori" (Hanzō's Bird). The bird belongs to Hanzō, a beautiful young man of the Nakamoto clan. An outcaste laborer with a wife and a child, Hanzō meets a young widow who lives outside the alleyway and becomes her lover. As a token of her favor, she gives him a bush warbler, a present from another lover, a man of low social status (but not of the outcaste class) who trained the bird to sing. At the opening of "Hanzō no tori," Oryū no Oba imagines the bird's voice:

Every time she heard the voices of the little golden birds coming to sip the nectar of the *natsubuyō* flowers that last for a single night, beginning to bloom in the evening and withering in the bright sun, Oryū wanted to ask if they were lamenting the night that vanishes like a phantom or celebrating the bright light of day. The voices of the little golden birds echoed in her ears like the voice of Tenko, the famous bush warbler kept by Hanzō. Every summer, Hanzō would let the bird that he tended so carefully out in the bracken on the far side of the hill so that old Oryū, confined to her bed, though nothing was particularly wrong with her, could hear the bird sing. (*NKZ* 5: 11)

In this rhythmical opening passage, with its recited patina and its fairytale elements (the invented flower that lasts for a single night), Nakagami pays homage to Tanizaki. Hanzō prizes the bush warbler above all else and brings it to Oryū periodically to cheer her with its beautiful voice. As in the *nō* play and *Shunkinshō,* Tenko offers Hanzō the gift of sound, of inventing his own stories and momentarily transcending his outcaste origins. The bird (and his desire for it) leads him out of the alleyway and into the arms of the widow of Ukijima. In addition, Hanzō trains the woman to "sing like Tenko" during a sexual climax. For a brief moment, Hanzō's horizons have widened.

Yet soon the parallels between the two Tenkos end. Having established Tenko as a precious object in *Sennen no yuraku,* Nakagami suddenly diverges sharply from Tanizaki's model and brings his tale to a disturbing close. Perhaps the greatest difference between the two works is the position of their central male characters. In *Shunkinshō,* Sasuke functions as both a character and an assistant to the narrator who fills in the gaps of Shunkin's story. This leads to Sasuke further objectifying his beloved as he manipulates the details of the story. But Hanzō has no control over the story in *Sennen no yuraku,* which unfolds in the mind of Oryū no Oba. In her loving descriptions of Hanzō's beauty and her ceaseless worries about whether he can survive another day in this world, Oryū no Oba makes Hanzō into an object and puts him in the position of Tenko, a highly valued commodity.

The conflation of Hanzō and the bush warbler is illustrated by a *menage à trois* between Hanzō, the widow, and the bird trainer. Unlike the veiled encounters between Shunkin and Sasuke, this scene is portrayed in graphic detail. After a friend is injured in the mountains, Hanzō comes to borrow money from the widow and meets the widow's other lover: the bird trainer who is humiliated to learn that Hanzō is now in possession of Tenko. In response, Hanzō taunts the man saying, "So you're the one who trained the bird to sing so beautifully" (*NKZ* 5: 26). The man's shame makes Hanzō want to punish him further. In the middle of a threesome, Hanzō and the widow bind the bird trainer's hands, and Hanzō nearly penetrates him from behind, reveling in the man's fear and his passivity.

When Hanzō awakes the next morning, however, his feeling of power is shattered. The bird trainer suggests that they return home together but Hanzō informs him that he will take the opposite route that leads back to the outcaste quarters of the alleyway. Abruptly, the man's attitude changes:

"I came here to borrow money for a friend who got hurt on the mountain," Hanzō told the man. Anxiously the man asked Hanzō if he could wait for him so they could go back together. But Hanzō explained that he was going round the pleasure quarters of Ukijima, up the hill and down into the alleyway. At this the man looked shocked and mumbled, "So you're from Nagayama," calling the outcaste area by another name, which he kept repeating to himself as if he couldn't believe that Hanzō came from that crowd of cattle skinners, *geta* menders, and basket weavers, and then suddenly as if he himself had shot up in status he remarked, "You're a good-looking guy." Hanzō shrugged off the comment with a "Thanks a lot," adding sarcastically that he would service him again sometime, but now he regretted not having taken the man from behind. It didn't matter if he played with women and they played with him, but he wasn't going to stand for a stranger from another place sleeping with him for his looks as if he were some gigolo. Hanzō spat. He hated being seen as a pretty-boy who had sold his body for a friend from his beloved alleyway, and spitting again, he started towards home up the steep path. It was about this time that a deep scar appeared on Hanzō's right cheek. He told everyone that he had gotten it when he fell on a knife in the mountains but Oryū thought that Hanzō had cut himself in anger at his own masculine beauty. (*NKZ* 5: 28)

At the moment when Hanzō reveals his alleyway origins, he is forced to recast the events of the previous evening. No longer can he view himself as the victor; the mark of outcaste status outweighs any event in the narrative, allowing even the lowly bird trainer to condescend. Hanzō suddenly recognizes himself as another exotic object of desire, a pretty-boy who had "sold his body for a friend from his beloved alleyway." His flippant comment to the man about his ability to train a beautiful voice now reflects back upon himself; Hanzō has taken the position of Tenko in the narrative.

In *Shunkinshō,* Tenko offers Sasuke a means to summon up the shadowy image of his adored Shunkin; in *Sennen no yuraku,* however, Tenko reveals to Hanzō that it is Hanzō, not the widow, who sings on demand. Tenko reflects the mechanisms of the *hō/seido*: it mediates between high and low (its beautiful voice was created by a man of low social status), and at the same time, it is equally instructive of the ways in which symbolic categories inevitably reassert themselves.

In fiction, Nakagami has brought the concept of the *hō/seido* to life. But he has clearly set an enormous challenge for himself. Returning briefly to "Monogatari no keifu," Nakagami criticizes Tanizaki for his reverent attitude and his fascination with a shadowy realm of aesthetics, but he also recognizes the power of the code in his own fiction. Gradually, in the course of his critique of Tanizaki, Nakagami begins to talk about himself:

> What characterizes those writers who rejected humanism and *belles lettres* was the recognition—whether conscious or unconscious—that they were enfolded in the arms of religion or the *hō/seido.* Of course, Tanizaki didn't discover this, it had already been discovered and thumbed through like an old book. To put it another way, this fact has been clear to our forbearers since the time of *Genji monogatari,* the first perfect flowering of the *hō/seido* that informs everything that is written in Japanese. The word "flower" always refers to the cherry blossom; the word "fish" means carp. From the viewpoint of modern popular culture it's absurd, but there is nothing "Japanese" that is not religious (Buddhist, Shinto, animist). The *hō/seido* enfolds religion. Tanizaki wasn't the only one who read the footprint of the Buddha in his beloved's feet; it's an automatic mechanism of the *hō/seido* that enfolds him. . . .
>
> Having written this much, I feel lost myself when I think of knocking Tanizaki down. The words "knock down" will extend to myself, a young writer of the *hō/seido.* When I call Tanizaki "pig" of the *monogatari,* I am calling myself "pig," too. The only way to differentiate me from Tanizaki, the bureaucrat of the system, is whether we feel pleased or disgusted by the cloying love of the *hō/seido.*[30]

Writing in a corner, Nakagami can neither fall back on the solutions of "humanism" nor can he simply reproduce the *hō/seido* in reverent fashion. It is fascinating to note that Nakagami began to publish portions of *Sennen no yuraku* in 1980, as if in reply to the concerns that he had raised so forcefully in the essay that was published in the previous year. Was *Sennen no yuraku* to be the fictional solution to the problem of an overbearing "code," a cultural system whose exclusivity and arrogance could be traced back to *Genji monogatari*? And if so, what would Nakagami discover in writing it? What form would his antidote to Tanizaki's realm of shadows take?

Nakagami Challenges the Hō/seido

At first, *Sennen no yuraku* promises overt transgression, each Nakamoto seeming more rebellious and violent than the last. Hanzō, the first Nakamoto, sleeps with every woman in the alleyway, even the woman who raised him as a foster child, and dies in a knife fight with a jealous husband. Miyoshi, the thief, seduces a woman and then murders her husband in a staged robbery attempt. Fumihiko, a visionary, steals a female shaman from the mountains and experiences mystical bliss through erotic practices. Oriental Yasu, the most violent Nakamoto, leaves the alleyway to start a colony in Latin America, after fleeing from the scene of his various crimes. Shin'ichirō, another thief, rapes one of his victims, and Tatsuo, the last Nakamoto, tries to escape the confines of the alleyway by fleeing to an Ainu ghetto in the north and exchanging identities with a young Ainu man. No matter what they do or how far they travel, however, the Nakamoto men die suddenly before they reach the age of 30.

The Nakamotos commit murder and rape on their way to spectacular ends, but Nakagami does not flesh out psychological portraits. Rather, the narrator Oryū no Oba portrays the Nakamotos as divine beings who are destined to grace this earth for only a short time. Miyoshi, the protagonist of the second chapter, "Rokudō no tsuji" (The Crossroads of the Six Realms), flees to the house of Oryū no Oba after committing murder. She washes his clothing and gives him shelter for the night. Later Miyoshi begins to suffer from night blindness; when he can no longer see well enough to work in the mountains he seeks out Oryū no Oba again, telling her that he would rather die than live a restricted life. Oryū's perspective on Miyoshi's guilt is made clear:

> Oryū no Oba understood Miyoshi only too well. If life that bubbles up ceaselessly like spawning larvae is blessed, so too is the life of the cicada that sings out its heart and dies. The baby who cries itself out and dies is innocent no matter what the circumstances of its birth, and Miyoshi was innocent, too, simply because he did not perceive that murder was a sin. . . . (*NKZ* 5: 61–62)

As with all the Nakamotos, Oryū no Oba believes that Miyoshi's blindness is not a punishment for misdeeds in this life but the end of a long chain of events set in motion by Miyoshi's ancestors; it is the coming to term of a curse in his Nakamoto blood. By removing guilt from Miyoshi, Nakagami signals his lack of interest in a realistic exploration of criminal motivations. The trajectory of "crime and punishment" cannot be traced in this world; rather, transgression takes on an abstract shape, and we cannot determine its causes in this world nor guess its results in the next. Further, rather than seeking to protect the Nakamotos, Oryū no Oba anticipates their demise. Or, as Mark Morris comments, Oryū no Oba oversees "the wreckage of the young male lives of the *roji*."[31] Her most lurid thoughts are reserved for Hanzō, whose imagined demise sparks sadistic delight: "Wouldn't he stir up some wild creature that would toy with him like a mouse, rip open his belly and pluck out his innards? The creature would chew him up so badly that it would be impossible to identify Hanzō's hair caressed by the wind, his lips that women had kissed, and even his arms. Oryū imagined terrible things" (*NKZ* 5: 23). In a similar fashion, Oryū watches Miyoshi standing outside the billiard hall, resplendent in a white suit, and compares him to candy that melts on a hot day. Rather than resist like defiant heroes, the Nakamotos barely have the vigor to survive as long as they do.

The passive nature of the Nakamotos suggests that the inexorable pattern of what Oryū no Oba calls "fate" (*inga*) will never be broken. Before birth and after death, the Nakamotos return to the point of origin, to the bloodline that creates and destroys them. As they approach death, they begin to shed the marks that distinguish one from another and return to what unites them—"the blood of the Nakamotos, tainted because it is so pure (*kiyoraka dakara koso yodonde iru Nakamoto no chi*)" (*NKZ* 5: 72) When Miyoshi dies, for example, Oryū no Oba sees a dragon flying up to heaven and she takes this as a sign that "one not of this world who was born with Nakamoto blood had died young and gone back to heaven. . . ." (*NKZ* 5: 62). The blood not only foretells the Nakamotos' early deaths, it is the single determining factor that shapes their personalities in this world. As Oryū no Oba muses, "The blood passed from one person to the next in a wave, cruelty and kindness flowing within. . . ." (*NKZ* 5: 71). Because it washes out differences and reduces six men to one, the Nakamoto blood belongs to the realm of myth, working on the principle of what Norma Field calls the "logic of identity."

In addition to the pure but tainted blood, Nakagami draws on another mythic archetype in *Sennen no yuraku*, the myth of the noble exile (*kishu ryūritan*). A young prince or divine being is forced into exile, undergoes a period of hardship, and finally regains his proper position in the world. The exile of Prince Genji in *Genji monogatari* conforms to this mythic pattern, as does Genji's eventual triumphant return to the city.[32] In an attempt to penetrate the secret of the Nakamotos, Oryū no Oba reads the *kishu ryūritan* pattern in their faces, imagining that they are descendents of the defeated Heike nobles who fled over the mountains to escape persecution, or noble wanderers who ceased their travels when they reached the alleyway and now devote their days to the pursuit of pleasure:

> As some in the alleyway claimed, the Nakamotos might have the blood of the warriors who'd been defeated at the hands of the Genji clan at Yashima with the aid of the Tankakuhime faction, founders of the castle that lay just a stone's throw away.
>
> Even in the alleyway, the Nakamotos didn't know how to break a sweat to make a living, they followed the dictates of the stagnant blood of those who had once settled in the alleyway and spent their days in music and dancing. As if nobody in the world needed to eat to live, they refused to put their backs into the task at hand, they'd

get fed up in the middle, and even if it meant going hungry, they'd wander off, play around, drink, and envelope themselves in the scent of a woman's powder. (*NKZ* 5: 42)

By making the Nakamotos into noble exiles and placing them at the top of an imaginary hierarchy, Nakagami not only practices what Barbara Babcock calls "symbolic inversion," turning accepted codes upside down, but he also ascribes noble, even divine, origins to all *burakumin*.[33] Through references to the *kishu ryūritan* pattern, Nakagami implicitly equates them with the emperor of Japan, another figure whose origins lie shrouded in the mists of time. In doing so, Nakagami also courts danger. By ascribing mythic and possibly divine origins to outcaste and emperor, he runs the risk of minimizing the unique and painful history of oppression suffered by the people of the alleyway. If, as Nakagami himself suggested, the emperor and the *burakumin* are two sides of the same coin (*ura* and *omote*), Nakagami seemingly engages in the same antics as did Tanizaki Jun'ichirō, falling into a posture of submission before the *hō/seido*.[34] Before we address the perils of the "logic of identity" in *monogatari* fiction, however, we will take one step back and briefly examine the reception of *Sennen no yuraku* in the years surrounding its publication.

The problem of static myths in Nakagami's work concerned a number of critics who wrote about the *monogatari* in the 1980s. To those who viewed Nakagami as a subversive figure who worked to undo the *monogatari* from the inside, certain repetitive patterns (the six deaths of the Nakamotos, for example) were an obstacle to overcome. Suga Hidemi, for example, noted that the *monogatari* genre tends to erect dualistic and rigid symbolic categories such as sacred/profane, high/low, male/female. He warned against tracing a *kishu ryūritan* archetype in Nakagami's work back to ancient *monogatari* (such as the *Taketori monogatari*) because this would ensure the defeat of the reader at the hands of a repetitive, mythic pattern. But when Suga first read *Sennen no yuraku*, he saw this pattern in evidence—the dualistic paradigms of beauty/deformity, sacred/profane, human/animal that binds the Nakamotos, eventually driving them to their early deaths. In the final chapter of *Sennen no yuraku,* however, Suga finds a means to transcend dualism. He notes that Tatsuo, the last Nakamoto, shows no fear of impurity, even declaring himself to be an animal. Furthermore, Tatsuo runs off and creates a double for himself, a young Ainu youth who later answers to Tatsuo's name. In his precocious behavior, Tatsuo begins to perform the same role as Oryū no Oba, who embraces the multiplicity of all things in the universe; by doing so, he finally breaks through a dualistic framework. Suga writes: "As Tatsuo merges with the young Ainu youth and then unites even with Oryū no Oba, he affirms both even and odd numbers, showing that he has thrown off the limitations of the self and become like Oryū no Oba herself—an endless infinite cycle of the seasons. . . ."[35]

In this analysis Suga skips over the deaths of the other five characters which are predicated on the explosive combination of pure but tainted blood (as well as Tatsuo's own death). Suga holds up *Sennen no yuraku* as an exceptional *monogatari* that can take itself apart from the inside out. Interestingly, his praise is linked to a rejection of the self; it is the "throwing off of the self" that dissolves dualism. Suga's work reveals the bent of the *monogatari* critic: the *monogatari* may be the stated focus of their work, but an implicit criticism of subject-oriented fictions (such as the *shishōsetsu*), in which the personal assumes the shape of the world, runs like a deep current through their work.[36]

In his book-length study of Nakagami, *Kishu to tensei,* Yomota Inuhiko also tackles the problem of repetition directly in a discussion of the *monogatari*. Like Nakagami and Fujii, he relates the *monogatari* to myth; in ancient times, repetition simply afforded a return to a primordial golden moment. Now modern people have rejected these repetitive rhythms "because no one needs the circular return of the epiphany of the *monogatari*."[37] Relegated to the fringes, the *monogatari* has become a twisted, perverse form. When Yomota turns to Nakagami's fiction, he poses the problem of how to avoid the sterility of repetition. One strategy is to "overturn the *monogatari* completely by allowing it to fall into a suspended state and create a space (*kūkan*) that is free from movement." This results in what Yomota calls the "felicitious circular pattern of *Sennen no yuraku* that moves in a space out of time."[38]

Yomota rightly describes a static space of the *monogatari* in his analysis; yet he, like other critics, searches for a path leading out of the maze. He locates an exit in the chapter entitled "Tennin gosui" (Decay of the Angel), which tells the story of Oriental Yasu, the utopian adventurer who goes to Latin America to start a new colony for the *burakumin*. Although Oriental Yasu does not succeed, Yomota discovers in his utopian fever the strength and the source of new tales. Rather than fall immediately into death, Oriental Yasu has the ability to move from here to there, to make the alleyway a ubiquitous space by transplanting it to Latin America, even as the alleyway of Shingū is entering into its final phase of decline. Yomota thus seizes on the one exception to the rule, allowing us to forget the tightly circumscribed orbits of the other five characters of the book.

The work of these critics illustrates the inherent difficulties encountered in reading Nakagami. Any critic needs a sense of movement, a reason for reading, and it is disturbing to realize that *Sennen no yuraku* may render one silent. But rather than search for an exit, we might begin our analysis by staying within the tightly circumscribed orbit of the Nakamoto stories, viewing their world from the inside out. We might ask why Nakagami Kenji worked so hard to master the "logic of identity" in the early 1980s, and what he expected to gain from his steadfast refusal to move.

The Pleasures of Defeat

Rather than negate the circle, Nakagami revels in the pattern, even teasing the reader by filling his stories with momentary spatial transformations, brief bursts of light and air made dramatic by their eventual eclipse. Two examples that involve Latin America reveal Nakagami's *modus operandi*. The first occurs before Oriental Yasu's departure for Latin America in "Tennin gosui," when he plays a record of tango music, briefly transforming the alleyway into the streets of Buenos Aires:

> When Oriental Yasu played the tango on his record player, he felt his blood heat up, and sliding open the paper door, he saw his familiar alleyway—with its piss-stained walls and thatched roofs (because people couldn't afford tile)—begin to look like the streets of Buenos Aires. He didn't remember when he had seen it but once he had slipped past a dog chewing on a cow bone that had rolled into the street, and he felt like he was heading for the mountains of Buenos Aires to dig for gold. Oriental Yasu soon caught the sound of children's voices outside, and opening the door, he saw not Buenos Aires but the alleyway where the children had attached a string to a clean cow skull and were dragging it around. Placing the skull by a wild rose tree, they made a trap out of thick straw rope and then hid in the shadows, trying to catch a dog that was running wild through the alleyway.
>
> But the crazy dog wasn't wild after all, it was a pet dog without a bell around its neck or a collar, so it made a good playmate for the children, running after the skull, putting a leg in the trap, and barking loudly. Stopping the record, Oriental Yasu left the little house heading for the dance hall at the bottom of Shiroyama, and he laughed because he knew Toraji's wife was watching him as he passed through the shadows behind the houses. Suddenly a memory returned to him of the women energetically washing something by the communal well at the entrance to the alleyway and he'd felt a wave of nausea when he heard that the white squishy stuff was fat and the rest was cow guts. (*NKZ* 5: 112–13)

In the beginning of the passage, the magic of transformation is at work. The music of the tango transports Oriental Yasu to Latin America, and the dingy contours of the alleyway melt into the imagined utopia. Yet suddenly the children's voices break into Oriental Yasu's reverie and his vision fades: he is not in Buenos Aires after all but in the alleyway. The sound of the children's voices sparks a memory of Oriental Yasu's own childhood. This physical sensation, which originates in his own body, tethers him to the alleyway much like the domestic dog that plays at being wild. Ironically, the brief transformation of the alleyway underscores its central role in the formation of Oriental Yasu himself. In the end, we hear nothing but speculative rumors about Yasu in Latin America; he dies "offscreen," as it were, his dreams of a utopia forgotten.

A second example concerns Shin'ichirō, the fifth Nakamoto, who also goes to Latin America in search of a new life. At first, it looks as if Shin'ichirō has been transformed in the course of his travels, his notions of the world changing dramatically:

> It was a country of opposites in every way. Thinking of opposites, for Oryū no Oba, there was the priest Reijo, and for Shin'ichirō, there was his sister prostitute. In truth, if you think about heaven and earth, life and death, up and down, right and left from the opposite point of view, then what's right here is left over there, what's up here is down there, and if you consider that the earth is round, there's no reason to believe in "up" or "down" at all. It was a country of transformation where one perverse person could call "day" "night" and "night" "day," and then spread confusion by muttering in the pitch black, "is it day because night is day, or is it day because day is night?" (*NKZ* 5: 157)

Geography is relative. In Latin America, at least, narrative transformations are possible and the *hō/seido* (law/system) loses its weight. In letters to Oryū no Oba, Shin'ichirō describes huge grasslands, a river that flows with silver, and people who glimmer like angels. For a time, Shin'ichirō feels free. When Shin'ichirō returns home, however, he reveals that his vision was false, telling Oryū that the land with the silver river was simply another place to live and that the angels were foul-smelling women. Like Oriental Yasu, Shin'ichirō experiences a momentary transformation before he returns to earth. These transcendent moments, accompanied by their inevitable falls, characterize the *monogatari* form. Interestingly, such transformations are often set in motion by the intrusion of an external realm: in Hanzō's case, with the widow of Ukijima and the bird, Tenko; in Oriental Yasu and Shin'ichirō's case, by the strange continent of Latin America. It is through contact with the outside that the protagonists can reflect on their own destiny carved in the narrow confines of the alleyway.

1 View of Shingū, 1911. Courtesy of the Shingū Public Library.

2 View of the "floating island" of Ukijima, Shingū, 1955.
Courtesy of the Shingū Public Library.

3 Transporting timber (*ikada*) on the Kumano River, 1955.
Courtesy of the Shingū Public Library.

4 Tabata Ryū and her husband Reijo in an undated photograph.

5 The Nakagami family, with daughter Nori, Tokyo, 1971.
Courtesy of Nakagami Kasumi.

6 Nakagami Kenji, circa 1975.
Courtesy of Nakagami Kasumi.

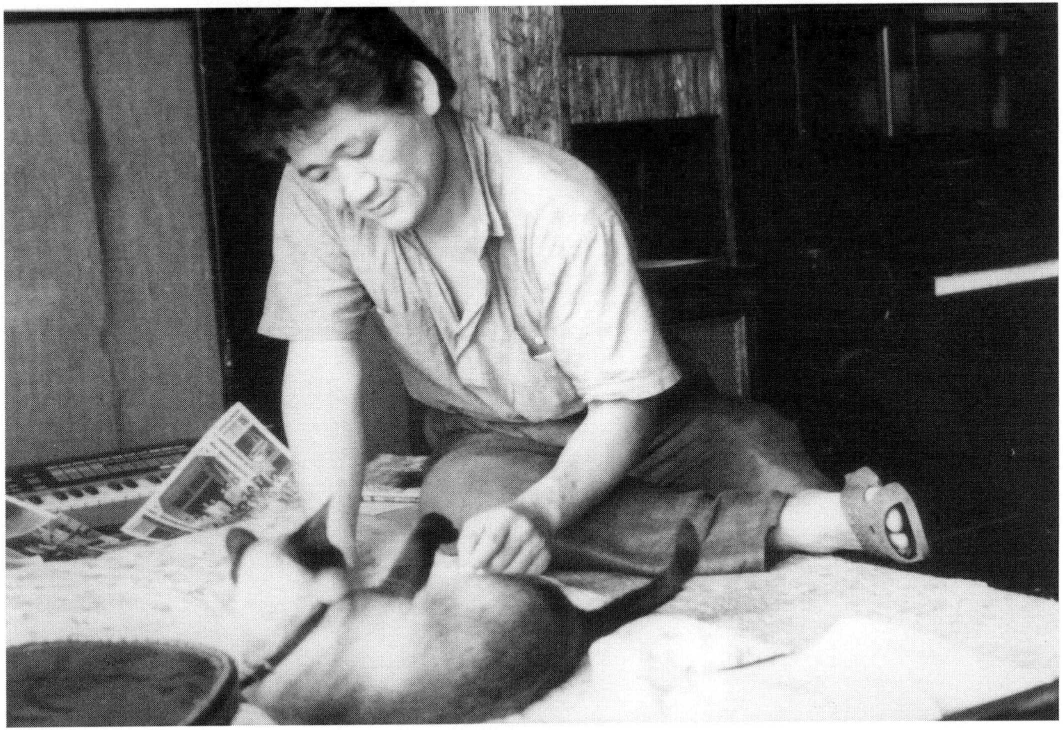

7 Nakagami Kenji visiting Shingū in the mid-1980's.
Courtesy of Nakagami Kasumi.

8 Nakagami Kenji participating in the Fire Festival in Shingū, mid-1980s. Courtesy of Nakamura Fūki.

9 Nakagami Kenji participating in the Fire Festival in Shingū, mid-1980s.
Courtesy of Nakamura Fūki.

10 Matsune Hisao during an interview in a Shingū eatery, 1993.
Author's photo.

11 (*from left to right*) Suga Hidemi, Watanabe Naomi, and Yomota Inuhiko, at the 1993 symposium sponsored by Kumano Daigaku and led by Karatani Kōjin entitled: "Sennen no bungaku: Nakagami Kenji and Kumano," Shingū, 1993. Author's photo.

12 The Kasuga district of Shingū, in 2004. Author's photo.

13 The Nakaue house in Noda, Shingū, 2004. Author's photo.

14 Staff members of the Shingū Public Library at an exhibit organized by the Nakagami Research Center, Shingū Public Library, Shingū, 2004. Author's photo.

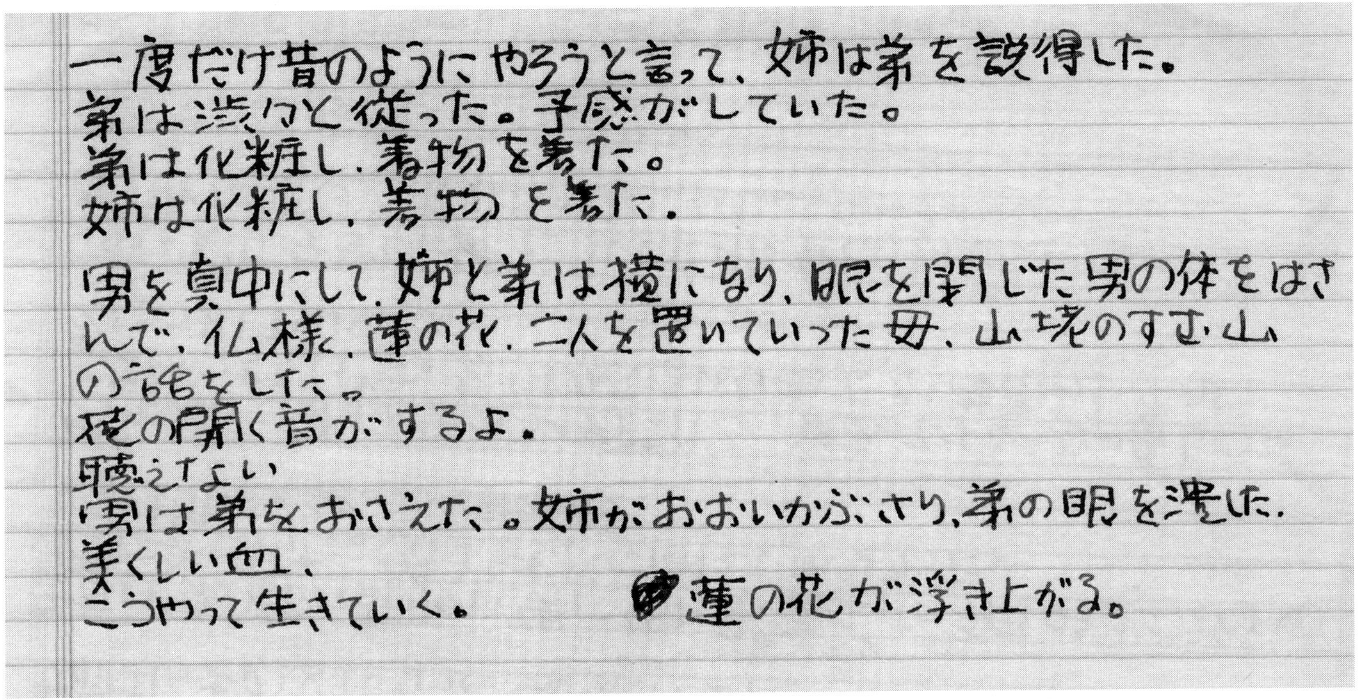

一度だけ昔のようにやろうと言って、姉は弟を説得した。
弟は渋々と従った。予感がしていた。
弟は化粧し、着物を着た。
姉は化粧し、着物を着た。

男を真中にして、姉と弟は横になり、眼を閉じた男の体をはさんで、仏様、蓮の花、二人を置いていった母、山姥のすむ山の話をした。
花の開く音がするよ。
聴えない
男は弟をおさえた。姉がおおいかぶさり、弟の眼を潰した。
美しい血。
こうやって生きていく。　蓮の花が浮き上がる。

15　Excerpt of handwritten scenario for a play based on the short story, "Futakami," written by Nakagami Kenji on yellow lined paper in a coffee shop in Greenwich Village, New York City, 1986.

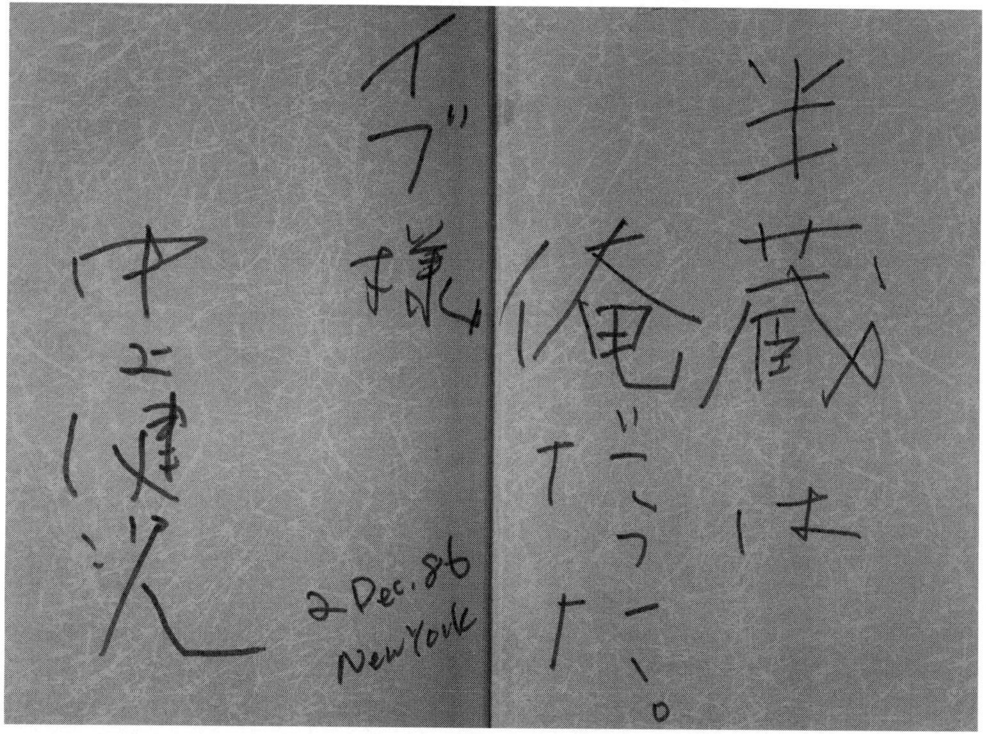

16 Handwritten inscription by Nakagami Kenji in a copy of *Sennen no yuraku*. "Hanzō was me." New York, 1986.

Nakagami takes joy in the rhythms of movement and in the eventual settling back to earth. We see a similar mechanism in Nakagami's treatment of the blood in *Sennen no yuraku*: "the tainted and thus sacred blood." The paradox of the blood—that it is only sacred because it is impure—spins an endless, self-referential riddle within the bodies of the Nakamotos.[39] Taking joy in this back-and-forth rhythm, Nakagami creates fictional characters who straddle the categories of pure/impure, sacred/profane, male/female, high/low. "Some have manly faces, some have womanly faces. . . ." (*NKZ* 5: 147). Hanzō, the first Nakamoto, manifests both male and female within himself. Dabbing his body with white powder, he is both pursuer and pursued, lover and beloved, giver and receiver of pleasure. Fumihiko, on the other hand, treads the boundary between the human and the animal; he is covered with hair at birth and alone can see the mythical bird-monster, the *tengu*. Nakagami uses paradox to create what Victor Turner terms a "realm of pure possibility."[40] The outcaste is a god; night equals day; the lotus pond of paradise lies concealed beneath the sewers of the alleyway. For a short time, paradox makes every category interchangeable, and a rational ordering of the world impossible.

Not only do the Nakamotos embody the resolution of opposites in their names and their blood, but they also manifest it in the very spaces that they inhabit and in others' perceptions of them. Using images of enclosure, Nakagami repeats the word *naka* (middle or through). When Hanzō walks through the alleyway (*roji no naka o aruku*) both men and women are stirred to passion (*NKZ* 5: 14). The Nakamotos drift along "in the scent of a woman's powder" (*onna no shibun no nioi no naka ni*; *NKZ* 5: 42). The word *naka* even links disparate space—*roji* and Latin America, in one instance collapsing the distance between here and there: "The silver river with a vein of silver in the river bottom that colored the water, was flowing through the alleyway, too [*roji no naka o nagareru*], and Shin'ichirō felt that he was in an infinite free land of pleasure, dozing with the taste of sweet dew on his lips" (*NKZ* 5: 149–50).

Stripped of psychological depth, the Nakamotos embody their own name, "origin of the middle" which refers to their beginnings, their dramatic ends, and their ability to feel tremendous pleasure. Reijo, the *roji* priest, grumbles, "No one should experience such pleasure in this life" (*NKZ* 5: 21). Caught between heaven and earth, man and animal, they absorb, resolve, and then perpetuate dualistic categories.[41] Given their in-between state, the Nakamotos seem perfect emblems of the powers of the *hō/seido*, giving an illusion of resistance and then relaxing into defeat.

Before we leave *Sennen no yuraku* entirely, however, let us consider its status as a twice-told tale that glances back not to Tanizaki or to the classical tradition but to a work that sits much closer in time—Mishima Yukio's tetralogy, *Hōjō no umi* (The Sea of Fertility, 1965–70), in which three divine beings (out of four), each with extraordinary marks of beauty, die at the age of 20, without knowledge of their own special status. The four works are united by the presence of an observer named Honda, whose life intersects but never merges with the highly poetic realm of the angels. Indeed, Mishima drives a wedge between knowledge and beauty in *Hōjō no umi* by making the sophisticated and knowing Honda into a bitter and ugly man. As Honda observes, "Fleshly beauty, spiritual beauty, everything that pertains to beauty, is born from ignorance and darkness and from them alone. *It is not allowed to know and still to be beautiful* [*sic*]."[42]

Trouble comes in the final volume, "Tennin gosui" (Decay of the Angel), when Honda encounters a young man named Tōru with the requisite physical markings of divine status, but "whose mechanism of his self-awareness was as apparent as if it lay behind a window."[43] In other words, Tōru stands on the verge of knowing his true identity. For the first time, the aged Honda entertains the possibility that Tōru, the final angel, is a counterfeit. Indeed, Tōru eventually learns the secret of his own special status, and consequently lives out his life in exile, unable to die and follow the other three angels into paradise.

Nakagami reveals his interest in Mishima in *Sennen no yuraku*, even borrowing the title of "Tennin gosui" for the chapter about Oriental Yasu. However, Nakagami waxes critical of Mishima's understanding of the *monogatari* form. In a *taidan* with Yomota Inuhiko, Nakagami faults Mishima for his failures as a *monogatari* writer because, in his creation of a false angel, Mishima misunderstood the dynamic of the *monogatari*. Nakagami states: "You have to believe in some aspect of the *monogatari*. *If the monogatari* is the return of the soul [*reikon*], meaning birth, death, and rebirth, you believe in the cycle. If *monogatari* is spirit [*tamashii*], or if it is simply the movement of material things [*mono*] as Origuchi [Shinobu] often preached, you believe in that. I don't think [Mishima] had enough faith in that kind of thing—kinetic energy, or *ki*, or spirit, or thing. In *Hōjō no umi*, he creates something more like loneliness."[44] Yomota expands on Nakagami's critique. According to him, Mishima's *Hōjō no umi* marked a radical disjunction in the fictional landscape of Japan. With the appearance of the imposter Tōru, the cycle of reincarnation ground to a halt and sacred stories ceased. In *Hōjō no umi*, Mishima had metaphorically declared the end of storytelling. In Yomota's view, however, Nakagami breaks this impasse with his own version of "Tennin gosui," and the cycle of storytelling begins anew.[45]

Sennen no yuraku adheres closely to Mishima's pattern of young beautiful creatures who must die, but Nakagami establishes one important difference between himself and Mishima. In contrast to Mishima's angels, whose beauty depends on ignorance, Nakagami posits that knowledge itself is a precondition for pleasure. The Nakamotos' pleasure is laced through with self-consciousness. Oryū notes that Hanzō lives with a sense of dread that is unnatural in a young man. Aware of the strange blood of the Nakamoto clan and of his own peculiar destiny, Hanzō becomes obsessed with the possibility that his child will be born with a deformity, as was Gen, his uncle with a misshapen hand. The other Nakamotos are similarly conscious of their family line. When Miyoshi begins to suffer night blindness, he immediately ascribes it to his tainted blood.

Tatsuo, too, knows that as a Nakamoto he will die, and he thanks the gods of the Ainu *roji* that his in-between status has kept him alive thus far. The Nakamotos recognize themselves as products of the logic of identity: they are characters in a *monogatari* that was set in motion long before they were born. When Fumihiko walks through the mountains with his shaman lover, he "suddenly had the feeling that he had wandered the mountains with this woman long ago" (*NKZ* 5: 82). As Fumihiko's self-conscious vision reveals, the Nakamotos' beauty is rooted in their ability to envision their unique ends. Nakagami's insistence on an open-eyed recognition of the pattern originates in his views on the *monogatari* as product of the *hō/seido*. If the "code" is a form of determinism, a seal that is imprinted on any text, then the narrative must express awareness of itself even as it loses its struggle for autonomy. Even the powerful Oryū no Oba must face the limitations of her own storytelling. Lamenting the fact that she can do nothing to manipulate the material she has been given, Oryū contemplates the death of Tatsuo, the last Nakamoto: "Oryū mused. If you're writing a story, you can put down the pen if things are getting ahead of themselves, or you can take a rest in the middle of telling a tale . . . but it's a different matter if the story has been set down in the faraway country of the Buddha, Oryū realized, weeping and sighing" (*NKZ* 5: 178). Oryū no Oba admits of the possibility of creating open-ended fictions (writing your own story), but not for herself. The story of the Nakamotos, a "twice-told" tale, has the weight of religious dogma because it was set down in the country of the Buddha. With her voice never wavering, Oryū stays firmly in character.

The story of Tatsuo is the final case in point. When Tatsuo returns to the alleyway after a sojourn in the Ainu ghetto in the North, he brings a young man who resembles him. Tatsuo's idea is to switch places with this young man—to defy the bloodline and defeat death—but his experiment is cut short by his own death in a violent alleyway fight. Soon, however, his double appears in the alleyway, calls himself Tatsuo, and attempts to take his place. The text holds up the tantalizing possibility that the ruse has succeeded. But Oryū no Oba, the vigilant narrator, sees through the switch: "The tainted yet pure blood of a Nakamoto had extinguished another of the Buddha's sins, but Oryū no Oba whispered to herself that the second Tatsuo only resembled the first Tatsuo who was born on the night that thunder crashed and the owl cried" (*NKZ* 5: 189). To Oryū, the Ainu youth will never be more than a poor copy, an approximation of a divine Nakamoto who cannot replicate the magical conditions of Tatsuo's birth. Unlike Mishima, who breaks the pattern in the character of the false angel, Nakagami follows the patterned movement of the *monogatari* through to the end.

In *Sennen no yuraku*, Nakagami confronts his readers with a set of unchanging coordinates. Like Tanizaki, he refuses to compromise, showing the unyielding force of the *hō/seido* from beginning to end. Perhaps Nakagami, too, longs for the shock of recognition that he belongs to a clan of brothers and that his story will mirror their own. At the same time, like Mishima, Nakagami does not practice sincere belief in his *monogatari* writing. He creates the perfect circle fully aware of the fact that he cannot dwell there himself. With its grinding focus on self-knowledge, *Sennen no yuraku* is a work that could only be written in exile. In Nakagami's case, it is forbidden to be beautiful and *not* to know. In its evocation of pleasure and its perfect circularity, *Sennen no yuraku* stands as a unique experiment in Nakagami's oeuvre, one that he would not repeat with the same optimism or bravado. Indeed, as we move toward the late 1980s, the potential for dynamic *monogatari*, forged in the collision between the "familiar" and the "strange," slowly dissipates. By the 1988 interview, Nakagami describes the impossibility of either dwelling in the *monogatari* or rejecting it out of hand. The writer's task is voiced in more muted tones:

> Storytelling has its basic rhythms. When you enter into this fixed rhythm you feel tremendous pleasure. It's like life in the *roji*. You wake up, go to work, come home, make love, drink, and go to sleep. There's perfect pleasure in the *monogatari*. If you leave everything up to the *monogatari*, it will carry you through. But then you don't make

any progress. You are left powerless. Once you wake up, though, it's incredibly painful. . . . And yet you can't completely resist the *monogatari* either. It's impossible. Try resisting the Bible. You can't do it. Take the story of Cain and Abel, for instance. It pops up both in fiction and in life. When you write about the relationship between brothers, you bump up against the story of Cain and Abel again and again. What can you do about this? Well, each story has an archetype [*genkei*] . . . actually the archetype is the same thing as an original crime [*genzai*] . . . in other words there's the archetype of Cain killing Abel, an archetype which is also the first crime. So because it's impossible to overturn these *monogatari*, you have to work closely with them, shift them a little, try to rearrange them. That's the only thing you can do.[46]

This statement, made ten years after "Monogatari no keifu" and the "discovery" of Kumano, shows the distance that Nakagami has come. Rather than agonize over the power of the *monogatari* or attempt to openly subvert it, Nakagami now admits the enormous difficulty of creating dynamic narratives. Instead of smashing the archetypes, his task is to shift them ever so slightly. In fact, the great achievement of *Sennen no yuraku* is its very subtle movements, its beautiful language within configured patterns. In *Sennen no yuraku* at least, Nakagami wandered out of the territory of realism and explored for a brief time the pleasures of mythic, transcendent, and imaginary spaces.

In the 1980s, Nakagami and others like him searched for a direction for modern Japanese literature that lay beyond the time-honored habits of realism. The *monogatari* served as a hedge, an effective way to resist the demands of a certain kind of literary production—whether socially realist or reformist. In its use of pre-existing patterns and stories, the *monogatari* may seem like a disguised form of praise of the *hō/seido*. But by staying perfectly still and following the pattern, Nakagami skillfully answers the *hō/seido* on its own terms, beginning with the premise of defeat. To put his actions in another light, we might quote Yamaguchi Masao's analysis of the *kishu ryūritan* myth in which the noble exile must "mediate between chaos and order by developing techniques of confronting chaos at the margins."[47] Armed with the "technique" of the *monogatari* in the early 1980s, Nakagami confronted the chaos that he saw both within and without himself. In order to carve out "room to move," he began to experiment with the colors and textures of modern literary prose. We now turn to Nakagami's myriad experiments with language as he worked to shift the rigid codes of Japanese literary and aesthetic practice.

FIVE

A Language of Kumano

The poet no longer has or aspires to native tenure in the house of words. The languages waiting for him as an individual born into history, into society, into the expressive conventions of his particular culture and milieu, are no longer a natural skin. Established language is the enemy. The poet finds it sordid with lies. . . . It is the writer's compelling task, as Mallarmé said of Poe, "to purify the language of the tribe." He will seek to resuscitate the magic of the word by dislocating traditional bonds of grammar and of ordered space. . . .

—George Steiner, *After Babel*

In "Tengu no matsu" (The Pine Tree of the Tengu), the third story of *Sennen no yuraku,* Nakagami illustrates the ways in which discrimination operates through language in the lives of the outcaste people. It is February, and the young men of the *roji* have been preparing for the annual fire festival by undergoing ritual purification, fasting, and sexual abstinence. That day, as they ready themselves to climb the mountain with burning torches, they encounter an unexpected setback:

It was painful for Oryū no Oba to witness the excitement of the young men every year at festival time. One, who had planned to ascend the mountain with a torch during the Fire Festival, had inadvertently wrapped the sacred rope around his waist not twice but four times [*yotsu*]. The word for "four" also meant a highly defiled person, death, or even a four-legged beast. Oryū first felt sad, then angry and disappointed when the others stumbled into the trap of words, chiding their friend, "No good! Do it again!" (*NKZ* 5: 77–78)

The young man's transgression can be traced back to a complicated web of numbers and words. Of the many names used to refer to the *burakumin,* perhaps the word *yotsu* has the greatest weight: it denotes four-footed creatures and it suggests that the *burakumin,* whose traditional occupations of slaughtering and leather-working brought them into close contact with animals, are animals themselves.[1] When the character for the number four is given its alternate reading *shi,* it becomes a homonym for death (*shi*). By wrapping the rope around his waist four times, the young man not only reveals his outcaste status but also transforms himself into a powerful harbinger of doom. The young men who participate in the fire festival know that their friend's defilement is made doubly potent by its connection to death.

The word *yotsu* is only one example of the "trap of words" that holds both majority Japanese and outcastes firmly in its grip. By scolding their comrade, the young men helplessly perpetuate the system that oppresses them. Throughout his life, Nakagami confronted the "trap of words" but he knew that he faced a more daunting problem than simply banishing discriminatory language. Rather, during the decade that he thought about the *monogatari,* Nakagami envisioned a subtle transformation of Japanese literature in terms of subject, diction, space, and even grammatical norms. This goal began to take shape for him in the late 1970s when, notebook in hand, Nakagami traveled around the Kii Peninsula, an area with a high *burakumin* population, interviewing the people in the small rural hamlets and byways. His account of the journey was published in serial form in the *Asahi Journal* beginning in 1977, and later in book form as *Kishū ki no kuni ne no kuni monogatari* (Tales of Kishū: Land of Trees, Land of Roots; 1986), each chapter corresponding to a place name: Shingū, Hongū, Arima, etc.[2]

Rather than a travel diary or an ethnographic account, *Kishū ki no kuni ne no kuni monogatari* formulates a grammar of space—or rather, it reveals how language shapes our perceptions of space and vice versa. In a chapter on Ise, the center of the Shinto religion, for example, Nakagami walks around the main shrine buildings, musing on the links between places and words. To Nakagami, the physical contours of Ise Shrine embody how words themselves are implicated in the creation of a symbolic hierarchy. At the very top of this spatial grammar tree, Nakagami reads the figure of the emperor. He elaborates:

> The rain was falling heavily and the bushes were wet. Listening to the rain and the water rushing through the ravine, I stood for a moment and then I began to walk around looking for a way to get over to the other side. Grass is grass, I thought. It seems to me that the essence of grass is not the thing itself, but simply the name that it has been assigned. Words exist. A word—grass—was being made wet by another word—rain—and appeared to be oozing a dark light in my field of vision that could only be called nature's eros. If words are controlled by the "emperor," or by a mechanism of the gods, then writing down the name "grass" brings it into the syntax and the purview of the emperor. But once one abandons the emperor's syntax, then what is "grass"? . . . In order to repudiate the emperor's realm through language, I will have to adopt another strange tongue, not the omnipresent recorded Japanese language of the "leaves that are words" [*koto no ha*]. Perhaps I must turn to the spoken word because it repudiates the written language. The contradiction of writing down the oral is enormous, but the cultural forms of the lower classes—popular sermons [*sekkyōbushi*], and *nō* drama in the form of Zeami's plays—could break away from the emperor's control of the written language because they were seen to be performing a mythic function. *Sekkyōbushi* and *nō* drama heartily shook the gap between god and beggar, emperor and commoner for the simple reason that these forms were free from syntax through the practice of recitation. At this point, I find myself at a loss for words. I am completely saturated with the poison of writing, with the poison of the written language. (*NKZ* 14: 609–10)

Clearly Nakagami's challenge as a writer is to create a written language that rings with the sound of the particular and local rhythms of Wakayama speech. He braces himself, considering that he might have to "adopt another tongue," or give up writing altogether. Eventually, he turns to the forms of *sekkyōbushi* and *nō* drama, which provide models for what he himself must do—get the recited word down on the page. Although he recognizes the "contradiction" inherent in writing down oral performance, Nakagami takes up the challenge of searching for new modes of representation. In the following pages, we will first explore how Nakagami defies the "trap of words" by writing about material life in the *roji*. Next we will turn to Nakagami's various innovations in short fiction in the 1980s, particularly works such as "Nokori no hana" (Late Blossoms, 1988); "Futakami" (Twin Gods, 1985); "Tennin gosui" (Decay of the Angel), the fourth chapter of *Sennen no yuraku*; and "Jūryoku no miyako" (City of Gravity, 1988). Finally, we consider a chapter from *Kishū ki no kuni ne no kuni monogatari* to contrast Nakagami's treatment of language in his nonfictional writing. Using specific passages of the prose, we will follow how Nakagami bravely confronted what he calls the "emperor's syntax."

Degrading Words

In the fiction of the 1970s and early 1980s, the *roji*, or alleyway of the *burakumin*, is a communal but segregated space overflowing with strong smells, vivid sights, and characteristic local sounds. In his depictions of the *buraku*, Nakagami also confronts stereotypes that the alleyway people are more primitive, violent, and libidinous than majority Japanese. In *Misaki*, for example, Akiyuki, a young laborer, steps into the sewage that flows down the ditches of the town and takes a look around:

> Listening to the banter of Yasuo and the woman, Akiyuki dug as deep as he could go. Damn, he liked to work hard with his body like this. It was the purest form of work. You start when the sun rises and quit when the sun sets. It was simple, even dirty, and sometimes you see stuff you never expect. Once they were cleaning out a big ditch next to a pig pen so they could build a stone wall. A puddle of pig piss lay at the bottom of the ditch. They got wet, soaked with it. The smell of the piss and all the other squishy filth almost overwhelmed the boss and the men but not him. Then it happened. A sausage in a condom floated past them down through the ditch. Everybody perked up. Somewhere in the apartments behind the pig

pen, or in the development, or in a house in town, Akiyuki guessed, a young widow was moaning in constant frustration. "If only she'd call on us," remarked Yasuo.[3]

The ditch, with its flow of squishy filth, represents the communal layer at the bottom of the world where all waste flows together and everyone's secrets are laid bare. Lacking the reflex of disgust, Akiyuki steps into the ditch, bearing witness to the fact that all human waste is equal and that he and his men do the "purest form of work." The condom that floats down the ditch serves as the point where waste and sexuality intersect. The makeshift penis does not need a body and as such it signals the boundless, fluid nature of desire; for the frustrated widow, any penis will do; and any one of the workers would be happy to oblige her. The incident reveals the leveling power of bodily life itself: one form of "flesh" (pork) can be substituted for another (human), and everything joins the stream of waste. Akiyuki's obvious delight in the ditch stems from his discovery of "things you never expect"—in this case the unveiling of equivalences between consumption, elimination, and desire.[4]

In *Misaki*, Nakagami uses the ditch to mine the rich potential of the lower realms. By *Sennen no yuraku*, however, Nakagami abstracts the physical space of the ditch to represent the forms of *roji* speech. Hanzō, the first Nakamoto, speaks in boasts and riddles that suggest exaggerated sexual prowess. He spins metaphors about his own prodigious sexual appetite, telling the women, "Inside this thing of mine that you love are thousands more just like it" (*NKZ* 5: 15). He further pushes the link between body and food, pushing metaphor to its furthest point and reveling in his ability to make talking another form of erotic play:[5]

"You're quite something, aren't you?" Oryū no Oba teased.

"I went to get my beans cooked and now they're so overdone their skins are peeling off," he replied, placing his hand on his crotch. "Some people have red ones, some people have white, but my mushroom is burnt to a crisp."

Catching sight of Oryū no Oba suppressing a laugh, he continued, "If only I let my wife do the cooking, she'd do a good job." (*NKZ* 5: 28)

In his use of metaphor, Hanzō recreates the communal phallus of the ditch by comparing himself to food that the women cook and burn. His extended metaphor is also a response to majority stereotypes about outcaste sexuality; as George De Vos notes, there is an attitude of curiosity on the part of majority Japanese who believe that the outcastes have heightened sexual desires and even different genitalia.[6] Through his word play, Nakagami challenges the reader, affirming the power of material life (we are food to be consumed), and implying that the outcastes do enjoy a heightened erotic life. Metaphor serves as a rebuke and a challenge to majority Japanese, a badge of verbal and physical fluency.

Like Hanzō, Oryū no Oba also experiments with metaphor, exaggeration, and word play. When Miyoshi tells Oryū that he is a good thief, Oryū quickly replies, "how do I know that you're good since you've never done it with me?" (*NKZ* 5: 54). Furthermore, she counters Hanzō's boasts about his phallus by pointing to her blood-smeared hands that have delivered many babies, and she warns him not to belittle women because a woman who gives birth is "stronger than a demon" (*NKZ* 5: 22). Language, too, simply mirrors the flows of material life: Oryū's polysemous speech testifies to the number of babies that she has brought into the world. As Miyoshi muses, "he never knew how many people he was talking to when speaking with Oryū" (*NKZ* 5: 54).

The exaggerated word play of Hanzō and Oryū corresponds to what M. M. Bakhtin calls the "familiar speech of the marketplace" with its emphasis on grotesque images of the body and its parody of official norms through laughter. According to Bakhtin, such playful speech has subversive possibilities; if present in high enough concentrations, it forms a "special collectivity" that in turn exerts its influence on orthodox speech.[7] If we accept Bakhtin's theory about marketplace speech, however, we must then determine how this special collectivity relates to groups outside of itself. What does this language signify to Nakagami's community, to the outside world, and to his own literary project?[8]

Slips of the Tongue

In *Sennen no yuraku*, Nakagami's vision of *roji* language is tied securely to the figure of Oryū no Oba, the old midwife and teller of the tale. According to Oryū no Oba, *roji* language is distinct from both standard Japanese and the local dialect of Shingū. The *roji* people are descendants of craftsmen who were brought to Shingū from another region of Japan to make leather goods for the daimyo, and they spoke a different dialect that has lasted down to the present day. In addition, *roji* language dates to a premodern, pre-technological age before Japan was saturated with the sounds of standard Tokyo language (*hyōjungo*). Nakagami highlights the distinct quality of *roji* language in "Tennin gosui" when Oriental Yasu plays Oryū no Oba a record in standard Japanese. Intrigued by the scratchy sound of the singer's voice, Oryū cannot catch the words: "The Japanese woman was singing in Japanese, but Oryū couldn't get a word of the song even though she spoke the same language. The words resounded in her ears like the chirps of a bird" (*NKZ* 5: 103). With the arrival of technology, Oryū becomes conscious that she and her countrywoman do not share the same language. Not only does the phonograph issue in a new age (*shinjidai*), it also sparks Oryū's determination to preserve *roji* language in the face of the "chirps of a bird."

Oryū's determination is rooted in her knowledge of history itself. The phonograph reminds Oryū of the violence unleashed against the *roji* people in the name of modernization. Oryū had heard the story from a woman who witnessed the events of 1871—the year that the Meiji government banned the terms *eta* and *hinin* and ordered that the outcastes be treated as common people.[9] She repeats what happened in the wake of the "Liberation Edict"—how the people celebrated wildly at first; how farmers from the surrounding areas came to attack them and drove them from their homes, killing a few in the process; how the violence spread through Japan.[10]

The "Liberation Edict" was one building block in the great project of nation-building that marked the Meiji period. As

Oryū relates, the farmers viewed the end of the caste system as a threat to their economic survival and they went on the attack. But the people of the *roji* also sounded a note of protest against assimilation when the "Liberation Edict" was read to them. In a mistaken rendering of *banzai,* the cry of support for the emperor, the people began to chant *banbai, banbai.* To Oryū, this unintentional error signaled an awareness of cultural identity on the part of her own people, and she believes that their continued existence depends on such slips of the tongue. *Banbai* is used by Oryū to transform images of grotesque realism (through blood and birth) into a tool of resistance:

> Even if they had been hunted down like monkeys, Oryū thought, more people would be born, they would build villages and towns, and these would overflow. Since her youth, Oryū had traveled around delivering babies and preaching that there was no reason to be ashamed of a child without a father; that it was better to be in a light place than a dark place, even if a child was retarded or not whole; that this world is better than the next; and that it's better to increase than perish. As her body grew less mobile Oryū sometimes felt that her attitude was a sin against the Buddha who had filled Reijo's sermons, but once she was confined to her bed, she would laugh to herself knowing that she had no reason to feel bitter over the loss of ten people who had died like monkeys because she had delivered a hundred more babies who said *banbai* into this world. (*NKZ* 5: 104)

Nakagami links images of the grotesque—the bloody hands of Oryū, the imperfect children, and the playful language of the *roji*—with the survival of a people. The word *banbai* moves from being a slip of the tongue to being the defining element of a culture that will preserve its own speech and stories. Moreover, it fractures what is seen as monolithic—in this case, language in praise of the emperor. As a single word, *banbai* relieves the downward pressure of discrimination and reveals what Henry Louis Gates describes as "masking," a theory of minority language that he bases on the work of George Steiner.[11] In *After Babel: Aspects of Language and Translation,*

Steiner discusses the tendency of language to mask more than it reveals. One must translate not only between different languages but also between works written in the same language, or even in a conversation with one's contemporaries.[12] Henry Louis Gates, in turn, expands upon Steiner's notion of "private language" to refer to the language of a minority group within a given culture. Following Steiner, Gates presents nineteenth-century African American poetry as a "private language" because it was written in dialect. This served two purposes: it solidified the ties of the in-group, and it served as a weapon against majority language—a role to which it was uniquely suited having been born from a marriage of English and lost African languages. But Gates believes that masking performs an even more subtle function: it encourages the African-American poet to become not only the "point of consciousness of his people" but also the "point of consciousness of the language."[13]

When Oryū rejects the notion of a dominant form of standard Japanese because her dialect is as valid as the "chirps of a bird," she, too, serves as the point of consciousness of the language. Through the word *banbai* and her many stories, Oryū no Oba emphasizes the role that language plays in the survival of a community, pushing back against the forces of assimilation. When considering the character of Oryū, we might also remember Nakagami's extra-literary activities in the late 1970s, taping the song of an old woman who lived around the corner and commenting to Matsune Hisao that the discovery of the real Oryū no Oba was worthy of Yanagita Kunio. Nakagami did not focus on *roji* language because he felt nostalgic or protective of his childhood home; rather, his interest in the patter of *roji* speech was quite pragmatic. There, in the place where he had been raised, he found the tools he needed to write fiction. Ironically, the forms of living *roji* culture that Nakagami worked to preserve are now kept in a room at the Shingū library, including numerous photographs and audiotapes. Nevertheless, on the pages of his fiction, we can trace how he put his discoveries to work.

Playing with Words

In order to determine whether Nakagami strays from certain stylistic conventions embedded in the modern *shōsetsu*, we now turn to a brief discussion of the form. I would argue that Nakagami's opponent in creating a "strange new tongue" is not the emperor's language per se but the contemporary *shōsetsu*. As the descendant of *genbun itchi* (the union of spoken and written languages), the *shōsetsu* is characterized by its adherence to standard grammatical norms, prescribed verb endings, and a homogenized literary vocabulary. Nakagami's interest in oral forms expresses his conviction that the standard written language, which has ceased to be open to the transforming powers of speech, is sorely in need of revitalization. Interestingly, Nakagami follows in the footsteps of Tanizaki Jun'icihirō, another writer who criticized *genbun itchi* style because it was too constricting; too heavily based on Western grammar in its explicit statement of subject; and most gravely, because it had destroyed the beauty of the "original Japanese language."[14]

In *The Rhetoric of Confession*, Edward Fowler gives one example of why the language of the *shōsetsu* might feel too restricting to Tanizaki and others. Fowler assigns the name "single-consciousness narration" to the dominant stylistic mode of the Japanese *shōsetsu*. According to Fowler, the comparatively fluid use of verb forms in Japanese lends what he calls an "immediate quality" to the texture of the narrative whether it is written in the first person or third person: we move in and out of a character's thoughts, and rarely is the story told through the eyes of an omniscient narrator. Fowler focuses on the *shishōsetsu*, the semi-confessional genre (in either first or third person), but he believes that single-consciousness narration is widespread in Japanese literature. Because the reader remains situated within the viewpoint of the main character, the Japanese *shōsetsu* boasts a strongly subjective writing style, and the reader tends to identify closely with the central character's perceptions.[15]

Noguchi Takehiko, in an analysis of the history of *genbun itchi* in the early modern period, suggests what might further be at the root of Tanizaki's and Nakagami's complaints about modern Japanese literary style: its Edo origins. Noguchi explores the origins of modern narration, namely the *ji no bun*, or narrated passages in contrast to quoted speech. He inquires about the motives of *genbun itchi* writers to tackle and revise what had become a moribund classical language. First, Noguchi mentions their experience of Western texts, wherein a reader could journey into the mind of a character and live the life of that character internally. Second, he presents the *kokkeibon*, a type of satirical Edo text characterized by large portions of colloquial dialogue and semi-colloquial background narration. Noguchi believes that Futabatei Shimei, who wrote *Ukigumo* (The Drifting Cloud, 1886–89), the first "modern *shōsetsu*," developed narrative style by transforming the patter of the *kokkeibon*'s narrator—who acts as a guide addressing readers directly from within the story—into the colloquial rhythms of the main character's thoughts.[16] Perhaps most important was the fact that this *kokkeibon* narrator spoke a colloquial Edo dialect. Noguchi states that this standard Tokyo dialect has dominated the *shōsetsu* since its inception, and that even when writers chafe against this convention by using regional dialect in passages of conversation or importing words that impart local color, *genbun itchi* style remains in place.[17] For the writer from other regions of Japan, this presents a challenge: how can one represent the local in the homogenized language of the *shōsetsu*? How can one resist the "patois" of Edo?

Voices of the Roji

During the 1980's, Nakagami began to experiment with narrative voice in ways that reveal his determination to transform language itself. In a number of short stories Nakagami creates a non-specific subject in the form of one or more old women thinking aloud as if they were reporting shared experience. In "Nokori no hana," for example, Nakagami experiments with a split narrative that moves back and forth between the perspectives of a young man and the old women who live in the *roji*. Most striking is the lack of a specific subject in the first paragraph of the story, which ends in two quoted utterances in broad Shingū dialect. In the opening of the story, Nakagami conveys the thoughts of someone or some group of people who are tending to the plants under the hot summer sun. Only in the second paragraph do we discover that the thoughts emanate from the old women of the *roji*. Translated quite literally, the passage reads:

> Like never before the hot days continued, and all the flowering plants on the benches wilted. Anybody would hold back, knowing that if one gave the plants water in the daytime, the hot water would burn the roots. So, the flowers were cajoled and comforted, withered flowers have such an air about them, but one was fretting over whether they could be saved from the heat.
>
> "Nothing to be done about it. I've had that plant for many years and it's given me lots of seed."
>
> "You gave me a seed from that one and it grew a different color flower at my place. But before I knew it, it grew back the same old color."
>
> The old women of the *roji* waited for the sun to set, and then filled a bucket with water, first ladling the water over the hot benches and then watering the plants. Mingling with the smell of the warm water, the scent of death wafted out from the middle of the petals and drifted through the air. (*NKZ* 10: 57)

The voice in the story's opening is deliberately vague. It meanders slowly, speaking in condensed poetic utterances that suggest the conservation of energy demanded by the heat. Although the *ji no bun* does not replicate the verb endings of *roji* dialect, Nakagami imbeds an exchange between two voices in Shingū dialect before he specifies who is speaking to whom. Nakagami strips the *ji no bun* to its bare essentials, creating a transcendent communal voice, as if the *roji* were speaking about itself.

The floating voice continues until the story turns a corner and a skeleton is discovered in the wall of one of the neighboring houses that is under construction. From this point on, the narrative enters a "tale within a tale" which tells the story of Jūkichi, a laborer who meets a mysterious blind woman and disappears under strange circumstances. When Jūkichi appears on the scene, the narrative focuses sharply on its central character and falls into single-consciousness narration. The switch in voice is abrupt; a rough seam between the communal voice and Jūkichi is clearly visible in an ambiguous phrase that turns on the word *jibun* (oneself), a signal that we have entered the domain of Jūkichi's mind:

> The old women gossiped in low voices among themselves, saying what good would it do to dig up the past now that the bones had turned up. They were more concerned because the house that had blocked the late afternoon sun was gone now and the plants would bake longer in the hot sun.
>
> One's fate was like a bit of paper falling to bits [*kami no yō ni kuzure ochiru no wa jibun no unmei datta*].
>
> The wild Jūkichi first saw the woman on a trip to the town of Nantō in Ise when he was taking leave of his migrant co-workers at the edge of town. Work at the temporary camp at Miyagawaoku had lasted for awhile, and his pay had been good. He'd won big at gambling, and now that he was carrying a sum of money bigger than he'd ever seen before, he could feel his village calling to him as he bounced around from work camp to work camp. Once he got back to his village, though, he understood that there was nothing of interest there. (*NKZ* 10: 60)

As the story progresses, the reader focuses on Jūkichi's perspective: Jūkichi brings the blind woman back to the *roji* where the two set up house and enjoy sex in isolation from the community. The woman's blindness makes her a "woman among women" to Jūkichi who is fascinated by her delicate movements and her sightless eyes. Nakagami once again pays homage to *Shunkinshō* by Tanizaki in which Sasuke, madly in love with Shunkin, his blind music teacher, first locks himself in a closet and then blinds himself in order to preserve his memories of his lover's beauty. Unlike Sasuke, however, Jūkichi is simply murdered (by whom is unclear) and left in the dark space behind a wall. Nakagami explodes the aesthetic dimensions of Tanizaki's fiction: the dark realm is not the realm of art where two symbiotic lovers dwell, but a hiding place for a corpse.

When we examine the various voices that tell the story, a number of interesting details emerge. Although the communal *roji* voice falls silent when Jūkichi first appears, it periodically intrudes to inform the reader about events beyond Jūkichi's ken. When Jūkichi goes to work, for example, the old women notice strange sounds of laughter coming from the house. They conclude that the blind woman is entertaining another lover, and they express their desire to warn the woman about Jūkichi's anger. In these interruptions, the communal voice expresses the general opinion that the love affair is shadowed by disaster. The old women represent the status quo of *roji* life, a counterweight to the obsessive passion being played out behind the walls of the house.

As one would expect, the story moves between its two main foci, the old women and Jūkichi; when Jūkichi is present, the women fall silent, and when the women are speaking, Jūkichi is gone. Gradually, however, a tension develops between the two voices of the story as if they were competing for control. After Jūkichi disappears, for example, the old women behave with subtle malevolence, refusing to tell what happened to Jūkichi and stating that it is best to leave the past undisturbed. As representatives of a communal consciousness unchanged by the passage of time, they survive long after Jūkichi's death. Predictably, the old women have the last word: "Jūkichi didn't return. The woman's laughter continued. The little chrysanthemums opened, and when their scent wafted from the houses down the alleyway, the old women and the neighbors grumbled, saying that it smelled like the fresh smell of sex between Jūkichi and the woman, and it made their heads ache" (*NKZ* 10: 67).

"Nokori no hana" ends where it began—with the old women dwelling on the flowers in the *roji*. Nakagami has not altered the *ji no bun* in "Nokori no hana," but he has created a narrative of contrasting, even jarring, perspectives. Further, he has raised certain doubts in the minds of his readers. Who tells the truth in this bizarre fable? Do the old women in fact control the tale, including Jūkichi's fate? Nakagami's experiments reveal his conviction that a heterogeneous voice is essential to the creation of a literature of the *roji* because one can only shift the codes of the *monogatari* by planting seeds of unreliability and doubt. To this end, Nakagami offers up the hapless Jūkichi, another "expendable male" who, in spite of his youth, cannot outlast the old women, the flowers, and the summer heat. As the story states: "One's fate was like a bit of paper falling to bits."

"Futakami" tells the tale of Yahei, a rough laborer who adopts an abandoned niece and nephew, Kiwa and Tatsuhiko. These children engage in odd games, with the sister teaching the younger brother to see visions. Once the children come to live with Yahei, a disturbing tale unfolds. Yahei sleeps next to the children and they begin to play games with his body, eventually bringing him to sexual climax. At first Yahei feels uneasy about breaking a taboo, but he soon concludes that he would destroy their innocence if he were to forbid their games. Yahei further becomes convinced that the little children are gods who have come to give him pleasure: "As Yahei worked on the mountain, where a fragrant wind blew across the slopes and touched his sweaty body, he felt certain that the caresses of the pure, sweet little things was a joy sent down to him from the gods. . . . He could have cried out—the wind gave him so much pleasure" (*NKZ* 10: 91).

In Yahei's mind, he serves as a tool of the gods who have chosen to manifest themselves as willful children. The story reads like an ancient creation myth in which the gods shape the cosmos from the body of a giant who in turn spawns other divine beings.[18] Yet reality intrudes when Kiwa's games grow too rough and Yahei reluctantly sends the children away. Years later, the children return grown to Yahei's house. Kiwa, now a beautiful young woman, insists that Yahei blind Tatsuhiko to prevent him from running away; she plans to dress her younger brother in women's clothing and teach him to see visions again. At the end of the story, the three live together once more: Kiwa as the cruel beauty, Tatsuhiko as a blind doll to be manipulated by the others, and Yahei as father and lover to them both.

As in "Nokori no hana," Nakagami moves back and forth between a communal narrative voice and Yahei. The communal voice of the *roji* provides the context to the story, its pragmatism contrasting sharply with Yahei's thoughts and behavior. The voice of the community also predicts trouble; it speaks in opposition to Yahei, waiting for him to make a mistake. At the end of the story, for example, the communal voice makes its opinion clear:

> No one knew where he had met Kiwa again. The day after Yahei greeted the neighbors with decorated gift boxes of soap, the women who kept their eyes on things were surprised by the sight of Kiwa briskly sweeping Yahei's house. Bringing a dish of mixed rice in return for Yahei's gifts, they went to Yahei's place and Yahei told them that Kiwa had come to keep house for him now that he was back. But a rumor quickly spread that she was Yahei's woman, and people also began to say that Yahei had been molesting Kiwa all those years ago. As everyone had predicted, Kiwa was a beautiful young woman. She continued on in Yahei's house and before long, Tatsuhiko appeared. The neighborhood women said that something strange was beginning in Yahei's house, and that Yahei had never taken care of the children for unselfish reasons—he'd only played with them, turning them into sex toys—and they imagined all different kinds of sex games going on. (*NKZ* 10: 95)

This realistic interpretation of events that occur in Yahei's house contrasts with the fantastic tone of Yahei's story, and suggests that Yahei, a man possessed, is a fundamentally unreliable protagonist. His fantasies of divine pleasure become mere perversion in the eyes of the community who read his story in historic not cosmic terms. The mythical qualities of the story are at once enhanced and made to seem more bizarre by the clear-eyed *roji* appraisal. At the same time, Nakagami uses both Yahei's voice and the voice of the community to tell a story on two different levels: "Futakami" is both a description of a man's experience of divine pleasure and a portrayal of incest at the end of a family line. It is the gap between the two perspectives—*roji* and Yahei—which propels the story back and forth between the poles of mythic dream and horror.

This gap testifies again to Nakagami's determination to disrupt the conventions of *shōsetsu* realism.

Finally, we return briefly to *Sennen no yuraku* in order to assess Nakagami's achievement in upsetting *shōsetsu* conventions. Technically, *Sennen no yuraku* presents the most difficult challenge to the reader with its long sentences and its unorthodox use of grammar and subject. According to the critic Iguchi Tokio, *Sennen no yuraku* is characterized by chaotic sentences (*chūshin kakuran no buntai*) that corrupt straightforward *genbun itchi* style. Readers can no longer follow a single perspective; rather, they are dragged through the distortions of Oryū no Oba's memory and the experiences of the strangely passive Nakamotos, their senses bombarded by strange smells, sights, and sounds.[19] Iguchi's comments suggest the degree to which Nakagami succeeded at writing rough-edged fiction, but he also overstates the case. Nakagami did not abandon narrative conventions altogether in *Sennen no yuraku*, and his sentences do not dissolve into chaos. Furthermore, Nakagami uses Oryū no Oba's perspective in more subtle ways than Iguchi suggests, as we shall see.

"Tennin gosui" tells the story of Oriental Yasu, who returns to the *roji* after the war and begins to gather a group of followers to travel to Latin American to found a new community. Oryū again identifies the "tainted but pure blood" as the source of Yasu's fever to begin anew. When Yasu tries to persuade a man named Saitō, a charcoal seller, to join the group on their way home together at the end of World War II, Saitō declines. Oryu states: "Saitō was like one of those commoners who had hunted down the alleyway people, killing them with bamboo spears, like monkeys. There was no reason that Saitō would understand Yasu's desire to start a new land, which originated in his pure but tainted blood, or his obsession to create a new Manchuria" (*NKZ* 5: 109). Before Yasu can leave on his journey, however, he is shot and barely escapes with his life. At the end of the chapter, he departs for Latin America, and Oryū no Oba eventually gets word that he has died there.

In the opening of "Tennin gosui" Oryū no Oba muses about the approach of winter. With the phrases "Oryū knew" and "Oryū thought," Nakagami anchors the reader in the mind of its central narrator. He uses the standard *-ta* verb ending in the first long sentence, indicating that Oryū no Oba is recollecting events of the past. An anonymous reader has suggested that Nakagami's use of *ta*-perfective endings simulates the use of *keri* in the classical *monogatari* form. The presence of *keri* in a text signals that we are at the feet of a narrator who is explaining something.[20] Once the narrative framework is set, however, Nakagami varies past-perfect endings with plain verb endings, lending immediacy to Oryū's thoughts and sensations. As we move past the opening sentences of "Tennin gosui," Nakagami uses plain endings (*konde miru, tsukande yaru*) that result in a heightened sense of physical sensation. Oryū floats above the earth, free of physical constraints, looking down at the world from a bird's-eye view.

> Oryū closed her eyes, tilted her head to the sound of the wind and then felt her ears fly up like a leaf swept up on the currents of the wind drifting endlessly to distant places. Everything she could see and hear was joy to her. Following a road through a stand of trees dappled by the sun, she emerged onto the edge of the hill above the alleyway, and there floating lightly in spirit form, she touched wonderingly the treetops glowing in the light. . . . A little white animal that had come running from the mountain down to the sea to lick the salt, Oryū stood on the beach, feeling the sea winds and thinking how wonderful it was to become a spirit and leave her motionless worn-out old body behind, and she turned to the other Oryū lying bedridden on the *roji* hill, whispering to her and laughing, "You've gotten to a fine old age. All you do is rest. Any aches and pains?" "No, I'm fine," the other Oryū answered. . . . Oryū no Oba was free. She could see or hear anything she pleased, even the instruments of the musicians from paradise who would come to greet her, even those who dwelled on the other side of the wave of incarnations. (*NKZ* 5: 101)

Oryū's spirit begins its travels aurally, her ears dancing up on the currents of the wind. She perceives the world with all her senses: she hears, she tastes, she feels, she sees. The sounds of music that float down from the clouds come from Amida's attendants who descend to the earth to receive the soul of the dead, yet Oryū is not ready for death.[21] In long, winding sentences, Oryū merges with the wind and the trees; she enters into a conversation with herself; she exists in two places at once. Free of her aged body, Oryū can see and hear what she pleases—her perspective encompasses the world.

When Oryū's spirit returns to her body, she resumes her narration of the Nakamotos' stories. As the text imparts details of the Nakamotos' lives, Nakagami engages a more direct narrative style. When Oriental Yasu first appears, for example, the story is told from Yasu's perspective, much as "Nokori no hana" shifts with the appearance of Jūkichi. The word *jibun* similarly anchors the narrative in the mind of its central character although it is written in third-person:

> Oriental Yasu had never thought himself [*jibun*] to be as handsome as Hanzō, and he had never been interested in what the alleyway women said about the manly Nakamotos. He couldn't care less about the doings between men and women. He had followed men trying to raise the flag in Manchuria and had gone to war. . . . When he got back, he couldn't contain his restlessness, and among those at the dance hall and the café, he chose the ones who looked like they could do something, and he invited them to accompany him to a new land. (*NKZ* 5: 107–8)

Through the direct reporting of Yasu's perceptions, we enter a single-consciousness narration. Through this convention, Nakagami imparts verisimilitude to the events of the Nakamotos' lives. Subsequently, however, the voice of Oryū again washes over the narrative, cleansing it of the immediacy of Yasu's perceptions and reminding the reader that we are in a story that transcends the specifics of one man's life and death. Nakagami sets up a tension between two visions of the world: the struggling Nakamotos, who are rooted in history, and the old woman Oryū no Oba, a narrator who both participates in and resides outside of the story.

Toward the end of the chapter, Oryū returns to earth, and turns her thoughts to the *roji*, past, present, and future. Oryū confronts her fear that "a thousand years of pleasure" will soon come to an end:

With such thoughts Oryū no Oba suddenly felt that she couldn't bear it and she entered the house and sat in front of the stove, which she always did when it was time to think. Peering into the stove where the fire had turned to ash, she mused that everything had gotten worse since the War; the sound of the men's voices chanting *banbai, banbai* was just a faint echo in her ears. As if to cleanse herself of these bad feelings, Oryū reviewed in her mind, "Oriental Yasu, or Yasuo, is the son of Yoshiaki; Yoshiaki is the son of Jinzaemon," and finally, all the warm memories of this world—of who had died and who would be born—came back to her body. As if willing herself back to the light after a brief descent into cold darkness, Oryū broke off a twig, shoved it under the pot and lit the fire again. Oryū was the *roji* itself, and no matter how old she got, as long as she had breath in her body, she would preserve this place where the babies tumbled into her hands and she bathed them for the first time before they reached their parents' arms. Like the virgin of a shrine, she would continue to take the *roji*'s pulse. But when she grew cold and couldn't move or think anymore, the children would lose their place, and those yet to be born would wander the world forever. Thinking of her own death, she cried, holding her hands out to the flames. (*NKZ* 5: 117)

Oryū's voice mutes the individual tales of the Nakamotos and reveals that *Sennen no yuraku*, with all its digressions, is a creation born in her mind. Realizing that the *roji* is on the verge of extinction, Oryū begins to recite the genealogy aloud to comfort herself: "Oriental Yasu . . ." This verbal recitation allows Oryū to literally "revive the memories of the warmth of this world that are felt by those who had died and those who are yet to be born. . . ." Because of her ability to experience the memories of the dead and the not-yet-born, Oryū's voice transcends or even reverses time. Yomota Inuhiko writes, "*Sennen no yuraku* is essentially a spoken *monogatari* (tale); at the same time it is a *monogatari* told by a narrator who is on the border between existence and nonexistence."[22] But we could go even further; through the character of Oryū, Nakagami creates a narrative that is thought or even dreamed aloud without regard to boundaries, tense, or person. Like the *nō* performer or *sekkyōbushi* narrator, Oryū exploits the fluidity of the word, turning it into an active agent that shapes both past and future. The word is the pleasure of a thousand years; it is Oryū herself, winding her way up on the currents of the wind.

Finally, *Sennen no yuraku* shifts the code of the *monogatari* because like "Nokori no hana" and "Futakami," it tells the tale from multiple, shifting points of view. Effortlessly, Nakagami moves from the action-driven stories of the Nakamotos to the poetry of Oryū's thoughts as she stirs the fire. In *Sennen no yuraku,* Nakagami does not fall back on what Karatani names "single-point perspective," nor does he remain in stream-of-consciousness mode. The book is challenging to read, as Iguchi suggests, partly because Nakagami moves so lightly on his feet. *Sennen no yuraku* draws us into a world apart; it is a piece of writing that is deeply engaged in the contemplation of its own performative nature.

Chinese Letters

Beginning in the late 1970s, Nakagami not only experimented with the language of fiction but he also wrote extensively about the process of writing it. In "Monogatari no keifu," for example, he addresses his complaints about the Japanese language in a more explicit form and hints of his deep alienation working in his native tongue. He turns to the cultural system that lies behind single-consciousness narration, contending that Japanese writers work within a cocoon of language and nurse illusions of a unique national literature (*kokubungaku*).[23] The views Nakagami expresses in this essay further illuminate his interest in disrupting the familiar and comfortable boundaries of the modern literary text.

The second section of "Monogatari no keifu" represents Nakagami's attack on the notion of *kokubungaku* as a literature that perpetuates myths about its own uniqueness. To illustrate the falseness of the term "national literature," Nakagami tells a story. Emerging from an inn in Shizuoka one day, his eye is caught by a sign in the *hiragana* script, the syllabic writing system based on Chinese characters that was in wide use in Japan by the tenth century.[24] At first the contours of the *hiragana* syllables that spell "strawberry" (*ichigo*) please him, but soon a wave of nausea sweeps over him. What troubles Nakagami is that behind the shapes of *hiragana* syllables he sees the shadows of the Chinese characters, and behind them the weight of Chinese civilization. How, he wonders, can we Japanese speak of a unique Japanese "national literature" when we work in a language filled with the fragments of another tongue? He elaborates:

> We use *kanji* [Chinese characters] and *hiragana* and *katakana*, which are derived from *kanji*, to write novels and criticism, to converse, and to dream. As long as we use Chinese characters that were invented in China, we don't have a distinct "Japanese spirit." We are Chinese, too, living under a Chinese system of thought. . . . What then is "Japanese national literature"? I have no idea.[25]

Nakagami's description of the Japanese as "Chinese" refers not to nationality but to an awareness that one's artistic and literary roots may lie outside of national literature. In subsequent pages, he illustrates this concept through a discussion of the writer Ueda Akinari, who explicitly recognized and highlighted the "Chinese" aspects of Japanese writing. This element is apparent in Akinari's supernatural tales, which are a dense web of references to both classical Chinese and Japanese texts.[26] To Nakagami, however, Akinari's ability to reproduce the dense language of the Chinese text represents more than skillful borrowing; it reveals that Akinari is aware of a world beyond the familiar contours of home. Nakagami reads Akinari's supernatural tales as a metaphor for the tenuous and difficult process of mediating between oneself and a foreign culture. He also notes Akinari's sensitivity to language: "The Chinese Akinari. What I mean by 'Chinese' is that in that period he was the one who was most aware of the strangeness of language itself. Aware of *sai* (difference) or *sabetsu* (discrimination), you could say."[27]

Nakagami traces Akinari's intuitive knowledge of "difference" to Akinari's mysterious birth (he was the son of a prostitute), and to his deformed hand. An inborn sense of alienation, along with Akinari's erudition, made him particularly suited to explore the mysterious and the strange. As he examined the distorted reflection of the Chinese in the mirror of the Japanese, he created what Nakagami calls "untouchable" tales (*fukashoku na monogatari*).[28] These "untouchable" tales are marked with a certain ironic detachment that Nakagami finds to be thoroughly modern. For example, in "Kibitsu no kama" (The Cauldron of Kibitsu), a story about a jealous wife who exacts revenge on her unfaithful husband, Nakagami is startled by the dispassionate tone of the prose and its lack of dramatic flair. He believes that this tone is purposeful, a sign that Akinari had voluntarily slipped from the attitudes of wonder and amazement that characterize the supernatural tale. Like Nakagami himself, Akinari had put distance between himself and his materials.

Perhaps the most interesting element of Nakagami's analysis of Akinari is how much it reveals about his own work. First, Nakagami clearly identifies with Akinari as a writer who knew about difference and discrimination. Second, his discussion of Akinari warns modern writers not to retreat into the cultural cocoon of the homeland; rather, the writer must embrace the foreign and reject the easy particularized realm of subjective personal experience. Again, Nakagami utilizes the premodern to criticize modern literary practices, and in his hands literary analysis becomes a tool of reform. Nakagami's advocacy of *sai* is simply another formulation of his desire to transform the language of the text.

In *Kishū ki no kuni ne no kuni* Nakagami takes a clue from Akinari, discovering *sai* not in full-blown supernatural tales but in the outcaste communities scattered along the Kii Peninsula. *Kishū* purports to be nonfiction, with Nakagami playing the role of reporter, yet a writer is clearly at work in its pages. Nakagami not only frames the spoken word on the page but he also emphasizes *ryōi* (strange marvels), as witnessed by his subjects.[29] In "Hongū," a chapter named after a small town in the mountains and the site of one of the three holy shrines of Kumano, Nakagami opens with a description of a nearby resort named Yunomine. A bubbling mineral spring known for its abilities to cure myriad illnesses, Yunomine has long been held to be the site of miracles. It was here that Oguri Hōgan who had fallen in love with Terutehime and had been murdered by her family, came back to life. It was here that Shuntokumaru sought his miraculous cure for leprosy.

Nakagami places Yunomine in its historic context in these pages—it is the point where the sacred waters of the spring and the impure body of the invalid meet; where death flows into life and life flows into death. But he also revitalizes the historic site by recording what he calls a contemporary *sekkyō-bushi* story. Nakagami interviews an old woman whose husband sought the restorative powers of the waters for what she describes as a wound from an accident and what Nakagami believes to be a case of leprosy. Through the medium of the old woman's speech, Nakagami links the sacred waters of Yunomine with the realm of his people, the outcastes of Kishū. Through the figure of the old woman, Terutehime, the faithful nurse and lover of Oguri Hōgan, speaks again.

The interest of the old woman's story lies in Nakagami's representation of the spoken and how even in a nonfictional text, he must struggle to capture the rhythms of oral speech. At first the narrator/reporter maintains an objective distance from his subject as he transcribes an account of her early life:

> The old woman's father was a gambler. "When there wasn't any rice, he gambled.and put food on the table." At the age of seven her mother died. Her father was a big man who could carry eighteen bags of coal He was strong enough to hoist nearly 200 kilos of cement and even hold down a bull. . . . "My mother died at Fukutani in Irokawa, in a hut in the mountains. She went crazy after she had us. One time they told me to go see her . . . she was singing a folk-song and dancing. I peeked through a chink in the wall. It was frightening." (*NKZ* 14: 557)

The story of the old woman begins with a clear demarcation between background narration and direct quoted utterance. Yet as the old woman's story progresses, the reporter cannot help entering the old woman's mind, giving a subjective cast to her experiences and filling in the edges around her speech. In the passage below, the boundaries between the objective narration and the old woman's speech break down as the reporter begins to speculate on the events of her life:

> At the age of thirteen she was sent to the cotton mill in Kishiwada to work. Down the Kumano River to Shingū. "It was 30 *sen* to take the boat, so instead I crossed over the mountains to Koguchi with a friend." According to the old woman, money wasn't the only deciding factor, she had gone that way to see her father who was in the mountains too. She spent a night in Koguchi. With her father, the gambler. "He bought me things," she said. Maybe her father had just won something. Or, from what we know about the cotton industry in those days, the father had probably sold his daughter into service and used the money to gamble, so perhaps he felt guilty. Maybe he'd found a comb that suited a young girl in one of his friend's stores. (*NKZ* 14: 559)

The use of conditional verb forms in the passage above (*darō*, *attarōka*) suggests that the narrator is extrapolating from the old woman's account and speculating on the motives of the young girl's father. As this occurs, the distinct styles of quoted utterance and narration blend, and the background narration—though not written in the verb endings that characterize broad dialect—mimics the rhythms of the old woman's speech. As he shifts back and forth, Nakagami subjugates the written narrative to the spoken, a tendency that becomes more pronounced as we reach the climax of the story: the illness of the old woman's husband. At this point, the reporter records the old woman's testimony in her local dialect, with few interjections, as if standard written Japanese could not do justice to her experience:

> The old woman said that her husband had a lung disease. It sounded like leprosy to me. I listened to her talk for a little while. "He was the boss at home. So when I told him to go to the doctor, he wouldn't go. But he did go to the springs at Yunomine. He had me burn moxa on his skin every day. It was around the end of December, no November, that he got a fever of 40 degrees [Celsius]. I called for the

doctor and he came on December 7th. Tomorrow, he said, I'll drain the abscess. On the 8th, he put down a dish and a stream of pus gushed out. I took it away and another dish filled up, then overflowed. The doctor bandaged it, my husband was shaking, his teeth chattering. When the sun came out, I went out to hang up the laundry, and he got angry wanting to know where I had gone. He was in such pain, he even cursed my father. They told him, you can go back to work after a couple of days, but when the day came, the pus was oozing out all over his shoulder. More and more pus. I cut the bandage thinking how odd it was. His sleeping things were soaked with it and it got all over me. Everything gone rotten. He had an abscess on his shoulder and he told me to squeeze it. I did and at first something like a broken tooth came out, and when I squeezed it again, something that looked like a piece of straw came out. That was the root of it. I took it to the doctor who said it was bone that had come loose. It was all because of that first wound. Because of that wound, he lost his nose, his ears rotted, his teeth fell out." Someone came and fumigated the house. The woman's husband was taken to a separate dwelling; he lived in darkness where no human eye could see him. "I worried, so I went to see him, but they said I was in danger." Before he got ill, her husband had walked to Yunomine with potatoes in his lunchbox. He was a man who loved cleanliness, so much so that before he went to work he powdered his armpits so that people wouldn't notice any smell. (*NKZ* 14: 559–60)

In the Japanese text, the woman's speech leaps out, slowing the reader down with its regional verb endings and expressions. The catalogue of the husband's disintegration reads like an oral eyewitness account of death encroaching slowly upon life. This account of the body's disintegration is reminiscent of Tanizaki's "Shōshō Shigemoto no haha" (The Mother of Captain Shigemoto, 1949–50), in which the narrator describes religious texts that advocate the contemplation of the rotting corpse to achieve salvation through impurity.[30] Similarly, in the dark mountains of Kumano, illness becomes a metaphor for the sacred in the form of the human body rotting before one's eyes. The leper is a living illustration of death in life, and life in death, a strange marvel of Kumano, or a miracle in reverse.

The old woman's testimony derives its power from its spoken origins; for Nakagami, *ryōi* is the word itself, unmediated and untranslated. Only this language can overturn discrimination (*sabetsu*) and begin to undo the "trap of words." In using regional cadences to catalogue the exact shape of the unclean, the text defies *sabetsu*—the viewing of a certain class of people as unredeemable. When Nakagami visits the main shrine at Hongū, for example, he sees evidence of *sabetsu* in a sign that prohibits "killing, pollution, and evil." To Nakagami, however, it is pointless to discuss a notion of the sacred that excludes the unclean; instead, he offers up the woman's voice as concrete proof that the sacred is rooted in the physical realities of the human body. The woman's voice persuades because it calls attention to its own striking difference. A transcription that bears little relation to written Japanese prose, it forces us to question how we read. As in *Sennen no yuraku,* Nakagami aims for the immediacy of the recited word, a form of the supernatural manifested in the world. Interestingly, Nakagami's attempts to disrupt standard prose bear fruit in a work that does not call itself a *shōsetsu,* a work in which Nakagami minimizes background narration (*ji no bun*) or dispenses with it altogether.

The final experiment in bringing alive a strange language on the page is "Jūryoku no miyako," the title story of a collection with the same name. Like "Nokori no hana," the story is another depiction of an encounter between a man and a woman that echoes Tanizaki's *Shunkinshō.* In "Jūryoku no miyako" a laborer named Yoshiaki encounters a strange woman who takes him home. Each day the woman suffers great torments because she is possessed by the spirit of a holy man (*ohito*) who is buried near the great shrines of Ise. Although sex with Yoshiaki briefly distracts the woman from the pain, eventually she begs Yoshiaki to blind her; this desperate act will free her from the torment of possession. As in *Shunkinshō,* blindness allows a character to deny reality and achieve freedom. In addition, the woman serves as a conduit linking this world to the next. But how does Nakagami fracture the narrative and bring *ryōi* alive through the voice of the *ohito*?

In "Futakami" and "Nokori no hana" Nakagami weakens the fabric of single-consciousness narration by inserting other voices that unsettle a straightforward reading of the story. In "Jūryoku no miyako" Nakagami carries this technique to even greater lengths and makes language itself suspect as though possessed by the spirits. For the most part, "Jūryoku no miyako" unfolds in Yoshiaki's field of vision as he begins to regard the woman with growing passion. Yet suddenly another voice breaks into the seamless depiction of Yoshiaki's experiences, challenging his dominant position; it is not the voice of the woman but the voice of the male spirit speaking through her body. The following literal translation preserves the immediacy of the spirit's utterances: "She said that her hands and feet hurt because the holy man [*ohito*], whose flesh had melted into a pile of rotting bones, lay in his grave at Ise, over the mountains and in the direction of the sea where the sun rose on the field each morning. He was groping her, saying as if this were only natural, "this is her ankle, this is the hollow of her knees, this her vagina." When he did this, the pain was transmitted to her body" (*NKZ* 10: 11).

Although Yoshiaki attempts to deny the existence of the spirit, the text says otherwise. The spirit moves through language, inflicting pain on the woman as he names the parts of her body. The words reverberate in the woman's chest, forcing Yoshiaki to listen. Nakagami uses *katakana* characters, usually reserved for foreign words, to represent the spirit's voice. The *katakana* stands out from the text, making the reader sound out the words, in order to capture the uncanny voice from beyond the grave. The spirit's moans seem incomprehensible, as if the page itself cannot contain them: his bones ache whenever it rains. As though reading a telegram in English, the reader must trace the message letter by letter: "I-t-h-u-r-t-s-s-o-m-u-c-h-s-t-o-p-t-h-e-r-a-i-n" (*itami ga hidoku naru kara ame o tomete kure*; *NKZ* 10: 20).

Like the body of the leper in the old woman's testimony in *Kishū*, the voice of the spirit brings *ryōi*, or strange marvels, to life in the text. In a reverse image of the dying leper, the decaying body of the corpse gains the power of speech: again, life bleeds into death and death bleeds into life. The power of *ryōi* is evident in the rotting flesh of the *ohito,* which has the power to manipulate the narrative through actual possession of the woman's body. The *ohito* represents Akinari's "untouchable" *monogatari,* the recited word that takes over the written narrative and defies the dictates of realism.

In the stories discussed above, Nakagami experiments with the language of the *shōsetsu,* a genre that tends to favor representations of the familiar and the known.[31] We might trace Nakagami's rejection of realism to intellectual trends in the 1980s, including the influx of European theories about writing (the postmodern toppling of the author), or even to Nakagami's interest in Latin American fiction. But Nakagami is not playing the postmodern raconteur when he creates texts filled with a chorus of voices. Rather, by challenging certain habits that have characterized the modern Japanese *shōsetsu* since its birth, Nakagami carves out space for alternate forms. With all the energy that he can muster, he muddies the surface of the *ji no bun.* It would be pointless to argue that Nakagami rejects *shōsetsu* style entirely but his experiments with *roji* language and his fascination with oral forms testify to his need to widen the scope of fiction writing—to bring other spaces and subjective viewpoints into common view. In *Kishū,* Nakagami once again suggests how *ryōi* saturates words:

> Kumano is a land that has been beaten down since the reign of Emperor Jimmu, a land wrapped in darkness. The names Kumano and Kumoriku [hidden country] are layers within this country of darkness. Mi-wa-sa-ki, U-gu-i, Na-chi, Ten-ma, Ka-tsu-u-ra, Ta-i-ji: if you take away the familiar Chinese characters and make these words into sounds alone, the strange shape of this defeated, darkened country emerges. Ko-za, Hi-me, Ta-ko, Wa-bu-ka, Su-sa-mi, As-so, the names of the towns go like this. These names sound like southern islands. (*NKZ* 14: 482)

As this rendition of place names suggests, Nakagami calls up the shape of the defeated country through its place names. He leads the reader to see the world from other perspectives—

whether from the sewer, the eerie realm of the spirits, or from a chain of southern islands. In his experiments with sound and grammar, Nakagami forcefully illustrates the need for a relativistic view of one's own language and culture, and he probes the construction of difference, the origin of *sabetsu*. In his hands, *sabetsu* is transformed from an instrument of oppression into the license to explore unfamiliar realms. Even *yotsu*, the derogatory term that pivots between the meanings of "four-footed" and "death," can be used to reconsider our deep fears about the physical processes of the body. The disgust inspired by the word "yotsu," Nakagami suggests, originates in our knowledge that we, like animals, are physical beings who must die, and we project this fear onto others. By allowing the "others" to speak and by keeping his ear to the ground, Nakagami fragments discrimination and unveils the dark, the impenetrable, and the unseen.

SIX

Violent Histories: The Snake and the Shaman

The imaginary had taken shape before his eyes.
–Nakagami Kenji, "Oni no Hanashi"

In three decades of writing, Nakagami Kenji explored the coordinates of *buraku* identity, created a fictional family saga, and pushed at the boundaries of Japanese literary language. A thread emerges in the work of a younger brother who struggles to resist a family or a community that threatens to engulf him. In the preceding pages we have explored the notion that masculinity itself is fragile; Nakagami's fiction is full of young men like Hanzō or Jūkichi who do not reach the age of 30. But we have not yet examined the ways in which masculinity is implicated in acts of violence. Nakagami's writing is peppered with graphic depictions of violence, which are often linked to sexual acts, and more often than not, violence is directed at the female body. In "Ja'in" (Snake Lust, 1975), Jun beats Kei; in *Karekinada*, Akiyuki rapes Kinuko; in "Tengu no matsu" (Pine Tree of the Tengu), the third chapter of *Sennen no yuraku*, Fumihiko ritually tortures his shaman lover at her request; and in "Ukijima" (1975), a laborer dispatches his lover (again at her request) in a pact of love suicide without killing himself.

The frequency of violence raises pressing questions: What end does the violent spectacle serve in Nakagami's work? Why is it such an integral part of Nakagami's writing? As readers, how do we approach Nakagami's predilection for feasts of eroticism and violence?[1]

Violence as Affirmation

In "Ima koko e" (In the Here and Now, 1985), Karatani Kōjin comments on the violent bursts that punctuate Nakagami's fiction. According to Karatani, Nakagami's promise lay not in writing "good *shōsetsu*" but in harnessing "something that was both violent and delicate" to create extreme fictions that transcend the parameters of the modern form.[2] He elaborates on the implications of violence in Nakagami's work: "What is violent about [Nakagami] is really the power of affirmation. And that power of affirmation is more destructive than any negation. What does he affirm? 'Here and now' (*ima koko*). 'Here and now' is transformation, variation, and the dissolution of good and evil. It opposes homogeneity, certainty, and discrimination."[3]

Karatani states that violence in Nakagami's work serves to affirm the present moment, or the ability to exist in one moment and no other. Being "present" in turn leads to the dissolution of such categories as death/life, illness/health, pleasure/pain, the basis for *sabetsu* or discrimination. In the same essay, Karatani mentions Nakagami's short story "Ja'in" as an example of how murderers and thieves "affirm difference." To Karatani, violent affirmation also gives Nakagami the freedom to create narratives that transcend the boundaries of a rigid Japanese literary and cultural system (*hō/seido*).[4] Taken to its logical conclusion, violence allows Nakagami to transform narrative itself.

In 1975, the same year in which "Ja'in" appeared, Nakagami issues a remarkable challenge to the Japanese classical canon. In the nonfictional preface to "Ukijima," Nakagami vows to undo the equivalences between celibacy and a "manly heart," and between woman and desire. Nakagami writes that he has based his story on a local Shingū folktale about a male snake that dragged young prostitutes into its lair in the marsh of Ukijima, a piece of land that still floats mysteriously in the middle of a swamp in Shingū today. What the reader must know, of course, is that the snake in Japanese legend appears more often in female form: transforming herself into a beautiful woman, the serpent seduces and then destroys her "victims." According to Nakagami, the female snake in Japan originated in Indian and Chinese prototypes that spread with the arrival of Buddhism. Nakagami intentionally returns to an earlier system of folk beliefs in which snakes were worshipped as the gods of swamps and ponds. By positing the male snake, Nakagami attempts to invert what he sees as a binding representation—the male as passive victim of the snake woman. He comments: "Are men saints [*hijiri*] who are sheltered by the Buddha and know nothing about filth? Are they virtue itself? What a stupid notion. And even if woman is a manifestation of the snake and is lustful, scheming, and wicked, man only came into this world with a thing dangling between his legs to go all the way with her" (*NKZ* 3: 61). Nakagami's stated goal is to counter the image of the lustful female snake with a male one—to reactivate the phallus between the legs and match the drive of the female snake. By having man go "all the way with her," Nakagami will realign the sexual dynamics of the text and thereby strike out at the deep patterns of the culture. Before we turn to the success of Nakagami's rewritings, we will touch briefly on changing visions of the female snake through time.

Perhaps the best-known depiction of the snake woman is the body of texts—*setsuwa* (didactic tales), *emaki* (illustrated scrolls), and *nō* drama—that surround the legend of Dōjōji temple, a version of which first appeared in the *Hokkegenki* (1004–43) and slightly later in the *Konjaku monogatari* (Tales of Times Now Past, c. 1120). The story tells of two priests who make a pilgrimage to the three holy sites of Kumano in the region of Wakayama. When they stop for the night in lodgings, the young widow of the house becomes infatuated with the younger of the two. That night she visits the younger priest's room, but he turns her away with a promise to return once he has completed his ablutions at Kumano. When the woman discovers that her prospective lover has returned home by another route to avoid her, she dies and is transformed into a monstrous snake. Slithering along the road, she catches up with her prey who has hidden himself beneath a great bell at Dōjōji temple. The snake coils her body around the bell, and generating great heat, reduces the young priest to a pile of ashes. The version of the story in *Konjaku monogatari* finishes with this admonition: "You see, therefore, the strength of evil in the female heart. It is for this reason that Buddha strictly forbids approaching women. Know this and avoid them. So the tale's been told and so it's been handed down."[5]

Nakagami correctly identifies the strain of much *setsuwa* literature: its deep misogyny and its fears of bodily defilement. But we might spend a few moments on Nakagami's claim that the female snake spread through Japan with the introduction of Buddhism, a foreign religion. In *Nihonjin no shisei kan* (Japanese Views of Life and Death), Yoshino Hiroko supports Nakagami's claim of a snake cult in pre-Buddhist Japan, but she states that this practice derived from ancestor worship. According to Yoshino, the snake was hermaphroditic, representing the phallus in its shape and the womb in its ability to shed its skin and periodically renew itself.[6]

Yoshino goes even further to suggest that the link between women and snakes predates the introduction of Buddhism. Expanding on the connection between the snake and female fertility in a discussion of the parturition huts or *ubuya* of ancient Japan, she rejects the notion that the early Japanese built these huts without doors and windows because they were fearful of impurity. Rather, Yoshino believes that the worship of snakes carried over into beliefs about birth: it was forbidden to peer into the *ubuya* because mother and child reverted to their original snake form at that moment.[7] In support of her thesis, Yoshino cites a myth from the *Kojiki* (Records of Ancient Matters, 712) in which Toyotamahime, the princess from the Dragon Kingdom beneath the sea, instructs her husband not to watch when she gives birth, saying: "All persons of other lands, when they bear young, revert to the form of their original land and give birth. Therefore, I, too, am going to revert to my original form and give birth. Pray do not look upon me."[8]

Another example of a pre-Buddhist link between snakes and women is the myth of the goddess, Izanami, who dies after giving birth to the fire god and descends into the underworld. Izanagi, the husband of Izanami, visits his wife and beholds a horrible sight: "At this time, maggots were squirming and roaring in the corpse of Izanami-no-mikoto. In her head was Great Thunder; In her breast was Fire-Thunder; In her belly was Black Thunder. . . ."[9] Yoshino suggests that the word "thunder" (*ikazuchigami*) can also be read as "fearsome spirit" and that it actually refers to Izanami's transformation into a snake.[10] As these stories suggest, the appearance of the snake is linked with moments of transition, from giving birth to the moment of death.

These literary sources and cultural practices suggest the remnants of what may have been a powerful role for the snake before the spread of Buddhism. Further, although the *setsuwa* compilers vilified the snake woman because they copied from continental models, later representations of the snake woman are not uniformly negative. Even in works that blame the snake woman for wrecking havoc on an innocent male, ambivalence comes into play. Susan B. Klein mentions a *nō* version of the *Dōjōji* play, *Kanemaki,* in which the figure of the snake woman is overlaid with a female founder of the temple, a diver who fished an image of Kannon out of the sea. Furthermore, the bell under which the priest hides is the object of the snake's hatred, but it eventually hastens her salvation when it rings in time to the chanting of the *Lotus Sūtra.* Finally, the snake woman herself is of indeterminate gender, because she appears in the form of a *shirabyōshi* dancer, a female entertainer who dresses in male garb.[11] Another tale that expresses sympathy for the snake woman is a medieval *setsuwa* entitled, "Onna musume o netami, te no yubi kuchinawa ni naru koto" (The Woman Who Became Jealous of Her Daughter and Whose

Thumbs Turned into Snakes). In a gesture of self-sacrifice, an older woman decides to give her own daughter to her new husband. She in turn retreats to a back room of the house and practices her religion. Unfortunately, the woman's repressed feelings of jealousy manifest themselves in a strange symptom: her two thumbs turn into snakes. No acrimony ensues from this malady and the story ends happily when the husband takes priestly vows and the woman and her daughter become nuns.[12]

Moving forward in time, Noguchi Takehiko discovers a note of sympathy for the snake woman even when she is at her worst. He describes the portrayal of the snake woman in Akinari's tale "Jasei no in" (The Lust of the White Snake, c. 1776), the title of which Nakagami shortened for "Ja'in." Akinari's tale tells of the love affair between Tōyō, the weak, studious son of a fisherman, and Manago, an ancient snake woman who has taken the form of a beautiful noblewoman.[13] "Jasei no in" adds a parodic element to the didactic legend of the Dōjōji temple, however. The female snake behaves wantonly, and Tōyō seems only too happy to surrender to her whenever she appears. In spite of the element of parody, however, Tōyō must repudiate Manago in order to survive. Snake-quelling takes on ideological overtones: Tōyō is first warned about the snake woman by Tagima no Kibito, a priest who belongs to the Yamato Shrine—which houses the god of the harvest and protects the nation from disaster. In order to save the hapless Tōyō from the snake woman, the priest lectures him on the necessity of cultivating a "manly heart" (*masurau kokoro*) free from passion.[14] Tōyō's father and brother also urge a "manly heart" upon him, the message being that Tōyō must reject the supernatural and the demonic for the linear, patriarchal order of the nation.

Although Manago is a repulsive creature, Akinari softens her portrayal by eliding her with the pathetic figures of abandoned women in *Genji monogatari*—Rokujō, Yūgao, and Suetsumuhana.[15] According to Noguchi Takehiko, Akinari sprinkled "Jasei no in" with literary references that would have been recognized by any reader of the time. In a depiction of a large pine tree in Manago's garden, for example, Akinari plays with the homonym of *matsu*, which as with the English word "pine" means both "pine tree" and "wait," conjuring up the image of the lonely woman who "pines" for her lover. While the story explicitly portrays the snake woman as a loathsome and foul creature, the language also reverberates with sympathy.[16]

These portrayals of the snake woman reveal that she has long been a symbol of what Nel Noddings calls "ambiguous evil." She is both an object of fear and of pity.[17] Nakagami's preface to "Ukijima," however, focuses only on the masculine question, stating that the phallic power of the male snake must be reinstated. We will turn to the work itself to see how Nakagami reworks the snake woman tradition and whether he successfully reworks the sexual dynamics of the story. "Ukijima" tells the story of Gonroku, a young man who carries heavy loads over the mountains for a living and who resides with wife and daughters in a house next to the Ukijima swamp. When Gonroku has money, he visits a child-like prostitute in a brothel above the swamp and she suggests that they commit suicide together. One night while making love, Gonroku strangles the prostitute, but when it is his turn to die, his passion cools and he returns home to wife and children.

In spatial terms, Nakagami at first seems successful in his portrayal of a male snake in "Ukijima." Situated next to the marsh, Gonroku's house might as well be in its center: when it rains, muddy water floods the house; and when it dries, a horrible stench permeates the walls. Like his model of old, Gonroku lies curled in his fetid hole ready to take his victim. Yet Gonroku's identity as snake is made suspect by the presence of a family in the house at Ukijima. Rather than serve as a hidden lair in which the snake devours his victims, the house in Ukijima grounds Gonroku in a domestic sphere from which he cannot escape. Gonroku lives with his wife, a heavy woman with sagging breasts, and two ugly daughters. The low placement of the dwelling by the marsh is recorded in the sickening odors of urine and rotten food that emanate from the mother and her children. Images of the marsh—with its evocation of the grotesque lower realms and the processes of excretion—are linked with the body of the mother whose role is to dominate and bind. On days when the smells fill the house, the mother scolds both husband and children violently, and Gonroku responds with blows.

In contrast to Gonroku's dirty domestic sphere, the prostitute occupies a higher realm in a brothel on a hill above the marsh. The high/low division of space is repeated in the body of the prostitute who has delicate proportions, in contrast to Gonroku's heavy wife. When Gonroku sleeps with the prostitute, he worries that the slender woman may not be able to withstand his onslaught. To Gonroku, the brothel is an escape from the ties that bind, a self-contained site where he can give free rein to fantasy.

In this site of fantasy, Gonroku resorts to extreme behavior to fulfill his desires. He murders the prostitute although she had envisioned a double love suicide. At first this brutal act seems to conform to the dynamics of male to female violence, functioning as an assertion of male autonomy. But certain passages contain ambivalent messages, as in the following depiction of Gonroku's thoughts:

> Loading raw materials and pulling them in the cart, he couldn't get the prostitute out of his mind. It had never happened to him before. By this time it seemed as though the woman would die of suffering. But there was power stored up in her thin arms, her slim waist and her slender legs. For a long time she would suffer, writhing and moaning and then falling completely limp. She would stay that way for awhile looking like a corpse. But then, as though life had returned to her, she would start to move her hands and arms. He wanted to see the woman suffering, and hear the involuntary moans that rose to her lips. She seemed like his wife but she was completely different. She was different from any other woman. She was different from any other prostitute. But he couldn't pinpoint why. (*NKZ* 3: 57)

It is here at the level of fantasy that the prostitute cancels out the identification between male and snake: she *is* the snake. In Gonroku's imagination, she writhes and twists with power "stored up" in her limbs. Like the ancient snake of the snake cult, the power of the prostitute lies in her flexibility to move back and forth between life and death and to renew herself periodically.

As portrayed in the passage above, Gonroku's desire for the prostitute takes the form of a scenario in which he watches the woman suffer: "He wanted to see the woman suffering and hear the involuntary moans that rose to her lips." At first we suspect sadism at work, but the passage above reveals that Gonroku actually needs the prostitute to carry out his own liberation. Gonroku requires that the woman be transformed—into a corpse, a snake, a being who dwells "over there" in the realm of death because it signals his own release—from the fetid snake hole and the realm of wife and children where no scenarios, no fluidity, no fantasies are tolerated.[18]

In the portrayal of Gonroku, we discover that Nakagami cannot rid the narrative of the snake woman because it would erase the figure of Gonroku who posits himself through her. An ambivalent projection of the male character's psyche, the snake woman is the source of many scenarios of both domination and submission. Furthermore, as her appearance signals the flowering of Gonroku's fantasy life, her death results in his despair. After he strangles the prostitute, Gonroku suddenly perceives the existence of a gap that separates this world from the next world, a gap that he can no longer bridge without her help. Cut off from the source of imagination, he realizes that he is lost and cries: "'Help me!' But the woman didn't move. How was he going to live from now on? How was he with this thing dangling between his legs going to survive now? the man asked himself. Separated by a membrane, over the edge of a mountain path, was that world. But he was on this side. He, with a body bigger than all the other mountain carriers, was here" (*NKZ* 3: 61).

The violent spectacle is followed by remorse and a declaration of helplessness. Again, questions arise as to the motive behind the murder. Did Gonroku kill the woman because she threatened to overwhelm his existence in this world? If so, her death signals the end of Gonroku's hopes for deliverance. "Ukijima" reveals the trap of the typical Nakagami protagonist who cannot bear what the snake woman represents, but who also cannot survive without her. Rather than create a triumphant male snake, Nakagami's story ends with Gonroku lamenting abandonment like a child.

The Snake Woman of "Ja'in"

"Ja'in" tells the story of Jun, a young delinquent who murders his parents in a moment of rage, and flees with his lover, Kei, to Tennōji, a popular site for love suicides. Jun falls in love with Kei when she comes to work as a waitress in Jun's coffee shop and he defies his parents by bringing Kei into the house and having sex with her there. Jun's mother repeatedly tells the lovers to "learn more of shame" (*NKZ* 2: 158), and she tells Jun that Kei is a "lustful snake" who merely wants him for his money.

If we read "Ja'in" through the lens of Karatani's notion of "violent affirmation," the story might well be a tale of liberation. Jun's parents are social climbers who have escaped their *burakumin* origins and have taken steps toward respectability. Jun's father has become a successful contractor; his mother has taken up the bourgeois hobby of the tea ceremony; and Jun has been given a coffee shop to run. What angers Jun, however, is not his parents' social mobility but their hypocrisy when they reject his lover Kei, a child of their old neighborhood. One might easily conclude that the murder has allowed Jun to escape the sterility of his parent's house and embrace desire in his lover's arms.[19]

A superficial reading might also lead one to think Nakagami successful at refashioning the dynamics of the archetypal tales and placing Jun in a position of power. Unlike Tōyō, the passive fisherman of Akinari's tale, Jun is the seducer, bringing Kei to live in the family house over the protests of his parents and making love to her to the sounds of jazz. Nakagami further reverses the older social equation: Manago, the snake woman is a noblewoman who showers Tōyō with gifts, while Kei is the impoverished daughter of an alcoholic woman from the *roji*. Furthermore, Jun rejects his mother's reading of Kei as a grasping snake; Kei has none of the ambitions ascribed to her by his own upwardly mobile mother. At the end of the story Jun turns toward Kei and notes, "large tears swam in those eyes that supposedly flickered with lust" (*NKZ* 2: 167).

"Ja'in" opens with a scene of carnage: Jun, the young delinquent, has just murdered his parents and placed their bodies in the family bathtub. Kei washes the bloody bathroom down with a hose. This tableau—the two dead bodies and the sensuous, naked body of Kei—illustrates the complicit relationship between violent outbursts and erotic climaxes in Nakagami's work. In the following passage, Jun muses over the causes of his crime, and at the same time, is unable to resist another outburst:

> Even now he thought the same way about it. He'd had no real reason to beat them with the ashtray—his body had just burst into flames. He brooded. The woman was completely naked. Was she a snake? Was she lust incarnate? . . . She sat down next to him exuding a scent of soap. "Jun," she said, "What are we going to do?" He remained silent. She lay down on the bed, pressing her body against his chest. His mother had been worried. He couldn't understand what it was about the woman that had made his mother nervous. At his age, what had he done? No, it was because of his age that he had done this. The woman wrapped her arms around his naked chest. He felt as if this had been his plan all along.
>
> "Burn down the house," he replied. The woman looked up at him blankly, but he didn't elaborate. She was a little deaf and he didn't feel like pressing her. Reaching for her nipples as she lay pressed against him, he found they were hard and he rubbed them between his fingers. The woman's eyes grew serene. He shifted her body to position her on top and when that didn't work, pulled her down beneath him. Too bad he hadn't put on any jazz. He got excited anyway and just when he was on the verge of exploding, the woman came. He felt his body go completely slack and he got out of bed. A missed chance, he thought. He grabbed the woman by the hair and shook her, thinking "you attached yourself to me, we've gone through all this and I bet you're planning to leave me." "Jun, Jun," she begged. He shoved her off the bed and pushed her face into the carpet, holding her by the hair. This is exactly what his father had

done to his mother, he thought. Then he let go. He wished it was a dream but he knew it wasn't. This was real. (*NKZ* 2: 166–67)

In the aftermath of the murder, Jun cannot identify a reason for his crime beyond the sensation of his body bursting into flames. Like a spark set to combustible material, Jun's violence seems spontaneous, an impulse born of pure rage that culminates in the bloody spectacle in the bath. Furthermore, one act of senseless violence segues into the next as Jun pins Kei down below him on the carpet.

Before we read Jun as violence incarnate, however, we might take a closer look at the story: is Jun as bold as he seems? In the murder scene from "Ja'in," the notion of "violent affirmation" is weakened by the fact that rather than suspend the reader in the present moment, the violent act is deeply embedded in a plot that unfolds in time. Hayden White defines narrative as: "the problem of fashioning human experience into a form assimilable to structures of meaning. . . ."[20] We might add that it is narrative that gives shape to time. Jun openly expresses interest in how his violent acts stem from his past and concurrently shape his future. After the murder, Jun asks a question that concerns his lover, Kei, in order to impose order on experience: "Was she a snake, was she lust incarnate?" Perhaps, Jun implies, the snake woman or lust itself explains his terrible crime. This question is a recapitulation of the mother's charges that Kei is a "snake woman" who seduced her son in order to improve her own position in life.

Rather than dispense with narrative design, Jun wants nothing more than to make sense of his violence by shaping it into a story with a beginning, middle, and an end. In fact, his violent treatment of Kei serves as a catalyst in the narrative; it is only when Jun holds Kei down that he makes the connection between himself and his father. Instead of lifting Jun into a defiant present moment, his own behavior makes him wish himself far away: "He wished it were a dream, but it wasn't. This was real." After he establishes the connection to his father, Jun travels back even further into the past to speculate on the causes of his own behavior. In another section of the story, Jun dredges up old memories of fights between his mother and father:

> Holding the knife in her hand, his mother glared at his father in silence. The father moved toward her. His mother didn't move to strike and his father grabbed her arm and knocked the knife out of her hand. Then he pushed her down and started kicking her. She moaned, scolded, and wept. His mother's parents burst in from next door. This happened over and over again. He didn't know whether it happened because of his father's womanizing, his mother's slovenliness, or just because they were poor. (*NKZ* 2: 161–62)

Jun digs back into the past, questioning the causes of violence in his own family, and seeking clues to his own actions. Although he cannot find answers, his questions enrich the texture of the narrative, sending out shoots and providing new possibilities for refining and retelling the story. Past and present violence illuminate the predetermined quality of Jun's story: Jun realizes that his own violent acts are the culmination of forces that were set in motion before he was born. His own story, he senses, has always been beyond his control. When Jun tells Kei that they will burn the house down, he "felt as if this had been his plan all along" (*NKZ* 2: 167). Later, Jun expresses a suspicion that even his meeting with Kei had been prearranged.[21]

Predetermination also characterizes the story of Kei. Jun first appears to view Kei as an innocent victim of his own family drama, particularly his struggle to wrest autonomy from his mother. Once again, however, ambivalent images gleam beneath the surface. Images of physical transformation and magical abilities link Kei with the snake woman of "Jasei no in." Kei has a deaf ear that she hides under a curtain of hair; when she shakes her hair, she frightens Jun. The deaf ear substitutes both for a vagina and a dumb mouth, a passage through which Kei is able to access a hidden past. As the shaman's blindness is traditionally a sign of her highly developed powers of sight, so too is Kei's deaf ear an instrument of memory and stories. Jun both desires and fears Kei because of the deaf ear; on purpose he speaks into the ear, knowing that he will confuse her. But in spite of his games, Jun realizes that Kei possesses a superior memory: "When it was time to close the shop or when they didn't have any customers, Kei reminisced about the past, but Jun didn't remember a thing" (*NKZ* 2: 152). Furthermore, Jun's confusion extends to an inability to navigate the alleyways where he was born: when he visits the *roji*, he cannot identify a single familiar landmark but must depend on Kei whose memory and link to the past make her the focus of Jun's obsessions. The passage below suggests parallels with the thoughts of Gonroku: "He was crazy about the woman—to the extent that he didn't recognize his feverish self. In the shop, the woman pretended not to know him. This bothered him and it made him feel effeminate. It had never happened before. . . . The way she changed the record, the movement of her fingers, her body when she took orders, the images were burned on his pupils" (*NKZ* 2: 156). In this passage, Kei initiates two disturbing transformations in the protagonist. First, Jun no longer recognizes his feverish self. Second, Jun feels effeminate (*memeshii*)—as if Kei were in control. Again, the snake woman holds up a mirror in which the protagonist views himself in startling ways. Like Gonroku, Jun becomes dependent on the vision and speech of the snake woman to transform his own position in the world.

Nakagami explores the link between gender and the violent spectacle in "Ja'in" but we cannot ignore the fact that the moment of realization for Jun comes as he pins Kei down on the floor. Given that the violent spectacle often involves a woman as its object, to what degree is violence an affirmation to Kei? Although the murder of the parents turns Jun's world upside down, the same claim cannot be made for Kei. Kei becomes the recipient of Jun's anger in a process of "displaced abjection" in which the subject (Jun) imitates those who have mistreated him by turning his rage on vulnerable members of his own group.[22] The problem of displaced abjection proves especially troubling because Kei is a member of the same oppressed minority as Jun; in fact, she occupies an even lower position in the social and economic hierarchy than he does.

Through his affair with Kei, Jun retreats into his room, escaping from the family through sex and jazz. In "Ukijima," Gonroku retreats to the rarefied space of the brothel where the woman waits for him in perpetual readiness. The fact that the protagonists' transformations each occur during a violent encounter with a woman in a space apart gives violence a thoroughly private character in Nakagami's texts. The dynamic of the violent spectacle—now reduced to a private fantasy—is thoroughly dependent on a certain context; it lacks any external momentum, it only refers back to the protagonist's mind. The private nature of Nakagami's violent spectacles again leads to the problem of displaced abjection because violence is concentrated on the body below one instead of outwards to confront a rigid cultural system. Nakagami intends to reverse the components of the equation—to free up male and female—but the woman in the room still projects the demonic and the dark. Although Nakagami would have male and female "go all the way" together, his protagonists keep the shaman and the snake woman pinned beneath them, as though to imagine the world through their bodies.

The limited scope of the violent spectacle—a spectacle based on the rhythm of the sexual climax and unable to move beyond the confines of the room apart—is replicated in the experience of the reader. We fall silent before violence in Nakagami's work because it draws us into the claustrophobic space in which the fantasy unfolds. We become passive spectators who watch and consume, viewing the world not through the eyes of the victim but through the eyes of the perpetrator. Yet the violent spectacle does not touch anything outside of itself; it simply perpetuates the hierarchies of a fixed cultural system, stranding the reader in darkness.

Shamans and Angels

The private drift of fantasy and displaced abjection continues to characterize Nakagami's portrayals of violence into the 1980s.

Yet there is a change in the work that dates from *Sennen no yuraku* as Nakagami turns his attention to refashioning feminine representations of the divine. The violence that characterizes his work in this period is no longer aimed at unraveling past family dramas, but rather takes on a ritualistic character in stylized erotic encounters, physical mutilation, and spirit possession. The ritualistic nature of violence in these works reveals Nakagami's heightened consciousness of his own project as a writer—to overturn deeply entrenched literary and cultural ways of seeing which have becomes formalized over the centuries. His exploration of the ritualistic act of violence is most pronounced in representations of a sister of the snake woman—the figure of the shaman (*miko*). In the short story "Fushi" (The Immortal, 1984) and the third chapter of *Sennen no yuraku*, "Tengu no matsu," Nakagami depicts ritualistic acts of violence as the inevitable result of an encounter with a supernatural or divine being in female form.

The rape or abduction of a shaman figure near a mountain pool appears with some frequency in Nakagami's work. In "Fushi," for example, a priest encounters a strange woman with tiny hands scooping water from a stream as he wanders the mountains and he rapes her repeatedly. In "Tengu no matsu," the young Nakamoto, Fumihiko, abducts a beautiful shaman beside a mountain pool and takes her back to his house in the *roji*. In his portrayal of the woman by the pool, Nakagami draws on a rich tradition of images and textual associations.

The mountain pool is a familiar topos in premodern literary and religious texts. In the *shugendō* tradition, a syncretic mix of Buddhist and native practices, for example, priests practiced austerities at mountain pools in their search for enlightenment. One early literary representation of the mountain pool in the *shugendō* tradition appears in the *Konjaku monogatari*, in the story of En no Gyōja, the mythic founder of the sect, who purifies himself there before descending from the heights to demonstrate his powers.[23]

In the Buddhist didactic literature, women were believed to defile sacred spaces and were barred from entering them.[24]

This prohibition crossed into all aspects of religious life. In the *Dōjōji* tale, for example, the priest cannot have sex with a woman on his way to worship at the shrine of Kumano, because doing so will not only break his Buddhist vows but also defile the deity of the shrine.[25] Man projects the shifting uncertainties of the body upon woman and makes her culpable for male desire. Beyond the constricting framework of early Buddhism, however, the tableau of the woman by the pool taps into another rich religious tradition—that of the female shaman. According to Barbara Ruch, this tradition was represented in many lesser-known sources, such as the songs from the *Ryōjin hishō* (c. 1170) and the *Kanginshū* (c. fourteenth century), as well as medieval paintings, eventually emerging in *nō* drama; however, these representations have been ignored by most historians. In "The Other Side of Culture," Ruch writes: "The importance of shamanism in ancient as well as medieval life has been underestimated and essentially ignored in contemporary historical discourse. Female dominated and individual oriented, it was in marked contrast with male-dominated and institution-oriented Buddhism."[26] Ruch has discovered evidence of various types of shamans in business in medieval Japan: wealthy cosmopolitan women in business for themselves, ascetic and virginal shamans, and others who fell into prostitution as they wandered the countryside advertising their skills. In an essay on "sacrilized courtesans" of the Muromachi period, Michele Marra focuses on the latter groups—shamans who practice a potent combination of sex and prophecy. Marra discusses holy men who had visions of bodhisattvas in the form of courtesans and also cites textual evidence that the powerful shaman figure was absorbed into the Buddhist order as the "celestial wife" of the priest.[27] These practices allowed Buddhist institutions to tap into the rich vein of the shaman tradition and at the same time exert control over a female tradition that challenged Buddhist hegemony.

In the modern period, the figure of the erotic shaman appears in slightly different form in *Kōya hijiri* (The Holy Man of Mt. Kōya, 1900), a tale by Izumi Kyōka. A priest travels to the mountains and encounters a beautiful woman, the daughter of a quack doctor, who has supernatural healing powers. She takes the priest to a mountain pool and bathes him. "And as the pain from my wounds ebbed away, I gradually lost my senses, as if the woman's body, so close to mine, had enveloped me in the petals of its blossoms."[28] Tempted to forget his vows, he longs to remain with the woman and enjoy the soft touch of her hands. Yet the priest changes his mind when an old man tells him that the animals he sees all around him are former lovers of the woman, and he continues his journey down the mountain.

Kōya hijiri maintains the traditional mode of linking woman with the body, desire, and the supernatural. As Charles Inouye has shown, the woman in the Kyōka story is linked to the pool of water, which in turn symbolizes both desire and death, and the priest barely escapes with his life. The priest resists seduction, but he has been thoroughly transformed by his desire for the woman. Like a talisman, he brings his longing for her back to the world and revisits it each time he tells his tale. Through a depiction of the supernatural woman in the mountains, Kyōka comments on the power of the tale, which unfolds around the listener like a dream. Through words the priest again experiences the touch of the woman's hands without giving up his vows or his human form.[29]

The woman by the pool in Nakagami's "Fushi" descends from the sorceress of Kyōka's tale. Yet rather than recreate the dream-like atmosphere of *Kōya hijiri*, "Fushi" returns to a more primitive time when an encounter between the human and the divine might result in sacrifice or death. Like *Kōya hijiri*, "Fushi" describes the journey of a wandering holy man (*hijiri*) into the mountains and his encounter with a beautiful woman by a mountain pool. Yet unlike Kyōka's priest, Nakagami's *hijiri* has sex with the woman, follows her on a supernatural journey into the mountains, and then plots to murder her. At the end of the story, the *hijiri* turns towards the woman and discovers that she has disappeared in a flock of crows, a sign that she was indeed divine or that she never existed at all.

Nakagami makes reference, particularly near the end of "Fushi," to Sakaguchi Ango's "Sakura no mori no mankai no shita" (In the Forest, Under Cherries in Full Bloom, 1947).[30] In Sakaguchi's story, a mountain man kidnaps and then becomes enchanted with a beautiful noblewoman from the capital. Acquiescing to the woman's every desire, the man procures fine goods and human heads to entertain his new wife. The story ends when the man carries the woman through a forest of blossoming cherry trees and she turns into a demon. In a bed of cherry flowers, the man strangles the demon, but when he turns to look again, she is gone. Through the woman, Sakaguchi makes the point that Japan, trapped in its hierarchical sets of relations and its fixed aesthetic obsessions, still worships phantoms—demons that appear to be beautiful woman but who dissolve into nothingness.

In "Fushi" Nakagami moves along a slightly different axis, deconstructing the equation of the celibate priest and the defiling sensual woman. At first the priest seeks to justify his own desires by invoking models of the priesthood: "even a scholar priest bound by high rank at the main temple would violate the commandments if he met a woman alone in the mountains."[31] Yet soon the story dispenses with this opposition altogether. The *hijiri* is not a devoted ascetic nor is the woman a fiendish representative of sexual desire. Rather, she becomes a manifestation of the mysterious landscape of Kumano itself—a place that has been worshipped by religious seekers down through the centuries—and she opens his eyes to its beauty. The *hijiri*'s desire for the woman becomes equivalent to a desire to penetrate the secrets of the land:

> Peering down from the cliff, she pointed with one of her childlike fingers. The wind blew through her hair and to the *hijiri*, her face was more lovely than anything that he had seen before. He found himself looking down the precipice as if captivated by her gaze. It was there that he had suddenly wanted to drink desperately from the waterfall, and there that he had been inspired to enter the falls and be lashed by the water.[32]

The *hijiri*'s desire for the woman takes the form of worship and he clings to her body, imagining that she is a manifestation of the bodhisattva Kannon who has come to save him, or an angel who has descended from above in a feathered robe. Rather than degrade her, his lust deifies her further. Her body becomes an object of contemplation, a mandala of the universe: "It was enough to do nothing, it was enough that this woman was breathing beside him, with her skin of peach blossoms bathed in morning light and her golden down—her red nipples, her navel which seemed to him the center of this world."[33]

Through the act of sex, the *hijiri* can briefly hold the angel to this world, but gradually, the *hijiri*'s desire to possess the woman transforms into a different desire; if he cannot keep her forever, he will destroy her. The figure of the angel is superimposed in the *hijiri*'s mind with a village woman whom the *hijiri* did murder. This woman had begged the *hijiri* to save her, calling him by the name of "holy man." Yet rather than elevate him, her words only reminded the *hijiri* of his bestial nature and he strangled her. The divine woman similarly threatens to strip the *hijiri*, not of his sainthood, but of his existence on earth as a wanderer and a beggar: "The *hijiri* was seized with an evil thought, . . . he saw a vivid image of himself wandering from village to village, from mountain to mountain, like a beggar or a thief, and he thought, *Shall I . . . jaarajaara . . . kill this woman?*—just as the *hijiri* he saw in his mind, unable to bear his own existence, had once killed a woman."[34]

In both cases, the women mock the *hijiri*'s illusions of authenticity and reveal him to be an outcast who belongs neither to the world of men nor to the realm of the gods. Both women represent an order—one sacred, one profane—from which the *hijiri* is barred. Although the *hijiri* does not succeed in killing the angel, the impulse to murder is born in the *hijiri*'s own "unbeareable" existence. If he cannot be a part of the symbolic order, he will destroy it. Murder also provides an antidote to meaning like the nonsense sounds *jaarajaara* that bubble up from the *hijiri*'s throat.

In "Tengu no matsu," an erotic encounter with a semi-divine being ends in an even greater cataclysm. Fumihiko, one of the young Nakamotos, goes to work in the mountains where he buys sex from a woman who is actually a shaman in training. Longing to see the woman afterward, Fumihiko follows a group of female shamans deep into the mountains and spies on them as they purify themselves in a waterfall, dance with bells, and sing to the gods. When he announces his presence, the women scatter; although they sleep with men for money and food, the presence of a man at the site of their devotions is defiling. Fumihiko carries away his lover, and tearfully she agrees to live with him. The two return to town where the woman urges Fumihiko to pierce her body with needles, a practice that results in her death at Fumihiko's hands. Despondent, Fumihiko commits suicide.

"Tengu no matsu" also upsets the paradigm of the man as ascetic pure being: here the woman is a devoted practitioner while the man cannot shake himself free of desire. When Fumihiko follows the shamans into the mountains, he defiles their sacred place of practice and is labeled an animal. Further, the woman's link to her community of shamans is revealed by the pain that she feels on rainy days coming to her from the mountains. She will use sex with Fumihiko to reproduce this pain and unite with the god. He in turn realizes that he is in the presence of the divine—that she is Amida in human form: "he sheds his clothes as if in prayer," and as she approaches her ecstatic climax, Fumihiko, too, "enters the vortex of pleasure" (*NKZ* 5: 90).

The shaman disrupts reality as we know it and rends the membrane that separates this world from the next. She draws Fumihiko in behind her when she leaves the mundane world for the "vortex of pleasure." This climax can lead only to the final disruption of death, the moment when the shaman enters into union with the god.[35] But can we read Fumihiko's suicide in a similar manner as a blissful union with a god? As in "Fushi," the shaman excludes the protagonist from the other realm. As a child, Fumihiko had visions of *tengu* (mythical bird-monsters) when he walked in the mountains, but no one believed him: "He didn't expect people to believe him when he recounted his visions; he himself thought that they were products of his own imagination" (*NKZ* 5: 88). Until this point Fumihiko has dwelled in a private world. But the shaman teaches Fumihiko that his visions do not belong to him alone; she, too, has the ability to see the *tengu*. This startles Fumihiko because it upsets his identity as the visionary outcast of the community. And rather than accept the revelation that both he and the woman have the power to see, Fumihiko suddenly concludes that she is a *tengu* who has assumed human form in order to deceive him. Following the old pattern, man and woman do not "go all the way together."

Fumihiko's suspicions place a barrier between him and the woman and prevent him from being swept away in her arms. Again, the woman represents a different order of experience, an extreme figure reaching for the divine. Fumihiko's desolation at the end of the story results from his realization that he has been barred from the symbolic order represented by the woman, and that he, like her needles or her masochistic practices in the mountains, has merely been a tool to hasten her own apotheosis. In desperation, Fumihiko tries to follow the woman to the other side, stepping through the veil that separates them, to his own death.[36]

In these two depictions of the shaman, Nakagami attempts to redress the balance of male and female by making the male into the active agent. But the shaman still stands at the intersection between this realm and the next. Through erotic encounters, the shaman draws the protagonist into her orbit, forcing them to reflect upon their own identities. As George Bataille writes, this is always true of the erotic: "Eroticism is one aspect of the inner life of man, . . . eroticism is that within man which calls his being into question."[37] When fear or hesitation holds the protagonist back, the shaman continues her journey, leaving him behind. It is these two movements—the disturbance of the self in the erotic encounter and the resulting abandonment—that spark violence on the part of the protagonists. In

"Fushi" the *hijiri*'s plot to murder the angel is fundamentally a strategy to prevent her departure. Similarly, Jun's treatment of Kei in the opening passage of this chapter stems from the transformations that she has wrought in him and his fear of eventual abandonment.

Once abandonment occurs, the protagonists of Nakagami's fictions return broken and defeated, even suicidal from their encounters with shamans. Again, Nakagami suggests that each story is the same: forever out of the protagonist's control. The *hijiri* in "Fushi" is haunted by a sense that he is a passive observer: "The *hijiri* . . . turned to ask the woman one more time if she would live with him in a village. There was no one there. The *hijiri* thought that he had known that from the beginning, too."[38]

A similar crack appears in Fumihiko's mind when he is suddenly struck by a sense of déjà vu as he and his lover walk through the mountains together. The passivity of Jun, Fumihiko, and the *hijiri* suggest that not only do they view themselves as puppets in a predetermined tale, but also that the shaman retains her power. Showing uncanny flexibility, she appears and disappears at will; she easily navigates the path between this world and the next. I would take issue with Nina Cornyetz's claim that "when Nakagami's protagonists reclaim the power of the snake's lust from the female archetype, they simultaneously deconstruct the conceit of coercion by erotically agentive, dangerous women."[39] Given the textual examples above, I do not believe that Nakagami has succeeded at this task. Cornyetz further identifies the misery of the abandoned protagonists, stating that these tales set up "resistances within resistances" and in the end, one reaches the "dissolution of the site of resistance."[40] But if the protagonists succeed at redressing the balance and if the site of resistance itself dissolves, why the abject misery and despair? Livia Monnet argues the case, in a more directly critical fashion, reading "Fushi" as a text that "brilliantly exemplifies the relation between representation, fantasy, and the reality of (sexual) violence, but at the same time, provides it, as it were, with the means to legitimate its own violent, masculinist textual politics."[41] In order to understand violence more fully in Nakagami's texts, we must explore the power of the female shaman. In what ways exactly does she exercise control?

Spinning Tales

The shamans of "Fushi" and "Tengu no matsu" draw strength not only from their abilities to entice and confuse through sex but also from their abilities as storytellers. In "Ja'in," for example, Kei misleads Jun by telling him stories about their early life together in the *roji* that Jun cannot remember. In contrast to Jun, who tries to make sense of his past, Kei uses stories to disguise connections between events. She tells Jun, for example, that she became deaf in one ear after her father beat her for stealing a fig from a plant on Jun's front steps; later, however, Jun discovers that Kei's mother beat her when she discovered her boyfriend molesting the young girl. To Kei, storytelling is survival, a means to obscure the remorseless clarity of violence.

The shaman in "Fushi" also disguises the connections between places and events that would make the narrative intelligible. When the angel takes the *hijiri* on a journey deep into the mountains, she dismisses his questions about the supernatural creatures that surround them, assuring him that they are merely wild boars passing in the night. Without her the *hijiri* would be lost, but she refuses a clear explanation for what he has seen. In "Tengu no matsu," too, the shaman prevents Fumihiko from learning too much about her practices by refusing to answer questions about her origins. To the confusion of the male protagonist, women both spin and disguise the tale in the same breath. These "female" narratives, with their blind spots and twists, do not correspond to Hayden White's definition of the word "narrative" (as fashioning experience into meaningful structures), a formulation that stresses its accessibility and its universality. The partly obscured web of women's stories in Nakagami's work suggests a different dimension to narrative altogether: it is never fully revealed in the broad light of day but unfolds in shadow in a series of revelations and reversals.[42]

The shadowy aspect of narrative is a further reflection of the ways in which the shaman mediates between the male subject and the divine. Violence toward these female figures thus becomes a means to wrest control of the narrative itself. By murdering the angel and piercing the shaman's body with needles, the protagonist attempts to take her place. This dynamic is highly suggestive in that it creates a metonymical link between the categories of female and narrative. Put more directly, it also suggests the justification for remaining mired in the symbolic systems of the past. Here we have the perfect justification for violence: the tale is feminine, it silences male speech, and must be thrown off like a heavy weight.

The most interesting aspect of this notion of a "feminine" presence shadowing Nakagami's work is the extent to which Nakagami promoted the idea himself. In "Monogatari no keifu," Nakagami discusses Tanizaki Jun'ichirō's masochistic tableau in which a man worships the feet of a beautiful woman. To Nakagami, the image is an apt metaphor for Japanese literature as a whole: the artist (male) is held captive by a narrative (female) that will punish and tease him. Masochism becomes the dominant mode of the writer who is under the spell of the *hō/seido*. But as we have seen in another chapter of this book, one learns far more by worshipping the *hō/seido* through masochistic play. Nakagami explains: "The picaresque, aestheticism, perversion, masochism, and fetishism reveal, whether consciously or unconsciously, the origins and the powers of the *hō/seido* much more than do more traditional pursuits. . . . From the viewpoint of humanism, it is hard to understand [the characters in the story "Shisei" (The Tattooer)], but Tanizaki doesn't write about human beings, he writes about puppets controlled by the system."[43]

Nakagami suggests that Tanizaki's fiction exposes the forms of the *hō/seido* more effectively than do other forms of writing. His interpretation of Tanizaki also illuminates a contradiction that marks his own representations of the feminine. On the one hand, as we have seen, the shaman is a divine intermediary who represents an avenue of escape to the protagonist; she is his key to the divine. On the other hand, however, the shaman reveals the presence of the *hō/seido* and she takes the form of a narrative (*monogatari*) that binds.[44] The contradiction between woman as divine medium and woman as binding *monogatari* illuminates the ambivalent portrayal of violence that we have discussed earlier in this chapter. The male protagonist, torn between his desire for release and a perceived threat to his own autonomy, strikes out even as he stands dazed and humbled before the divine. In fact, as we have seen, Nakagami's protagonists, in spite of their violent behavior, assume a passive position before the figure of the shaman. Could we then compare Nakagami's protagonists to those in Tanizaki's fiction who assume an abject position before the foot of a beautiful woman? Might not Nakagami's violent gestures simply conceal an attitude of masochism?

In *The Forms of Violence*, Bersani and Dutoit question why human beings are drawn to violence in art, whether they celebrate or repudiate it. Their answer is that although violence produces disgust in the spectator, it also produces excitement, which is tinged with a sexual element. Oddly enough, the excitement that the observer feels upon beholding a violent scene is not based on identifying with the figure who gives pain. Rather, the observer feels pleasure because he/she identifies with the suffering victim, vicariously experiencing that person's pain as masochistic pleasure. Bersani and Dutoit go even further; the excitement felt by the observer, often masked as sympathy, is a means to destabilize the self, which is the primary goal of masochism.[45]

Gilles Delueze paints a different picture of masochism and sadism by drawing a distinction between the languages that characterize the writings of Sade and Sacher-Masoch. Although both Sade and Sacher-Masoch aim for Thanatos, the death instinct, Deleuze believes that they strive for this goal in dramatically different ways. The sadistic text uses language to demonstrate that "reasoning itself is a kind of violence": the libertine lectures his victims, drafts a constitution, or engages in a debate. The goal of the sadist is to pursue the ultimate negation of all laws and states of being. In contrast to the sadist, the masochist tends to use language that is persuasive and dialectical, the primary goal being to persuade a reluctant partner to abide by a contract that guarantees the maintenance of a strict inequality. Only then can the masochist safely enjoy disavowal—"*radically contesting the validity of what is.*"[46]

Both interpretations of masochism, destabilization, and disavowal reject the hard shape of the world for an imaginary realm of pleasure. Interestingly, Nakagami finds both aspects of masochism in the work of Tanizaki. In fact, Nakagami implies that Tanizaki pursues the destabilization of the self to extremes. According to Nakagami, Tanizaki's essay on Japanese aesthetics, "In'ei raisan" (In Praise of Shadows, 1933–34), is an extreme expression of this selfless masochism: it stubbornly obstructs reality in favor of an ideal realm—the domain of the shadowy Japanese room ruled by the tiny pale woman with crescent eyebrows and blackened teeth.

In "Monogatari no keifu" and in his fiction writing, Nakagami attempts to distance himself from Tanizaki, but he fails to do so. Nakagami also uses eroticism to transcend the boundaries of the self and disavowal appears in the presence of narrative secrets that cloak reality. In fact, Nakagami shows the ambivalence of the masochist who is drawn into the orbit of the shaman but halts, terrified, at the edge of the abyss. Violence serves as an attempt to change this equation by introducing sadism into the dream-like world of narratives such as Izumi Kyōka's *Kōya hijiri*. The impulse is to regain control over the boundaries of the self and empty out the shadowy room. But as we have seen, the violent impulse results in the opposite as the protagonists experience despair, defeat, and death.

In the fiction of the 1980s, the figures of the snake woman and the shaman become the targets of a concentrated form of violence as if Nakagami believed that he could deconstruct these powerful archetypes by force alone. Violence also illuminates the problem of masculine expendability, the fear that one can be literally chewed up and thrown away—the actual fate of the protagonist in one final story, "Oni no hanashi" (A Demon Tale, 1984). The vulnerability of Nakagami's male characters prevents him from unseating the snake woman. In fact, vulnerable male protagonists lead Nakagami to create ever more powerful imaginary female beings. The tenacious hold of the snake and the shaman also speaks to the literary dilemma that Nakagami faced: as a writer of *monogatari*, Nakagami worked with the materials of premodern tradition, straining to bend them into new forms. The cataclysmic violence of his fictions simply reveals the enormity of the challenge he faced. In view of the cycles of desire and disappointment that we have seen, however, violence falls short of its aims. After rape, murder, and matricide, not much has changed: the snake woman and the shaman still hover over Nakagami's shoulder, filling up the shadowy spaces of the imagination.

Conclusion

In 1978, Nakagami Kenji, aged 35, traveled from Tokyo to Shingū, where he made a short film of the Shingū alleyway, which was in its final stages of "urban renewal." Panning down narrow alleyways with a 16-millimeter camera, Nakagami's lens lingered on the small houses, the close-fitting roofs, the potted plants, and the sweets displayed in the local shop. With images of a neighborhood that was soon to be destroyed by the wrecker's ball, Nakagami created a visual record of the place that had nourished his fiction. The alleyways shaped Nakagami's ideas about identity—they provided a reservoir of legends and stories, they presented a vision of community that at times degenerated into nightmare.

The 1978 footage, among the last recorded images of the *buraku* that Nakagami had known as a child, is widely available today in the 2001 film tribute by Aoyama Shinji entitled *Roji e: Nakagami Kenji no nokoshita fuirumu* (To the Alleyway, Nakagami Kenji's *Roji* Film). Aoyama had heard about the lost footage and had finally located it among a number of things that Morimoto Yūji was storing for Kumano Daigaku. At the suggestion of Nakagami Kasumi, Aoyama began to spin his own film around Nakagami's segment. In *Roji e,* Aoyama shot footage in places that appear or look as if they might appear in Nakagami's fiction: an old dance studio, a mountain path, a beach. Izuchi Kishū, the narrator, stands or sits in these places, reading aloud passages from Nakagami's fiction in Shingū dialect, although the passages do not always match the scenes. Through the technique of the still life (Izuchi remains motionless while reading), Aoyama forces the reader to consider the relation between text and place. Do we experience the place through the text or the text through the place? How does Izuchi's reading transform our experience of both text and place?

Aoyama further goes on to test the viewer. At one point, Izuchi stands on a parking structure gazing down at contemporary Shingū, a large flat provincial town with no remnants of the *roji* in sight. Standing with his back to the camera, Izuchi represents the perspective of the viewer who searches for a physical space that would substantiate the flow of Nakagami's words. Or, as described earlier, such images attest to Izuchi and Aoyama embarking on "a real journey to a nonexistent place" (*nai basho ni iku*), the *roji* of Nakagami's fiction. Suddenly, in the middle of contemporary Shingū footage, Aoyama splices in Nakagami's film, as if he were finally surrendering to the viewer's desire to see the *roji* itself. We experience an eerie slippage, viewing the old neighborhood through Nakagami's own eyes in 1978: An old woman stands in the street; a boy rides past on a bicycle; a dapper, young Matsune Hisao poses for the camera.

Nestled at the center of Aoyama's film, Nakagami's footage represents a sliver of a lost world, but what world? Vivid images attest to how Nakagami loved the old neighborhood with its peculiar insular ways and its local speech and its stories, but also how his art sprang from the burning and destruction of that same space, the process by which it was erased. To Nakagami, the act of representation begins in the anticipation of loss or its aftermath when the person, place, or thing slips from view. Rather than write to recover from loss, however, Nakagami writes to trace the effects of absence rippling into the world: the arc of Icarus falling, the *roji* people scattering, the shaman crossing to the other world. In both the early realistic works and the later mythical tales, Nakagami was mesmerized by the power of rupture itself—the moment when something valuable or desired is violently torn away. It is the magnitude of this preoccupation that makes the reader pause, and at times, look away. The effects of loss also differ along gender lines (men lose and women take away) and at times, Nakagami's writing seems to spin out of control as if to encode violence itself as a form of longing.

Seen against the auditory backdrop of Izuchi's reading, the alleyway footage embodies in ghostly form the complex roles played by one postwar Japanese writer. Nakagami Kenji was a vocal writer of the margins who chafed against the elitist tendencies of high modern Japanese literature. At the same time, he was a member of a circle of writers and intellectuals who wield great influence in Japan today. Nakagami's position in Japanese literary circles might best be described in terms of simultaneity—he held both the positions of outsider and insider at once. Given his stature, how do we begin to trace Nakagami's legacy to modern Japanese literature?

In the summer of 2004, Nakagami's family and friends gathered to mark the thirteenth anniversary of his death, the last time that formal Buddhist rites would be held for him in the Buddhist calendar of mourning. To mark this occasion, Kumano Daigaku planned a symposium in his honor on August 7, 2004, and Tsushima Yūko was invited to give a special lecture the night before. Early in the weekend, the cast of speakers began to gather: Karatani Kōjin, Watanabe Naomi, Asada Akira, Aoyama Shinji, Tsushima Yūko, and Takazawa Shūji. In addition, Margherita Long, an assistant professor at University of California, Riverside, was invited to give a talk to open the symposium. The title of the panel was "Nakagami Kenji to kindai bungaku no owari" (Nakagami Kenji and The End of Modern Literature). It was based on a book by Karatani with the title *Kindai bungaku no owari* (The End of Modern Literature) and it aptly remarked the close of an era to those involved.[1] In a spacious tatami room at the Greenpia Resort above Shingū, Long opened the event by reading her paper on Nakagami's relation to Tanizaki Jun'ichirō. Twelve years had passed since the first posthumous symposium in 1993 in which I had been invited to give the opening talk. I noted with interest that Kumano Daigaku had kept up the practice of inviting one non-Japanese female academic from the West to bring a different point of view to the proceedings.

After Margherita Long had presented her paper, the other participants began to comment, both on her talk and on the effects that globalization was having on national world literatures. The discussion continued for a couple of hours, and there were moments of excitement, especially when director Aoyama Shinji criticized citizens of wealthy nations who flock to see films about the third-world poor. I found myself contrasting the two events that were separated by more than ten years time. The 2004 discussion seemed fairly sedate compared to the first symposium in 1993, when the participants, still raw from Nakagami's death, argued for approximately three hours. I also found myself marveling at the form of the *taidan*, which had suited Nakagami perfectly. A hardscrabble exchange of ideas, the *taidan* is a collegial but contentious performance in which the participants score points on each other. It has the spontaneity of a verbal performance but it allows participants to revise their comments extensively for publication. The *taidan* could not be more different from the formal presentations and polite exchanges of academic conferences in the West. How well did I remember my own case of nerves sitting on a stage in the Shingū welfare center in 1993, listening to my talk being criticized by my fellow panel members who had had the opportunity to read it beforehand. Afterward, Yomota Inuhiko, who had been the recipient of some rough talk himself, told me not to complain; in his words, "you survived the first round."

In spite of my own discomforting memories, however, I recall that Margherita Long did a good job both in presenting her ideas and in responding to critiques of her feminist approach. Inspired by her example, I even asked a question at the end of the panel discussion. "More than a decade has passed since Nakagami's death; how has he changed in the ensuing years for you? And more importantly, how do the people in this audience read him today?" Karatani began by stating that Nakagami had often called him in the middle of the night, telling him to drop everything and come to Shingū. Looking around at his present surroundings, Karatani had to conclude that Nakagami was still on the other end of the phone. In a more serious vein, Karatani continued, "The dead age, too, and Nakagami has grown smarter over time." Watanabe Naomi, the author of *Nihon kindai bungaku to sabetsu* (Modern Japanese Literature and Discrimination, 2004), a major study of literature and the *buraku*, responded that meeting Nakagami had changed the course of his life's work. After Kumano Daigaku events, he would return home and "think about something new."[2] Tsushima Yūko, who had spoken at great length the previous night about the fierce rivalry and the mutual recognition between the two writers, had little to add. The thirteenth anniversary panel struck a solemn note at times, as if the participants were overtly conscious that the event marked the end of a period of mourning as marked by the Buddhist calendar and that we would be attending formal rites for the dead.

It was not surprising, given the panel format and the fame of certain panel members, that the young people in the audience remained silent. The symposium had attracted approximately 80 people, most in their early or mid-twenties. Two of Nakagami's three children, Naho and Suzushi were there, too; Naho, an accomplished potter, had given a workshop that morning. Some participants had traveled long distances to attend and had paid the weekend conference fee. Over the course of the weekend, I tried to learn what had drawn this audience to Shingū, particularly the younger people to whom the publication of the 15-volume *Nakagami Kenji zenshū* (Collected Works of Nakagami Kenji) in 1996 must seem like old history. One member of the audience was Mobu Norio (b. 1978), a young writer from Osaka, who had taken his penname from a rap group (presumably one which included the word "mob"). Barely a month later, Mobu would win the 131st Akutagawa Prize for "Kaigo nyūmon" (Introduction to Nursing, 2004), a story about his grandmother that he mentioned to me in connection with Nakagami's *Sennen no yuraku*.[3] Other representatives of a younger generation were also present: Okuizumi Hikaru, another Akutagawa Prize winner, who had done a live "rap" performance the night before with Itō Seiko, celebrating Kumano through puns and double entendres; Aoyama Shinji, the creator of the *roji* film; and a young woman who gave me a journal entitled *Gōu II* that was published by Kumano Daigaku. In the course of conversations, I tried to learn why younger readers of Nakagami had gotten on the train to Shingū as I had first done many years ago. Why do they read Nakagami Kenji?

No matter how we view it, Nakagami Kenji was not and will never be a popular author, but his name is widely known, and he holds an undisputed place in the modern Japanese literary canon. From the participants at the symposium, I gathered that many of the young people who attended the symposium had first encountered Nakagami's fiction in the Akiyuki works, particularly *Karekinada*. Aoyama Shinji, for example, had first read *Misaki* in high school but he hadn't understood it. He rediscovered Nakagami in university and couldn't stop reading. Another young man at the symposium, in contrast, had never attended university and he worked in a low-paying job. He had discovered Nakagami on his own, a common story in this self-motivated group that included many young men and a number of young women, too.

Nakagami modeled the fact that anyone can be a writer, even without a university degree or good social connections. More importantly, he demonstrated how the writer should be attuned to the material at hand; Mobu Norio, for example, used the story of his own Osaka grandmother combined with his experience as a musician (various lyrics are embedded through the text). A common theme was that younger readers of Nakagami found the work to be fresh and the style intriguing, not like the literature they had read at school. In addition, Nakagami offered a different kind of literary lineage to these readers, stretching back to Sakaguchi Ango, to Izumi Kyōka, and then back into the oral performance tradition. Okuizumi's funny rap-style performance had even drawn a link between Nakagami's writing and contemporary urban culture.

Younger readers were also interested in Nakagami Kenji as a person, and many attended an exhibit in the Shingū Library. They wanted to see the artefacts of a writer's life: the photos, the handwriting, and the signed book copies. For the thirteenth anniversary, Kasumi had even lent the Shingū library a suit-case, a pair of 1970s vintage sunglasses, and a pair of brown leather shoes. These daily-life artifacts drew interest (Mobu Norio modelled the glasses) and they revealed something about Nakagami's reception in Japan. The characteristics of his writing make us want to "see for ourselves," whether it means going to Shingū, or simply immersing ourselves in a mountain of Nakagami material, primary and secondary. His handwritten manuscripts in particular pique interest. Nakagami usually wrote his first draft by hand on large sheets of *genkōyōshi* (manuscript paper), often after considerable thought. He then went back over his work, correcting it in his rounded hand. Looking at his drafts, often with characters crossed out and lines to notes in the margins, one senses the physical intensity of the act of writing. The sheets of handwritten manuscript take on even more value because so few still exist, at least to public view. (The 1988 fire in the Hachiōji house destroyed many of them. Very recently, however, a portion of the original handwritten manuscript of *Sennen no yuraku* was found in the personal effects of Kaneda Tarō, one of Nakagami's deceased editors. The discovery made the newspapers.)[4] It is no accident that samples of Nakagami's handwritten drafts appear on the book flaps of each volume of the *Nakagami Kenji zenshū* and even on the DVD of Aoyama's *Roji e* itself.

One element of the myth surrounding Nakagami is, of course, his untimely death at age 46. As a writer who always seemed in the process of becoming, his early death leaves us wondering where he might have gone next and what he might have done had he lived. His death indelibly shapes our reading of the fiction. I, for one, began to read his texts differently when, in the aftermath of Nakagami's death, I translated *Misaki*. Beneath the patter of Akiyuki's musings, I began to sense the realm of the spirits, haunting the talk of the every day. *Misaki*'s treatment of the force that the dead have on the living further revealed to me the depth and scope of Nakagami's writing. Nakagami's death in 1992 set in motion a long period of mourning, during which critical discourse on Nakagami was hardly dispassionate or rational. Open fights broke out about who could read Nakagami properly. The thirteenth anniversary served to mark an end to this period of controversy and concentrated activity, and seemingly ushered in a period of relative calm. We can now anticipate with pleasure the work on Nakagami that is to come.

Nakagami began a discussion about difference in Japan that has continued to this day both in Japan and the world. We need to expand our scope of study to incorporate more of the historical, social, and literary frames of *buraku* discourse, as Anne McKnight and others are currently doing. As Watanabe Naomi and Edward Fowler have shown, there is a wealth of raw material both in Japan and abroad. Furthermore, Nakagami is a Japanese writer who should be better known outside of his own country. He belongs to a global community of writers who explore representations of difference and he should be read in this context more fully. Nakagami may not be known abroad to the same degree as Yoshimoto Banana or Murakami Haruki, but more translation of his works into English and other languages will shift the balance. The reception of *Snakelust*, Andrew Rankin's translation of "Ja'in" and other stories, and *The Cape*, my translation of *Misaki* in 1999 gives a good indication of the potential interest in North America. Films such as Yanagimachi Mitsuo's 1986 *Himatsuri*, which enjoys an international reputation, and Aoyama's *Roji e* will spread his name further. Nakagami's major works are well-translated into European languages and his name now appears on many more undergraduate syllabi than it did ten years ago. My undergraduates react strongly to his fiction, both positively and negatively, a clear sign that Nakagami's works do not go out of date. Still, we need more translations of his work into English.

Sitting in the audience at the thirteenth anniversary symposium in 2004, I realized that what I miss about Nakagami (as others do, too, I believe) is the sound of his voice, whether in person, through a microphone, or even recorded on video or film. Nakagami had a way of broaching an issue in simple terms, and then adding layers to it, exploring its tensions and contradictions, always making the difficult point and pushing conversation forward. He was acutely aware of the power of the human voice, its rhythms and crescendos, its emotive range. What characterizes Nakagami's fiction is its seemingly tangible connection to the physical body of one who is speaking. During the course of writing this book, I began to feel that I could finally understand the import of Nakagami's project more than ten or twenty years after the fact. Nakagami once wrote that Arthur Rimbaud was "too young" when he wrote his greatest work—but perhaps this is the central point. Nakagami Kenji, too, was a young writer who wrote fully in and of the time in which he lived. One page of Nakagami's prose brings back his engagement in "that time" in all its vibrancy, poetry, and danger. It is to feel wholly present in such moments that we turn to Nakagami's fiction even as we ourselves move inexorably through time.

Appendix

The following is the full version of the *kudoki* song that appears in Chapter 3.

It happened in Nishijin, Kyoto,
the brother, Monten, was twenty-one
the sister, Okiyo but nineteen;
Monten fell madly in love with Okiyo
Taking to his bed
his passion consumed him
three meals a day became two
two meals a day became one
till no food could pass his lips

"Okiyo, Okiyo," twice, three times a voice called
"Yes, yes, mother," Okiyo answered, "What do you want?"
"Your brother is ill, go and see him."

Okiyo went to Monten's house
lightly sliding the indigo paper-paneled door
three steps forward, one step back
putting her hands forward, she pressed her head to the floor

"Monten, how do you feel?
Shall I call the doctor; shall I be your nurse?"
Monten replied:
"I don't need a doctor; I don't need a nurse

"A single night would cure me
with two pillows and three quilts
if only you would sleep with me
I beg you, Okiyo"

Greatly startled, Okiyo replied:
"What are you saying, Monten,
aren't we brother and sister
If people hear, they would damn us"

"If our parents hear,
they would kill us
what shame we'd feel before our friends
you have a lovely wife
and I a good husband"

"My husband is just nineteen
a wandering monk
but if you kill him
I'll be your wife—
for one night, two nights, three nights."

Withdrawing, Okiyo went to prepare
she put up her hair, made-up her face
from the heirloom chest she took
a white gown of rough silk to wear beneath
a black robe of rough silk to wear on top
Winding a fashionable *obi* with circle patterns around her waist
She tied it, patted it once with her hand
And swirled it to the back.

With the latest style of straw sandals on her feet,
and a long bamboo flute in her hand
she concealed herself beneath a large straw hat
and crossed Seta Bridge, playing a tune

There Monten saw a figure approaching
"That must be Okiyo's husband
if I kill him, she'll be mine!"
Aiming his revolver, Monten fired
Then he heard a woman's shriek
"Ah, who goes there? Forgive me!" Monten cried.
He ran to the body and raised the hat
only to see it was Okiyo who had planned this all along:
"My sister has deceived me,
but if I die here, we'll die together as one,"
so said the brother
in Nishijin, Kyoto.

Reference Matter

Notes

Introduction

1. Personal interview with Nakagami Kenji, New York City, October, 1988.

2. Kanai, Karatani, Kōno, Yasuoka, et al., 34–36.

3. See, for example, Nakagami, *Nakagami Kenji hatsugen shūsei*. In this six-volume collection of discussions and lectures edited by Karatani Kōjin and Suga Hidemi, we see how Nakagami sat down with writers and critics from across the literary and political spectrum and how he talked.

4. Neary, "Burakumin in Contemporary Japan," 55.

5. See Sumii, *The River with No Bridge*. I am indebted to my former student Aileen Cruz who wrote a thesis on this writer.

6. See Oda, Pak, Tanaka, Wetherall, and Honda, 1–8. Although Japan is party to a number of human rights decrees, such as the Convention on the Elimination of All Forms of Racial Discrimination (ICERD), Diène's team states that there is no legal recourse for victims of discrimination in employment or marriage. Diène also reports that there is substantial evidence that such discrimination continues (a recent survey in Osaka found that 78% of people stated that marriage to a *burakumin* would be undesirable). See Diène, 11.

7. See McLaughlan, "Japan's Burakumin: An Introduction," 1.

8. Noma and Yasuoka, eds., 189.

9. Ibid., 204. Nakagami's dismissal of the position of the victim also illuminates his harsh criticism of atomic bomb literature. See Treat, 108–9.

10. Personal interview with Nakagami Kenji, October 1988.

11. Satō Hiroaki pointed this out to me. It is too easy to imagine *roji* as a marked space. Nakagami does, however, use Nagayama, the local term for the *buraku*.

12. Hirano, "*Roji* no motsu imi: Nakagami Kenji ron," 288. Also note that later in the essay, Hirano concludes that Nakagami's *roji* is not the space of the victim; rather, it is "a base for pinning down all of reality, a sign of Nakagami's strength." Hirano, 292.

13. Fowler, "The *Buraku* in Modern Japanese Literature," 34.

14. Cornyetz, 11.

15. In a funny comment on Nakagami's borrowings (and on how Japanese readers blur text and life), Matsune Hisao, Nakagami's informal mentor in Shingū, complained during our 1993 interview about Hanzō, the main character of *Sennen no yuraku*, "I knew Hanzō, but he wasn't quite as beautiful as Kenji made him."

16. Personal interview with Nakagami Kenji, October 1988.

17. This discussion was held in conjunction with a screening of the film at Yale University, April 2005, under the aegis of Aaron Gerow, a specialist in film studies.

18. See Bakhtin, *The Dialogic Imagination*, 263. Both Nakagami and Matsune brought up the question of a special *roji* language during the interviews. Interestingly, according to Nakagami, men inside the *buraku* use softer, more feminine forms of speech.

19. The activities of Kumano Daigaku bring Tokyo writers and intellectuals to Shingū every year in August for an annual symposium. See also Nakagami, *Nakagami Kenji to Kumano*, edited by Watanabe Naomi and Karatani Kōjin, a recent collection of Nakagami's own forums in Shingū and symposia that occurred after his death.

20. Gates, 178.

21. See Karatani, Yomota, Watanabe, Suga, and Zimmerman, 155–56.

22. Recently Otsuka Eiji published a lost fragment of *Nankai kisen* in *Shin genjitsu*, a popular culture journal that he edits. He describes *Nankai kisen* as being somewhere between "script and *shōsetsu*." See Otsuka, p. 171.

Chapter One

1. Personal interview with Nakaue Chisato (1917–1999). I conducted an hour-long interview with Nakaue Chisato in her Shingū home in July 1993, a year after her son had died. During the first part of the interview, she recited a folktale. In his biography of Nakagami,

Takazawa Shūji states that Chisato was the youngest of eight children with a different father from her siblings. In my interview she described her family saying, "When my father was alive he traded cattle and made a good profit. He built a house and had things all set up but he died soon after I was born. That's when we lost everything." For more details on Chisato's background, see Takazawa, *Hyōden Nakagami Kenji*, 103–4.

2. Biographical details are taken from the 1988 interview. Other facts come from my 1993 interview with his mother, Nakaue Chisato. Details from Takazawa Shūji's biography as noted.

3. Personal interview with Matsune Hisao, July 1993, in a local eatery in Shingū. After breaking with Chisato, Tomezō had three children with another woman in Shingū whom he married. He also had another daughter out of wedlock. These biographical elements are reflected in *Misaki* and in other early stories.

4. Personal interview with Nakagami Kasumi, June 2004.

5. Personal interview with Matsune Hisao, July 1993. In the 1988 interview, Nakagami also mentioned Tokugawa-period occupations for the Shingū *burakumin,* in particular dyeing cloth, fixing *geta* (wooden clogs), *yama shigoto* (mountain work), and gold working (the last job reflecting the coinage needs of the feudal daimyo). For a complete description of the history of Nakagami's neighborhood and how it expanded from Nagayama to encompass Noda and Ukishima (local pronunciation), see Wakamatsu and Mizuuchi, 55–93.

6. Personal interview with Matsune Hisao, July 1993.

7. Personal interview with Nakagami Kenji, October 1988.

8. Neary, 60. For a detailed overview of activism among the *burakumin* themselves, see Fowler, "The *Buraku* in Modern Japanese Literature," 1–39.

9. Takazawa, *Hyōden Nakagami Kenji,* 8.

10. Ibid., 7–8.

11. Ibid., 38.

12. Personal interview with Nakagami Kenji, October 1988.

13. Personal interview with Nakaue Chisato, July 1993. In addition, see Nakagami Kenji, "Sakka to nikutai" in *Tori no yō ni kemono no yō ni,* 85, for one example of Nakagami's version of his mother's dislike of his profession. In contrast, during my interview with her, she stated that Kenji had confided in his mother as a teenager that he wanted to go to "writing school" and she had kept his secret though she had had her doubts. In her words "I didn't know whether he

could do it or not, but I didn't want to disappoint him, so I just said, study as hard as you can." Whether this is simply hindsight, or the raw memories of a mother who has just experienced the loss of her son, we will never know. Chisato died in May 1999, at the age of 82.

14. In 1980 Hirano Hidehisa, himself from the *buraku*, reported in an essay on Nakagami that he had traveled to Shingū and interviewed a man in charge of Dôwa affairs who reported, "The problem now is what happens with discriminatory attitudes that don't tend to surface easily." Umezawa, Hirano, and Yamagishi, eds., 270.

15. Personal interview with Matsumoto Iwayo, May 1998, in a coffee shop by Shingū station.

16. Personal interview with Matsune Hisao, July 1993.

17. Personal interview with Nakagami Kenji, October 1988.

18. Takazawa, *Hyōden Nakagami Kenji*, 152–53. In 1986 Nakagami took me to see what he said was a last forgotten block of the *roji*. The car stopped at the opening to a narrow street with three or four small houses. Outside were washing machines and potted plants. I was never able to find the street again.

19. See Nakagami, "Hon'yaku shita shi," *NKZ* 14: 461. In contrast, his mother said that he did well in every subject.

20. Tamura, 61. Also see discussion between Nakagami and Tamura that mentions Yamamoto Ai: "Dōsō no goro no Kenji-kun" in Karatani and Suga, eds., *Nakagami Kenji hatsugen shūsei* 1: 313–16. Also, John Dower suggests how writing about everyday things became a tool to democratize the postwar educational system. See Dower, 250.

21. Tamura, 61.

22. Takazawa Shūji estimates that he received 30,000 yen monthly from his parents, and periodically another 20,000 from his oldest sister, a generous amount for the mid-1960s. See Takazawa, *Hyōden Nakagami Kenji*, 10.

23. See Takazawa, *Hyōden Nakagami Kenji*, 17. Also Cornyetz, 158.

24. Personal interview with Nakagami Kenji, October 1988.

25. Personal interview with Nakagami Kasumi, June 2004.

26. "Jūkyūsai no chizu" appeared in the June, 1973 issue of *Bungei shunjū*. Kawade shobô issued it in book form in 1974.

27. Ibid.

28. Conversation with Suzuki Riki, November 2003. Suzuki Riki also gives an interesting account of the creation of *Nichirin no tsubasa* (Wings of the Sun, 1984) which was written over a two-week stretch,

first at a house owned by Karatani Kōjin and then at a house belonging to the owner of a popular literary (*bundan*) bar. In Suzuki's words: "My biggest work with him was *Nichirin no tsubasa*. . . . There were three of us. Nakagami to write the manuscript, me to produce a fair copy, and Mochizuki, a helper who was hired to drive the car and make meals. On the last day, Mochizuki and I were waiting for Nakagami to finish his work. We prepared special dishes and sake (he had not had a drink for a week), twenty minutes passed but there was nothing from him. Thirty, forty, sixty minutes passed but still nothing from him. I entered his room to find that he was still writing. After ninety minutes had passed, I asked, 'Nakagami-san, are you O.K.?' He assured me that he was and that he would finish in ten minutes. Twenty minutes passed and still no sign of him. I dared to ask him what was happening. Then he handed me the manuscript he was writing. I was astonished. Instead of concluding, the novel went off in new directions. . . . I told him that this is super but this is the beginning of another story! Please make a conclusion to this story! He agreed and after ten more minutes, *Nichirin no tsubasa* was completed. He had been writing the opening of *Sanka* [Hymn, 1990] as the conclusion to *Nichirin no tsubasa*." Email correspondence with Suzuki Riki, January 12, 2007.

29. Personal interview with Nakagami Kasumi, June 2004.

30. Ibid.

31. Akiyama, 109. In particular, Akiyama holds Nakagami up to compare him to the "introverted generation," the *naikō no sedai*, including Furui Yoshikichi and others.

32. Nakagami, *Nakagami Kenji zenshū*, 1: 400–1. All subsequent references to this source will be cited in the text as *NKZ*.

33. Kleeman, 20. See Kleeman for an insightful discussion of Nakagami's early fiction, particularly in the late 1960s and early 1970s.

34. Isoda, 1643.

35. Ibid. Jay Rubin suggests that Murakami felt himself to be a member of a different generation, even though the two writers were only three years apart in age. See Rubin, *Haruki Murakami and the Music of Words*, 231. For an analysis of the notion of Murakami as the inventor of "curious worlds," see Hirata, *Discourses of Seduction*, 43–47.

36. Isoda, 1643.

37. Going back to the early postwar days, for example, we see this attitude even in the aftermath of a draining war. The literary scene was galvanized by debates over the role of politics and literature

(*seiji to bungaku*)—thinly disguised ruminations on the role played by intellectuals during the war—or debates on the meaning of the subject itself. See Usui, ed.

38. Nakagami, *Tori no yō ni*, 88.

39. Tsushima, 347.

40. Faye Kleeman discusses how Nakagami was grouped with other writers of the *fūdo* in the same era such as Fukazawa Shichirō and Minakami Tsutomu. See Kleeman, 17–18.

41. Honda, 786.

42. For an illuminating discussion of the concept of *nikutai* in postwar Japan, see Slaymaker, 8–30.

43. In fact Nakagami was forced to share the first prize with Okamatsu Kazuo (b. 1931). An anonymous reader of this manuscript noted that the prize is given to veteran writers at times.

44. "Wakarinikui bungakushō sakuhin no miryoku," *Asahi Journal* 18 (1976): 48.

45. *Akutagawashō zenshū*, 10: 440.

46. The group, which according to Isoda Kōichi "put the everyday back into fiction." Isoda, 1625.

47. *Akutagawashō zenshū*, 10: 441. One wonders what novel is Nakamura talking about—the mother in *Misaki* is not bedridden!

48. Karatani et al., eds., *Gunzō Nihon no sakka*, 144–45. Eto Jun's review was published on February 24, 1977.

49. Quoted in Ōe, "Sengo bungaku o dō uketometa ka," 579. Needless to say, Ōe mocks Etō's tone, stating "I'm not going to say something vague such as 'Etō Jun's theory of style is in decline, but. . . .'"

50. Portions of the trial are transcribed in Kamei, ed.

51. Noma and Yasuoka, eds., 212.

52. Ibid., 197.

53. Ibid., 184.

54. Ibid., 206–7.

55. Ibid., 210.

56. Ibid., 210.

57. Karatani and Suga, eds., *Nakagami Kenji hatsugen shūsei* 1: 141.

58. Noma and Yasuoka, eds., 208.

59. See Karatani and Nakagami, *Kobayashi Hideo o koete*, 10.

60. Karatani would receive the Gunzō New Prize for an essay on Natsume Sōseki in 1969; his first collection was published in 1972, *Ifu suru ningen* (Those Who Dread). Nakagami at this point was a

member of *Bungei shuto* and had not yet made his "debut" with "Ichiban hajime no dekigoto," which was published in 1969.

61. Nakagami, *Tori no yō ni*, 28.

62. Karatani, *Sakaguchi Ango to Nakagami Kenji*, 109.

63. Kobayashi, "Chūyō," 203–5.

64. Karatani and Nakagami, *Kobayashi Hideo o koete*, 12.

65. Ibid., 12.

66. Karatani, *Origins of Modern Japanese Literature*, 69.

67. Karatani and Nakagami, *Kobayashi Hideo o koete*, 56.

68. Ibid., 100–1.

69. Ibid., 31.

70. Ibid., 29.

71. Kobayashi's notion that the I-novel (*shishōsetsu*) grew from a soil that was filled with "too many old and outmoded kinds of fertilizer in the cultural ground," scatological as it may be, is based on this essentialism. In fact, Karatani speaks eloquently about how Kobayashi's vision of a native soil is no longer possible in the world today. External culture can no longer be a series of "multiple designs"; we must look at history itself. We must deal with Marx's idea of *kōtsū* (intercourse); there is no essential center anymore to be infiltrated; all is a product of exchange. Karatani and Nakagami, *Kobayashi Hideo o koete*, 20 and 29. For the Kobayashi essay, see Anderer, trans. and ed., *Literature of the Lost Home*, 70.

72. Karatani and Nakagami, *Kobayashi Hideo o koete*, 139–86.

73. A term he borrowed from the critic Hasumi Shigehiko.

74. Karatani and Nakagami, *Kobayashi Hideo o kotete*, 42.

75. Etō, 16.

76. See Hirata, *Discourses of Seduction*, 82.

77. Karatani, *Sakaguchi Ango to Nakagami Kenji*, 118–19.

78. Karatani and Nakagami, *Kobayashi Hideo o koete*, 78.

79. Karatani, *Sakaguchi Ango to Nakagami Kenji*, 125.

80. Personal interview with Nakagami Kenji, October 1988.

81. Watanabe, "Shijifosu no yō ni yamai to tawamurete," 204–19.

82. The eulogy was later published in *Bungakukai* (October, 1992). The American professor who sent the fax was Paul Anderer. Nakagami had spent half a year at Columbia University in 1986.

83. Tsushima, 344.

84. Ibid., 344.

85. Ibid., 346.

Chapter Two

1. Asamori, 77.

2. One exception to this is Mark Morris who states perceptively that Nakagami is "a deflected poet of abjection." See Morris, "Gossip and History," 49.

3. Asamori, 75.

4. Takazawa, *Hyōden Nakagami Kenji,* 47.

5. Karatani and Nakagami, *Kobayashi Hideo o koete,* 50.

6. Nakagami, *Nakagami Kenji zenshū* 14: 460. All subsequent *zenshū* citations will appear in the text.

7. Yomota Inuhiko mentions these two Japanese poets specifically; as a poet Nakagami was not working in a vacuum. See Yomota, "Nakagami Kenji no shoki no shi ni tsuite," 9.

8. Tanikawa, 5.

9. Takazawa, *Hyōden Nakagami Kenji,* 46.

10. Yomota, "Nakagami Kenji no shoki no shi ni tsuite," 11.

11. Nakagami notes that the word *kisetsu* (season) may or may not be a reference to Rimbaud's *A Season in Hell. NKZ* 14: 38.

12. For a lively account of Rimbaud's life, see Steinmetz.

13. I am grateful to Gretchen Schultz for pointing out the congruencies between Rimbaud and Nakagami's provincial origins. For a chronology of Rimbaud's life, see Hubert Creekmore, "A Rimbaud Chronology" in Rimbaud, *A Season in Hell,* vii–xx.

14. Anderer, trans. and ed., *Literature of the Lost Home,* 100.

15. Nakagami stated that he had read Rimbaud in Kobayashi's translation and had never found another translator who drew him the same way. See Karatani and Nakagami, *Kobayashi Hideo o koete,* 50–51.

16. Translation in Lawler, 45.

17. René Etiemble, *Le Sonnet des Voyelles* (Paris: Gallimard, 1968), 233, as quoted in Lawler, 43.

18. Cohn, 128 and 132.

19. Lawler, 46.

20. Rimbaud, 65.

21. Ibid., 13. Steinmetz believes that this poem describes Rimbaud's ship journey to England with Verlaine when the lovers were fleeing Verlaine's family. See Steinmetz, 135.

22. Rimbaud, 87.

23. Ikumi Kaminishi has suggested to me that Nakagami may be drawing on a local folk belief about a paradise (*potalaka*) that lay just

off the shores of Nachi; in medieval times, pilgrims would row their boats to the spot and throw themselves into the water. The paradise also has the Buddhist name Fudaraku and is associated with Kannon. See Inoue Yasushi, 206–23. Also note Nakagami's early story entitled "Fudaraku" about the brother's suicide (*NKZ* 1: 449–71).

24. Rimbaud, 50.

25. Girard, 79.

26. See Takazawa, *Hyōden Nakagami Kenji*, 29. Also note the resemblance between Akihiro (明弘) and Akiyuki (秋幸), the protagonist of the 1970s "Akiyuki series."

27. Noma and Yasuoka, eds., 183.

28. Personal interview with Nakagami Kenji, October 1988.

29. Watanabe, *Nakagami Kenji ron*, 204–5.

30. The rhythm of walking in "Umi e" also resembles Irisawa Yasuo's poem entitled, "On Love," which begins with the following lines: "We walk / we approach / we talk to one another / we walk and we talk / We talk to each other / about our love / about the future / about our lack of freedom. . . ." Irisawa, 44.

31. Take the classic example, *An'ya kōro* (*A Dark Night's Passing*) by Shiga Naoya in which the protagonist Kensaku returns to the countryside after his nerves become jangled in Tokyo.

32. Nakagami might also be inferring masturbation in this passage. One of Rimbaud's early fragments reads, "At the foot of dark walls, beating skinny dogs," a reference to schoolboy masturbation. See Rimbaud, *Collected Poems*, 175.

33. Woolf, 422–23.

Chapter Three

1. See a transcript in Karatani and Watanabe, eds., *Nakagami Kenji to Kumano*, 80–85. The lecture was one of a series of events sponsored by the Buraku Seinen Bunkakai (Buraku Youth Culture Group), founded in 1978 by Nakagami, Matsune Hisao, and others. The full version of the song that I have translated in the Appendix is actually a slightly longer version of the old woman's song that appears in its entirety in *Karekinada* (*NKZ* 3: 415–19). The song is of the *kudoki* type, involving a long narrative that is put to song. See Takazawa, *Nakagami Kenji jiten*, 17. A reader of this manuscript also noted the resemblance to a story by Akutagawa Ryūnosuke entitled "Kesa to Morito" but I have yet to discover whether the story and song share a common *setsuwa* root. My ideas about the importance of incest in

Nakagami's work grew out of a panel at the Annual Meeting of the Association for Asian Studies and other talks given in 2001. These ideas were first published in Zimmerman, "Nakagami Kenji (1946–1992)," 245–59.

2. Nakagami may be right about the generational argument. James Twitchell notes the large number of English brother-sister incest ballads at the end of the eighteenth-century, but he discovers no examples of father-daughter incest, or mother-son incest in the popular ballads. As in the Shingū song, the audience sympathizes with the rebellious young lovers but in the end expects the punishment of death for their misdeeds. See Twitchell, 62.

3. Karatani and Watanabe, eds., *Nakagami Kenji to Kumano*, 90.

4. Fujino, 132. For an informative discussion in English about Social Darwinism and nation-building, see Bourdaghs, 47–76.

5. Sōtō Zen temples either kept a separate register for outcaste parishioners or modified the *kanji* in posthumous names to indicate outcaste status (using radicals for "leather" or "beast"). There is also historical evidence that priests practiced special funeral rites for outcastes, lepers, and the mentally ill even before the advent of the Tokugawa period. These rites were aimed at severing the ties between the dead spirit and the community in order to prevent spirits from taking revenge. The belief was that these inflictions were a direct result of karma from a previous life and were thus deserved. Evidence of Sōtō temples providing background information from necrologies dates to as late as 1984 when a temple wrote a letter in support of marriage for a young woman whose parents had lived near an outcaste enclave but had not been members of the community. For an excellent study, see Bodiford, 1–27.

6. De Vos and Wagatsuma, 139.

7. I am grateful to Mako Yoshikawa, novelist and scholar, for pointing out to me the links between incest and ethnicity when we were at the Bunting Institute in 1999. See Yoshikawa, 358–76.

8. Sticking close to the thoughts and perceptions of his main character, Akiyuki, Nakagami practices what Edward Fowler calls "single-consciousness" narration, a stock *shishōsetsu* technique in which the readers view the world through the eyes of a single character despite a third-person narration. See Fowler, *The Rhetoric of Confession*, 30–31. For a look at the diverse roles the *shishōsetsu* form has been assigned in modern Japanese literature, see Suzuki, *Narrating the Self*.

9. *Shiga Naoya zenshū*, 2: 446, as cited in Fowler, *The Rhetoric of Confession*, 207.

10. Fowler, *The Rhetoric of Confession*, 298.

11. Yomota, *Kishu to tensei*, 151.

12. Karatani, afterword to *Chi no hate*, 605.

13. Hidaka, 71–72.

14. Morris, "Gossip and History," 47.

15. Kleeman, "Nakagami Kenji," 152.

16. See the *taidan* between Karatani and Nakagami, *Kobayashi Hideo o koete*, for an example of how a younger generation of intellectuals appraises the legacy of their intellectual elders.

17. See Yomota, *Kishu to tensei*, 151. Yomota Inuhiko also compiled a list of mistakes to be avoided when reading the Akiyuki fictions: "locating details of the author's life in the story of Akiyuki, feeling empathetic identification, seeing the union of a young man with water, fire, the forces of nature, reading the return of the gods to a godless world" (Ibid., 158).

18. Karatani, Afterword to *Chi no hate*, 605.

19. Karatani, *Sakaguchi Ango to Nakagami Kenji*, 213.

20. I make the same point in my Ph.D. dissertation. See Zimmerman, "A Language of Rebellion" 227. It is interesting to note that Volume Three of Nakagami's *Collected Works* includes *Misaki* and *Karekinada* in one volume, as if the editors Karatani Kōjin, Asada Akira, Yomota Inuhiko, and Watanabe Naomi recognized the practical advantage of presenting the works in sequence.

21. The term *kare* traveled to Japan in the Meiji period to fill a need for third person pronouns in translations from European languages. But, according to Yanabu Akira, the word "kare" did not play the same role in Japanese as it did in other languages; rather, it was a "demonstrative pronoun that originally referred to something external and distant to both listener and speaker." See Yanabu Akira as cited in Levy, 253. Or, as Indra Levy states in a discussion of *kare* in Meiji-period translations, *kare* plays the "role of the unspecified" (Ibid.). When translating *Misaki* into English, I found that the term "he" didn't work at all because it could be used to refer to any male character in the story. Short of using italics or a capital "H," which made Akiyuki sound like a divinity, I had to find a better solution for English readers: with trepidation, I gave Akiyuki back his proper name. In "House on Fire," because the story was about a father and son, I called the male character, "the son," a strategy that didn't

work in *Misaki*. In *Misaki*, the use of the word "son" begs the question, "Whose son?"

22. Nakagami, *The Cape and Other Stories from the Japanese Ghetto*, 104. All page references are to my own translation.

23. Anderer, *Other Worlds*, 15.

24. The use of incest to make a desperate appeal to the father appears in literature of the American South as well. In *Autobiography of an Ex-Colored Man* (1912), for instance, the hero falls in love with a white woman only to discover that she is his sister by their white father. Sitting near the woman in a concert hall, the speaker states, "I would have given a part of my life to touch her hand and call her sister." See Sollors, 303.

25. For a Freudian analysis of brother-sister incest, see "Between Repetition and Recollection: Allen Tate and William Faulkner" in King, 119.

26. *Akutagawashō zenshū*, vol. 10 (Tokyo: Bungei shunjū, 1982), 437.

27. Freud, 22.

28. The suggestion is made more obvious in *Karekinada*, which describes the time when Mie and Ikuo lived together alone in their mother's old house, and rumors floated through the alleyway that the young siblings were acting like husband and wife (*NKZ* 3: 292–93).

29. *NKZ* 3: 364.

30. See, for example, "House on Fire," a related story in Nakagami, *The Cape and Other Stories from the Japanese Ghetto*, 148.

31. See King, 118.

32. Murakami and Nakagami, 17.

33. See Miller, 148–70.

34. The classic story runs: the white planter's son, in a desire to escape what he feels to be a quasi-incestuous union with a woman of his own race and class, pursues a black woman, only to discover that she is his half-sister by his father, the white plantation master. In one fell swoop he commits both incest and miscegenation, poisons to a society erected on the institution of slavery. See Sollors, 319–20.

35. Nakagami's story is a mixture of history, oral legend, and myth. Nakagami himself learned that a warrior named Suzuki Magoichi fought against Nobunaga but later surrendered and took an oath of loyalty along with six members of his group. See Nakagami, *Kishū ki no kuni ne no kuni monogatari*, 144–45. The account of Magoichi's surrender to Nobunaga is corroborated by an extant letter of 1577 to the Saiga fighters (*monto*) from Oda Nobunaga, stating that he has

received their loyalty pledge and will forgive them. See McMullin, *Buddhism and the State in Sixteenth-Century Japan*, 123. During a visit to the Seikaku temple in Arima, however, Nakagami discovered a different version of Magoichi's story from the chief priest of the temple. According to this account, Magoichi fought Nobunaga, put out a rumor about his own death, and quietly went over the mountains to Arima where he lived in hiding. It was Magoichi's legacy as a *kakurebito*, a "hidden person," that fascinated Nakagami. In the legends of noble exiles who fled to far-flung regions to escape persecution, Nakagami discovered a possible origin for the *burakumin* of the Kii coast. Recently, Karatani Kōjin has suggested that Nakagami's vision might have been more historically accurate than he knew at the time. Nakagami had first learned of the story of Suzuki Magoichi through the 1960s writings of Shiba Ryōtarō but had no evidence of any direct historical link between the Saiga fighters and the *burakumin*. But there was a link: in the 1570s, Nobunaga, furious at the Saiga fighters, denigrated them to outcaste status and gathered all the Jōdo temples of Wakayama under the rubric of *kegare-ji* (defiled temples). See Karatani, *Sakaguchi Ango to Nakagami Kenji*, 203. In his fascination with Magoichi, Nakagami seems to have intuited the importance of the Saiga fighters before he had the history to prove it.

36. *NKZ* 3: 371.

37. Ibid., 438–39.

38. Ōe Kenzaburō, "The Day He Himself Shall Wipe Our Tears Away," 3–110.

39. I am indebted to Marleigh Ryan who asked me during a lecture in June 2000 about how the experience of World War II had affected Nakagami's community and his family.

40. See *NKZ* 3: 282 and 302.

41. Hidakaō, 71.

42. Alan Tansman writes eloquently about the use of rhythm in *Karekinada*, analyzing what brings the text to life. See Tansman, 257–88.

43. Like many plot elements in Nakagami's fiction, the water cult is based on historical fact. In 1975, a couple sequestered themselves in a house with the man's mother and his younger brother and sister. In order to purify themselves, they refused food, drank large amounts of water, and beat each other. Unfortunately, the younger sister died. Nakagami had attended middle school with the woman. See Nakagami, *Kishū ki no kuni ne no kuni monogatari*, 20.

44. Morris, "The Untouchables."

45. See *NKZ* 6: 104. Hamamura Ryūzō's anarchistic attitude is given historical roots in the course of the novel, too. Ryūzō and Sakura feel the effects of the High Treason Case of 1910 (*taigyaku jiken*), a supposed plot to overthrow the Emperor in which a group of leftist Shingū locals were imprisoned and/or executed, including Ōishi Sakunosuke, a well-respected doctor who had treated those in the *buraku*. The government, in an attempt to root out socialism, charged high treason, basing their evidence on remarks by Kōtoku Shūsui in Tokyo that were reported back to the Shingū group by the doctor. In *Chi no hate*, Nakagami makes Ōishi Sakunosuke Sakura's uncle. In the novel, Sakura and Ryūzō experience the sting of the government's lingering prejudice against Shingū residents. When the Emperor comes for a visit, the two men are not allowed to view the parade. See Nakagami, *Chi no hate*, 302. For a thorough account of the High Treason Case, which details its implications for Japanese literary history, see Rubin, *Injurious to Public Morals*, 156–62.

Chapter Four

1. Special because outcaste priests were of lower status than other priests, and had to wear robes of different colors. See De Vos and Wagatsuma, 88–99. For a discussion of the relationship between the Jōdo Sect and the outcastes, see Amstutz, 24 and 28.

2. Nakagami first met Matsune in 1975 after he had moved to Tokyo. Nakagami was sitting in a coffee shop in Shingū writing in the dim light when Matsune approached and introduced himself. Having read the young Nakagami's poems in the local paper and knowing both of his parents, Matsune had long wanted to meet the young writer. That day the two men moved to a bar whereupon Matsune reportedly burst into tears. Matsune reported: "I'd had such a tough time and here was this marvel from the *buraku* who was making a name for himself . . . then just as suddenly as they'd come on, the tears dried up. Nakagami looked stunned." During the late 1970s and into the 1980s, Matsune and Nakagami met frequently in Shingū, mutually profiting from the contact. Matsune, a haiku poet, found a companion with whom he could discuss literary issues and the *buraku*. Nakagami in turn found a faithful supporter who knew a great deal about the neighborhood. Eventually, Matsune would engineer a meeting between Nakagami and his biological father. Personal interview with Matsune Hisao, July 1993.

3. In fact, Mark Morris attributes the "discovery" of Oryū no Oba to Nakagami's reading of William Faulkner. For a comparative analysis of Nakagami's work, see Morris, "Gossip and History," 35–50.

4. Shirane, 4.

5. Konishi, 256.

6. Field, 25.

7. Fujii Sadakazu as cited in Field, 314.

8. Fujii and Nakagami, 173. The discussion was originally published in the July 1985 issue of *Kokubungaku: kaishaku to kyōzai no kenkyū*.

9. Ibid., 199–200.

10. Ibid., 183.

11. Karatani, *Origins of Modern Japanese Literature*, 167.

12. Fujii and Nakagami, 193.

13. Ibid., 176.

14. Lippit, 4. Lippit writes: "*Monogatari* is a genre of retelling former *monogatari* – all *monogatari* are twice-told tales. . . ."

15. Enchi, 108.

16. Karatani, *Origins of Modern Japanese Literature*, 162.

17. Nakagami borrows the term *hō* from Hasumi Shigehiko. For one of Hasumi's early treatments of the *hō*, see Hasumi, 121–39.

18. Ken Ito made this suggestion to me when he served as discussant of a panel entitled "Through Blind Eyes: Visions of Ecstasy in Modern Japanese Literature," Association of Asian Studies Annual Meeting, Washington, D.C., April 1998.

19. Karatani and Nakagami, *Kobayashi Hideo o koete*, 142.

20. For an informative essay on Kobayashi and a translation of key essays, see Anderer, trans. and ed., *Literature of the Lost Home*, 1–15 and 67–93.

21. Ibid., 70.

22. Ibid., 82.

23. Karatani and Nakagami, *Kobayashi Hideo o koete*, 143.

24. Anderer, trans. and ed., *Literature of the Lost Home*, 88.

25. Ibid., 89.

26. Ken Ito analyzes how Tanizaki sketches the shadowy realm where the two lovers dwell, particularly the use of a "multilayered" discourse that combines the testimony of a narrator/researcher, the account of a servant and a "historical document" about Shunkin's life. According to Ito, the use of these disparate sources increases the verisimilitude of the narrator, making him appear objective and drawing the reader in. See Ito, 175 and 181.

27. Karatani and Nakagami, 146.

28. For a synopsis of *Tenko*, the play, see O'Neill, 188–89.

29. Karatani and Nakagami, *Kobayashi Hideo o koete*, 147.

30. Ibid., 147–48.

31. Morris, "Gossip and History," 40.

32. For a discussion of the *kishu ryūritan* myth, see Shirane, 4.

33. Barbara Babcock defines "symbolic inversion" as "any act of expressive behavior which inverts, contradicts, abrogates or in some fashion presents an alternative to commonly held cultural codes, values, norms be they linguistic, literary or artistic, religious, social, or political." Babcock, ed., 14.

34. Personal interview with Nakagami Kenji, October 1988.

35. Suga, 96.

36. Iguchi Tokio also discusses the rejection of the self in *Sennen no yuraku*. See Iguchi, 42.

37. Yomota, *Kishu to tensei*, 155.

38. Ibid., 156. For a discussion of mythic rituals, also see Enaka, 215.

39. As Rosalie Colie has stated, "redirecting thoughtful attention to the faulty or limited structures of thought, paradoxes play back and forth across terminal and categorical boundaries. . . ." See Colie, 7–8.

40. Turner, 106.

41. In *Edo to aku*, Noguchi Takehiko discusses retribution and punishment in the opening chapters of the *Hakkenden* (The Tale of Eight Dogs, 1814–41). Noguchi inquires into the death of the evil female character Funamushi, concluding that in the absence of any formal mechanism of transgression and retribution, Bakin simply approached the problem through animism, the idea that "grasses, trees and animals all come from the same root." In a non-anthropocentric universe, the woman Funamushi suffers the same fate as her namesake, the sea louse—to be trampled to death underfoot. One's name signifies one's destiny. See Noguchi, *Edo to aku*, 41.

42. Mishima, 76.

43. Ibid., 77.

44. Yomota and Nakagami, 293–94.

45. Ibid., 205–310. The original discussion was published in February 1986 in *Bungakukai*.

46. Personal interview with Nakagami Kenji, October 1988.

47. Yamaguchi Masao as quoted by Karatani, *Origins of Modern Japanese Literature*, 162.

Chapter Five

1. For the etymology of the word *yotsu*, see De Vos and Wagatsuma, 4. The word *yotsu* has such powerful implications that a person need only hold up four fingers to signify *buraku* status. The writer Yasuoka Shōtarō mentions another nonverbal aspect of the word *yotsu*: the word is uttered with a chilly laugh to dispel pollution. Noma and Yasuoka, eds., 176.

2. Nakagami, *Kishū ki no kuni ne no kuni monogatari*.

3. Nakagami, *The Cape*, 25–26.

4. In a study of grotesque realism in the work of Rabelais and late European medieval culture in general, Mikhail Bakhtin discusses the process of "degradation," a move downward through space that sets regeneration in motion. He writes: "To degrade is to bury, to sow, and to kill simultaneously, in order to bring forth something more and better. . . . [Degradation] therefore relates to acts of defecation and copulation, conception, pregnancy and birth. . . ." Nakagami clearly practices degradation in this passage but rather than relate to conception and birth, we simply remain in the stream of waste. Bakhtin, *Rabelais and His World*, 21.

5. Hanzō's use of sexual metaphor resembles what Henry Louis Gates describes in African American literature as a "precise feel for metaphor, which virtually creates a thing through its naming but which equally allows that thing to stand for itself." Gates, 175.

6. De Vos and Wagatsuma, 138.

7. Bakhtin, *Rabelais and His World*, 16 and 188.

8. Bakhtin addresses this issue himself when he discusses the subversive possibilities of laughter. Bakhtin posits the effect of laughter in literature as an internal revolution rather than an external one: "This carnival spirit offers the chance to have a new outlook on the world, to realize the relative nature of all that exists, and to enter a completely new order of things" (*Rabelais and His World*, 34). But Bakhtin is vague on how this new and critical historical consciousness might relate to or affect the external world.

9. Other derogatory terms for the outcastes that can loosely be translated as "full of filth" and "non-human." See De Vos and Wagatsuma, 4.

10. Nakagami, *Sennen no yuraku*, 128.

11. Gates, 167–95.

12. Steiner, 1–47.

13. Gates, 178.

14. For an illuminating discussion of Tanizaki's experimentation with language, see Suzuki, 175–86.

15. Fowler roots single-consciousness narration in Japanese grammar itself, stating that in English, "the use of past tense . . . creates sharp differentiation between utterance and narration," whereas in Japanese the lack of such differentiation gives a spoken immediate quality to the text which in turn "encourages identification with the character." He further believes that these tendencies are enhanced by a "written reportive style" in Japanese in which the speaker only reports on what he or she has actually experienced (there being another class of words for the experiences of others). This in turn enhances the immediacy of the text and furthers the dominance of single-consciousness narration whether written in the first or third person. See Fowler, *The Rhetoric of Confession*, 38. See also Karlsson, 75–140, for a formal analysis of narrative perspective particularly in the Akiyuki works.

16. To Noguchi, the term "third-person narration" refers not to an omniscient narration but to a representation of the thoughts of the central character, which mimics the rhythms of speech. As Noguchi himself notes, this is possible because Japanese verbs are not specific as to person, unlike verbs in English. A third-person narrative can, however, easily attain the immediacy of the first-person narrative in English through grammatical markers. Noguchi, *Kindai shōsetsu no gengo kūkan*, 32.

17. Ibid., 7.

18. See the Indian creation myths, for example, in Leeming, ed., 29–30.

19. Iguchi, 44–48.

20. Richard Bowring describes the function of *keri* in the following way: "The narrative marker 'keri' in 'arikeri,' which signifies something like 'now then there is/was,' is presentational in tone and draws attention to the fact that someone is explaining something." Bowring, 58.

21. The scene of Amida descending with musician attendants is depicted in the *raigō zu* (welcoming descent) paintings of the late Heian and Muromachi Periods.

22. Yomota, *Kishu to tensei*, 52.

23. Karatani and Nakagami, *Kobayashi Hideo o koete*, 155–68.

24. Samson, 129–32.

25. Karatani and Nakagami, *Kobayashi Hideo o koete*, 154–55.

26. "Kibitsu no kama," a story from Akinari's *Ugetsu monogatari* (Tales of Moonlight and Rain, 1776), for example, draws plot details and turns of phrase from the *Nihon shoki* (Chronicle of Japan, 720), the *Wuzazu* (A Fivefold Miscellany, a Ming collection), the *Jiandeng xinhua* (New Tales for Lamplight, another Ming collection), and *Genji monogatari*. See Ueda, 241–45. According to Noguchi Takehiko, through borrowing and patching, Akinari was able to give his tales several dense layers of meaning. See Noguchi, *Akinari gengi*, 48.

27. Karatani and Nakagami, *Kobayashi Hideo o koete*, 164–65.

28. Ibid., 159.

29. Earlier in the book, Nakagami writes of *ryōi*: "traveling around Kumano one enters a world of strange marvels (*ryōi*), a skeleton dangling upside down from a cliff, its tongue still chanting the sūtras. . . ." (*NKZ* 14: 486).

30. Tanizaki, *The Reed Cutter and Captain Shigemoto's Mother*, 159.

31. Anderer, *Other Worlds*, 14–15.

Chapter Six

1. My interest in violent spectacles originated in a 1993 symposium on Nakagami in Shingū during which I commented on the problem of violence directed against women, stating that women play the role of a "bridge linking this world and the next" and that it was time to read Nakagami from a different point of view. My comments, and the responses of my co-panelists, were published in Karatani, Suga, Watanabe, Yomota, and Zimmerman, 138–68 and also reprinted in Karatani and Watanabe, eds., *Nakagami Kenji to Kumano*, 176–215. For a spirited critique of subsequent views on violence by male critics in the *bundan*, see Monnet, 13–15. Monnet expresses surprise at how Japanese male critics disposed of the topic of violence by lamenting a plethora of "feminist critics," and locating bisexuality or fluid gender roles in Nakagami's fiction. Also see Cornyetz, 182–85, for a nuanced reading of the snake woman in Nakagami's oeuvre.

2. Karatani, *Hihyō to posutomodan*, 84.

3. Ibid., 85.

4. Ibid., 88.

5. Ury, trans., 96.

6. Yoshino, 36–37.

7. Yoshino also mentions practices surrounding birth that have survived to this day. In certain rural villages in Okinawa and other

regions, for example, the infant, viewed as a serpent at birth, is not allowed to wear garments with sleeves until a certain ceremony has been performed signaling transformation into a human being. Yoshino, 40–44.

8. *Kojiki*, 156.

9. Ibid., 63.

10. Yoshino, 129–30.

11. Klein, 306–7.

12. The tale appears in *Chūsei setsuwa shū*, 225–28.

13. Ueda, 161–84.

14. Ibid., 178.

15. Noguchi, *Akinari gengi*, 52.

16. Ibid., 53–56.

17. Noddings, 56.

18. In *The Language of Psychoanalysis*, Laplanche and Pontalis discuss the complicated relationship between fantasy and desire. They write that fantasies are not merely a form of wish fulfillment on the part of the subject but are scripts or scenarios that can be dramatized and thus demand the active participation of the subject. "[Desire] is not an object that the subject imagines and aims at, so to speak, but rather a sequence in which the subject has his own part to play and in which permutations of roles and attributions are possible." See Laplanche and Pontalis, 318.

19. This reading of violence is similar to one made by James Baldwin in a discussion of the character Bigger Thomas in Richard Wright's *Native Son*. According to Baldwin, violence not only provides an escape from oppression but is equated with the assertion of masculine identity: "To flee or not, to move or not, it is all the same; his doom is written on his forehead, it is carried in his heart. In *Native Son*, Bigger Thomas stands on a Chicago street corner watching airplanes. . . . he dies, having come through violence to a kind of life, having redeemed his manhood." Baldwin, 22.

20. White, 5. In *The Forms of Violence*, a psychoanalytic study of violence and narrative, Leo Bersani and Ulysses Dutoit also focus on giving order to experience when they define narrative as "hierarchical orders of recognition in which one event is foregrounded over another." See Bersani and Dutoit, 10.

21. In *The Forms of Violence*, Bersani and Dutoit discuss the implications of the placement of violent events in a story. Their subject is the Assyrian Palace reliefs of the seventh through ninth centuries A.D.,

which have been heavily criticized by Western art historians for their depiction of violent carnage. Yet Bersani and Dutoit believe that what alienates these art historians is not the depiction of violence but its random presentation and lack of narrative cohesion. In contrast to the reliefs that depict violent acts indiscriminately, Bersani and Dutoit believe that Western art attempts to isolate and tame violence within carefully structured stories. See Bersani and Dutoit, 8–39.

22. This term is taken from Stallybrass and White, who define it as the dilemma of violence that is projected downward in carnival practices in Europe which have long been viewed as a site of resistance to high culture. They write: "Carnival often violently abuses and demonizes weaker not stronger social groups—women, ethnic and religious minorities in a process of displaced abjection." See Stallybrass and White, 19.

23. Ury, trans., 82–83. Another is the story of Mongaku, the irascible but charismatic priest, who is depicted in episodes of *Heike monogatari* (The Tale of the Heike, fourteenth century). Determined to practice austerities for 21 days, Mongaku plunges into the cold waters of Nachi Falls in Kumano in the twelfth month and nearly dies, but is saved by Fudōmyōô, the guardian of esoteric Buddhism and later, the gruff protector of folk tradition. McCullough, trans., 178–79.

24. Barbara Ruch writes: "Theologically women were viewed as inherently flawed, as both defiled and defiling. . . ." Ruch, "The Other Side of Culture," 505.

25. Ury, trans., 96.

26. Ruch, "The Other Side of Culture," 523.

27. Marra, 55.

28. Charles Inouye, 46.

29. See Charles Inouye, 141–55, for an extended discussion of the origins, the import, and the imagery of *Kōya hijiri*.

30. See Jay Rubin's excellent translation of Sakaguchi in *The Oxford Book of Short Stories.*

31. Nakagami, "The Immortal," 432.

32. Ibid., 437.

33. Ibid., 438.

34. Ibid., 439.

35. Bataille, *Erotism*, 16.

36. Susan Napier takes yet another approach, embedding "Fushi" in postwar literary history. While she states that Nakagami decon-

structs his literary heritage, she also believes that he touches on a common theme of abandonment in postwar Japan. Or, in her words: "The absence of women implies the absence of many things as well: love, hope, the past and even, finally, the future." See Napier, 79.

37. Bataille, 29.

38. Ibid., 442.

39. Cornyetz, 184–85.

40. Ibid.

41. Monnet, 27.

42. Frank Kermode discusses the shadowy aspects of narrative: "we may like to think, for our purposes, of narrative as the product of two intertwined processes, the presentation of a fable and its progressive interpretation (which of course alters it). The first tends toward clarity and propriety ('refined common sense'), the second toward secrecy, toward distortions which cover secrets. . . ." See Kermode, "Secrets and Narrative Sequence," 87. Also see Atsuko Sakaki's insightful discussion on the role of narrative secrets in Tanizaki's *Manji*. Sakaki, 224–28.

43. Karatani and Nakagami, *Kobayashi Hideo o koete*, 144.

44. Nakagami is not the only one to ascribe to this problematic equivalence between woman and *hō/seido*. In the 1993 symposium on Nakagami's work, Watanabe Naomi made a similar connection when he stated that violence against women in Nakagami's work is merely a displacement of violence against the *monogatari* itself. See Karatani, Suga, Watanabe, Yomota, and Zimmerman, 155–56.

45. Bersani and Dutoit, 38.

46. Fetishism, a component of masochism, for example, functions upon the principle of disavowal because it opens up new possibilities of belief that stave off reality; in this case, the child can continue to believe that the mother has a penis. Deleuze, 31.

Conclusion

1. Karatani, *Kindai bungaku no owari*.

2. See Watanabe, *Nihon kindai bungaku to sabetsu*.

3. Mobu, 386–422.

4. "Nakagami Kenji *Sennen no yuraku* no nama genkō mitsukaru." *Asahi shinbun* (online), 5 June 2007. http://www.asahi.com/culture/news_culture/TKY200706050350.html. Accessed 6 August 2007.

Bibliography

Akiyama Shun. *Hon no kao hon no koe.* Tokyo: Fukutake shoten, 1982.

Akutagawashō zenshū. Vol. 10. Ed. Ishikawa Tatsuzō et al. Tokyo: Bungei shunjū, 1982.

Amstutz, Galen. *Interpreting Amida: History and Orientalism in the Study of Pure Land Buddhism.* Albany, NY: State University of New York Press, 1997.

Anderer, Paul. *Other Worlds: Arishima Takeo and the Bounds of Japanese Fiction.* New York: Columbia University Press, 1984.

——, trans. and ed. *Literature of the Lost Home: Kobayashi Hideo – Literary Criticism, 1924–1939.* Stanford, CA: Stanford University Press, 1995.

Asamori Mizuho. "Kenji to no deai—shoki shihen yori." *Nakagami Kenji tokushū: Kumano-shi* 39 (1995): 74–78.

Babcock, Barbara, ed. *The Reversible World: Symbolic Inversion in Art and Society.* Ithaca, NY: Cornell University Press, 1978.

Bakhtin, Mikhail. *The Dialogic Imagination.* Trans. Caryl Emerson and Michael Holquist. Austin, TX: University of Texas Press, 1981.

——. *Rabelais and His World.* Trans. Hélène Iswolsky. Bloomington, IN: Indiana University Press, 1985.

Baldwin, James. *Notes on a Native Son.* Boston: Beacon Hill Press, 1955.

Bataille, George. *Erotism.* Trans. Mary Dalwood. San Francisco, CA: City Lights Books, 1986.

Bersani, Leo and Ulysse Dutoit. *The Forms of Violence: Narrative in Assyrian Art and Modern Culture.* New York: Schoken Books, 1985.

Bodiford, William. "Zen and the Art of Religious Prejudice: Efforts to Reform a Tradition of Social Discrimination." *Japanese Journal of Religious Studies* 23/1–2 (1996): 1–27.

Bourdaghs, Michael. *The Dawn That Never Comes: Shimazaki Tōson and Japanese Naturalism*. New York: Columbia University Press, 2003.

Bowring, Richard. *Murasaki Shikibu and the Tale of Genji*. Cambridge, UK: Cambridge University Press, 1988.

Buraku kaihō kenkyūjo, ed. *Buraku mondai jiten*. Osaka: Kaihō shuppansha, 1986.

Chūsei setsuwa shū. Vol. 23 of *Nihon Koten Bungaku*, ed. Nishio Kōichi and Kishi Shōzō, 225–28. Tokyo: Kadokawa shoten, 1977.

Cohn, Robert Greer. *The Poetry of Rimbaud*. Princeton, NJ: Princeton University Press, 1973.

Colie, Rosalie. *Paradoxica Epidemica: The Renaissance Tradition of Paradox*. Princeton, NJ: Princeton University Press, 1966.

Cornyetz, Nina. *Dangerous Women, Deadly Words: Phallic Fantasy and Modernity in Three Japanese Writers*. Stanford, CA: Stanford University Press, 1999.

De Vos, George and Hiroshi Wagatsuma. *Japan's Invisible Race: Caste in Culture and Personality*. Berkeley, CA: University of California Press, 1966.

Deleuze, Gilles. *Masochism: Coldness and Cruelty and Venus in Furs*. Trans. Jean McNeil. New York: Zone Books, 1989.

Diène, Doudou. Addendum to the report "Racism, Racial Discrimination, Xenophobia, and All Forms of Discrimination." Mission to Japan, Commission on Human Rights, United Nations. http://daccessdds.un.org/doc/UNDOC/GEN/G06/103/96/PDF/G0610396.pdf. Accessed 24 July 2007.

Dower, John. *Embracing Defeat: Japan in the Wake of World War II*. New York: W.W. Norton, 1999.

Enaka Naoki. "Sen no yuraku / man no yuraku." *Hihyō no toriāde* 20 (1982): 196–217.

Enchi Fumiko. "Love in Two Lives: The Remnant." In *Japanese Women Writers*, trans. and ed. Noriko Mizuta Lippit and Kyoko Iriye Selden, 97–111. Armonk, NY: M.E. Sharpe, 1983.

Etō Jun. *Bungaku no genzai: renzoku taidan*. Tokyo: Kawade shobō shinsha, 1989.

Field, Norma. *The Splendor of Longing in the Tale of Genji*. Princeton, NJ: Princeton University Press, 1987.

Fowler, Edward. *The Rhetoric of Confession.* Berkeley, CA: University of California Press, 1988.

———. "The *Buraku* in Modern Japanese Literature: Texts and Contexts." *Journal of Japanese Studies* 26 (2000): 1–39.

Freud, Sigmund. *Totem and Taboo.* London: W.W. Norton & Co., 1950.

Fujii Sadakazu and Nakagami Kenji. "Monogatari to wa nani ka." In *Nakagami Kenji hatsugen shūsei,* vol. 2, ed. Karatani Kōjin and Suga Hidemi, 172–200. Tokyo: Daisan bunmeisha, 1995.

Fujino Yutaka. "Buraku mondai to yūsei shisō." *Buraku kaihō kenkyū* 100 (1994): 125–43.

Gates, Henry Louis. *Figures in Black: Words, Signs, and the "Racial" Self.* Oxford, UK: Oxford University Press, 1987.

Girard, René. *Violence and the Sacred.* Trans. Patrick Gregory. Baltimore, MD: Johns Hopkins Press, 1977.

Gluck, Carol. *Japan's Modern Myths: Ideology in the Late Meiji Period.* Princeton, NJ: Princeton University Press, 1985.

Hidaka Shōji. "*Karekinada* kara *Chi no hate* e." *Kokubungaku* 36 (1991): 69–97.

Hasumi Shigehiko. "Monogatari to shite no hō." *Gendai shisō* (August 1977): 121–39.

Hirata, Hosea. *Discourses of Seduction: History, Evil, Desire, and Modern Japanese Literature.* Cambridge, MA: Harvard University Asia Center, 2005.

———. *The Poetry and the Poetics of Nishiwaki Junzaburō: Modernism in Translation.* Princeton, NJ: Princeton University Press, 1993.

Honda Shūgo. *Monogatari sengo bungaku ronsō.* Tokyo: Shinchōsha, 1966.

Iguchi Tokio. *Monogatari ron hakyoku ron.* Tokyo: Ronsōsha, 1987.

Inouye, Charles Shirō. *The Similitude of Blossoms: A Critical Literary Biography of Izumi Kyōka (1873–1939), Japanese Novelist and Playwright.* Cambridge, MA: Harvard University Asia Center, 1998.

Inoue Yasushi. "Passage to Fudaraku." Trans. James T. Araki. In *The Oxford Book of Japanese Short Stories,* ed. Theodore W. Goossen, 206–33. Oxford, UK: Oxford University Press, 1997.

Irisawa Yasuo. *Shi shūsei 1951–1994.* Tokyo: Seidosha, 1996.

Isoda Kōichi. "Shōwa gojū nendai no bungaku." In *Nihon kindai bungaku daijiten,* ed. Nihon kindai bungakukan, 1623–44. Tokyo: Kōdansha, 1984.

Ito, Ken K. *Visions of Desire: Tanizaki's Fictional Worlds*. Stanford, CA: Stanford University Press, 1991.

Kamei Tomu, ed. *Sayama jiken e no kokuhatsujō*. Tokyo: San'ichi shobō, 1978.

Kanai Mieko, Karatani Kōjin, Kōno Taeko, Yasuoka Shōtarō, et al. "Tsuitō Nakagami Kenji." *Bungakukai* (October 1992): 128–80.

Karatani Kōjin. *Han bungakuron*. Tokyo: Kōdansha, 1991.

——. *Hihyō to posutomodan*. Tokyo: Fukutake shoten, 1989.

——. *Kindai bungaku no owari, Karatani Kōjin no genzai*. Tokyo: Insukuriputo, 2005.

——. *Origins of Modern Japanese Literature*. Trans. and ed. Brett de Bary. Durham, NC: Duke University Press, 1993.

——. *Sakaguchi Ango to Nakagami Kenji*. Tokyo: Ōta shuppan, 1996.

——. Afterword. *Chi no hate shijō no toki*. By Nakagami Kenji. Tokyo: Shinchōsha, 1993.

Karatani Kōjin and Nakagami Kenji. *Kobayashi Hideo o koete*. Tokyo: Kawade shobō shinsha, 1979.

Karatani Kōjin, Suga Hidemi, Watanabe Naomi, Yomota Inuhiko, and Eve Zimmerman. "Sennen no bungaku: Nakagami Kenji to Kumano." *Bungakukai* (October 1993): 138–68.

Karatani Kōjin and Suga Hidemi, eds. *Nakagami Kenji hatsugen shūsei*. 6 vols. Tokyo: Daisan bunmeisha, 1995–99.

Karatani Kōjin and Watanabe Naomi, eds. *Nakagami Kenji to Kumano*. Tokyo: Ōta shuppan, 2000.

Karatani Kōjin et al., eds. *Gunzō Nihon no sakka: Nakagami Kenji*. Vol 24. Tokyo: Shogakukan, 1996.

Karlsson, Mats. "The Kumano Saga of Nakagami Kenji." Ph.D. diss., University of Stockholm, 2001.

Keene, Donald. *Seeds in the Heart: Japanese Literature from Earliest Times to the Late Sixteenth Century*. New York: Henry Holt & Co., 1993.

Kermode, Frank. *The Sense of an Ending: Studies in the Theory of Fiction*. Oxford, UK: Oxford University Press, 1966.

——. "Secrets and Narrative Sequence." *Critical Inquiry* 7, no. 1 (1980): 83–101.

King, Richard. *A Southern Renaissance: The Cultural Awakening of the American South, 1930–1955*. Oxford, UK: Oxford University Press, 1980.

Kleeman, Faye. "Nakagami Kenji" in *Japanese Fiction Writers Since World War II*, ed. Van C. Gessel, 143–53. Detroit, MI: Gale Research, 1997.

——. "The Uses of Myth in Modern Japanese Literature: Nakagami Kenji, Ōe Kenzaburō, and Kurahashi Yumiko." Ph.D. diss., University of California, Berkeley, 1991.

Klein, Susan Blakely. "When the Moon Strikes the Bell: Desire and Enlightenment in the Noh Play *Dōjōji*." *Journal of Japanese Studies* 17 (1991): 291–322.

Kobayashi Hideo. "Chūyō." In *X e no tegami/watakushi shōsetsu ron*, 203–5. Tokyo: Shinchōsha, 1962.

Kojiki. Trans. Donald L. Philippi. Tokyo: University of Tokyo Press, 1968.

Konishi, Jin'ichi. *A History of Japanese Literature*. 3 vols. Trans. Aileen Gatten. Princeton, NJ: Princeton University Press, 1986.

Laplanche, Jean and Jean-Bertrand Pontalis. *The Language of Psychoanalysis*. Trans. Donald Nicholson-Smith. New York: W.W. Norton & Co., 1973.

Lawler, James. *Rimbaud's Theater of the Self*. Cambridge, MA: Harvard University Press, 1992.

Leeming, David, ed. *The World of Myth: An Anthology*. Oxford, UK: Oxford University Press, 1990.

Levy, Indra. "Sirens of the Western Shore: Westernesque Women and Translation in Modern Japanese Literature." Ph.D. diss., Columbia University, 2001.

Lippit, Noriko Mizuta. "Watakushi Katari and Monogatari: Women's Self-Expression and the Tradition of the Monogatari in Modern Japanese Literature." In *Proceedings of the Second Midwest Research/Pedagogy Seminar on Japanese Literature*, 3–18. West Lafayette, IN: Purdue University, 1993.

Long, Margherita. "Nakagami and the Denial of Lineage: On Maternity, Abjection, and the Japanese Outcast Class." *differences: A Journal of Feminist Cultural Studies* 17, no. 2 (2006): 2–32.

Marra, Michele. "The Buddhist Mythmaking of Defilement: Sacred Courtesans in Medieval Japan." *Journal of Asian Studies* 52 (1993): 49–65.

McCullough, Helen Craig, trans. *The Tale of the Heike*. Stanford, CA: Stanford University Press, 1988.

McLaughlan, Alastair. "Japan's Burakumin: An Introduction." *Japan Focus*. http://www.japanfocus.org/products/details/2075. Accessed 4 January 2006.

McMullin, Neil. *Buddhism and the State in Sixteenth-Century Japan*. Princeton, NJ: Princeton University Press, 1984.

Miller, J. Hillis. "The Two Relativisms: Point of View and Indeterminacy in the Novel *Absolom, Absolom.*" In *Relativism in the Arts*, ed. Betty Jean Craige, 148–70. Athens, GA: University of Georgia, 1983.

Mishima Yukio. *The Decay of the Angel*. Trans. Edward Seidensticker. New York: Knopf, 1974.

Mobu Norio. "Kaigo nyūmon." *Bungei shunjū* (September 2004): 386–422.

Monnet, Livia. "Ghostly Women, Displaced Femininities, and Male Family Romances: Violence, Gender and Sexuality in Two Texts by Nakagami Kenji." *Japan Forum* 8 (1996): 13–34.

Morris, Mark. "Gossip and History: Nakagami, Faulkner, García Márquez." *Japan Forum* 8 (1996): 35–50.

——. "The Untouchables." *New York Times Book Review*, 10/24/99.

Murakami Haruki and Nakagami Kenji. "Toshi to han-toshi." *Kokubungaku* 30 (1985): 6–30.

Nakagami Kenji. *The Cape and Other Stories from the Japanese Ghetto*. Trans. Eve Zimmerman. Berkeley, CA: Stone Bridge Press, 1999.

——. *Chi no hate shijō no toki*. Tokyo: Shinchōsha, 1983.

——. *Fūkei no mukō e*. Tokyo: Tōjusha, 1983.

——. *Himatsuri*. Tokyo: Bungei shunjū, 1987.

——. *Hōsenka*. Tokyo: Sakuhinsha, 1980.

——. *Izoku* (uncompleted). Tokyo: Kōdansha, 1993.

——. *Ja'in*. Tokyo: Kadokawa shoten, 1976.

——. *Jūhassai, umi e*. Tokyo: Shūeisha, 1977.

——. *Jūkyūsai no chizu*. Tokyo: Kawade shobō shinsha, 1974.

——. *Jūryoku no miyako*. Tokyo: Shinchōsha, 1988.

——. *Karekinada*. Tokyo: Kawade shobō shinsha, 1977.

——. *Keibetsu*. Tokyo: Asahi shinbunsha, 1992.

——. *Keshō*. Tokyo: Kōdansha, 1978.

——. *Kiseki*. Tokyo: Asahi shinbunsha, 1989.

——. *Kishū ki no kuni ne no kuni monogatari*. Tokyo: Asahi shinbunsha, 1986.

——. *Kumano shū*. Tokyo: Kōdansha, 1984.

——. *Misaki*. Tokyo: Bungei shunjū, 1976.

——. *Mizu no onna*. Tokyo: Sakuhinsha, 1979.

——. *Nakagami Kenji zenshū*, Eds. Karatani Kōjin, Asada Akira, Yomota Inuhiko, Watanabe Naomi. 15 vols. Tokyo: Shūeisha, 1996.

——. *Nichirin no tsubasa*. Tokyo: Shinchōsha, 1984.

——. *Sanka*. Tokyo: Bungei shunjū, 1990.

———. *Sennen no yuraku*. Tokyo: Kawade shobō shinsha, 1982.

———. *Snakelust*. Trans. Andrew Rankin. Tokyo: Kodanasha International, 1999.

———. *Tori no yō ni kemono no yō ni*. Tokyo: Hokuyōsha, 1976.

———. *Tōyō ni ichi suru*. Tokyo: Sakuhinsha, 1981.

———. *Yume no chikara*. Tokyo: Hokuyōsha, 1979.

———. "The Immortal." Trans. Mark Harbison, In *The Showa Anthology*, ed. Van C. Gessel, 426–42. Tokyo: Kodansha International, 1985.

Napier, Susan J. *The Fantastic in Modern Japanese Literature: The Subversion of Modernity*. London: Routledge, 1996.

Neary, Ian. *Political Protest and Social Control in Pre-War Japan: Origins of Burakumin Liberation*. Atlantic Highlands, NJ: Humanities Press, 1989.

———. "Burakumin in Contemporary Japan." In *Japan's Minorities: The Illusion of Homogeneity*, ed. Michael Weiner, 50–78. New York and London: Routledge, 1997.

Noddings, Nel. *Women and Evil*. Berkeley, CA: University of California Press, 1989.

Noguchi Takehiko. *Akinari gengi*. Tokyo: Seidosha, 1989.

———. *Edo to aku: hakkenden to bakin no sekai*. Tokyo: Kadokawa shoten, 1991.

———. *Kindai shōsetsu no gengo kūkan*. Tokyo: Fukutake shoten, 1985.

Noma Hiroshi and Yasuoka Shōtarō, eds. *Sabetsu sono kongen o tou*. 2 vols. Tokyo: Asahi shinbunsha, 1984.

Oda Makoto, Pak Kyongnam, Tanaka Hiroshi, William Wetherall, and Honda Katsuichi. "The Diène Report on Discrimination and Racism in Japan." *Japan Focus*. http://www.japanfocus.org/products/details/1882. Accessed 7 August 2007.

Ōe Kenzaburō. "The Day He Himself Shall Wipe Our Tears Away." In *Teach Us to Outgrow Our Madness*, trans. John Nathan, 3–110. New York: Grove Press, 1977.

O'Neill, P. G. *A Guide to Noh*. Tokyo: Hinoki shoten, 1953.

Otsuka Eiji. "Nankai kisen gekiga gensaku ni tsuite." *Shin genjitsu* 3 (April 2004): 161–76.

Rimbaud, Arthur. *A Season in Hell and The Drunken Boat*. Trans. Louise Varèse. New York: New Directions, 1961.

Rimbaud, Arthur. *Collected Poems*. Trans. Oliver Bernard. London: Penguin Books, 1962.

Rubin, Jay. *Haruki Murakami and the Music of Words*. London: Harvill Press, 2002.

——. *Injurious to Public Morals: Writers and the Meiji State*. Seattle, WA: University of Washington Press, 1984.

Ruch, Barbara. *Mō hitotsu no chūseizō: bikuni, otogizōshi, raise*. Kyoto: Shibunkaku shuppan, 1991.

——. "The Other Side of Culture." In *The Cambridge Encyclopedia of* Japan. Ed. Richard Bowring and Peter Kornicki. Cambridge, UK: Cambridge University Press, 1993.

Sakaguchi Ango. "In the Forest, Under Cherries in Full Bloom." Trans. Jay Rubin. In *The Oxford Book of Short Stories*, ed. Theodore W. Goossen, 187–205. Oxford, UK: Oxford University Press, 1997.

Sakaki, Atsuko. *Recontextualizing Texts: Narrative Performance in Modern Japanese Fiction*. Cambridge, MA: Harvard University Asia Center, 1999.

Samson, George. *A History of Japan to 1334*. Stanford, CA: Stanford University Press, 1958.

Shiga Naoya. *A Dark Night's Passing*. Trans. Edwin McClellan. Tokyo: Kodansha, 1976.

Shimazaki Tōson. *The Broken Commandment*. Trans. Kenneth Strong. Tokyo: University of Tokyo Press, 1974.

Shirane, Haruo. *The Bridge of Dreams: A Poetics of the Tale of Genji*. Stanford, CA: Stanford University Press, 1996.

Slaymaker, Douglas. *The Body in Postwar Japanese Fiction*. London: RoutledgeCurzon, 2004.

Sollors, Werner. *Neither Black Nor White Yet Both*. New York: Oxford University Press, 1997.

Stallybrass, Peter and Allon White. *The Poetics and Politics of Transgression*. Ithaca, NY: Cornell University Press, 1986.

Steiner, George. *After Babel: Aspects of Language and Translation*. Oxford, UK: Oxford University Press, 1975.

Steinmetz, Jean-Luc. *Arthur Rimbaud: Presence of an Enigma*. Trans. Jon Graham. New York: Welcome Rain, 2001.

Sumii, Sue. *The River with No Bridge*. Trans. Susan Wilkinson. Rutland, VT and Tokyo: Charles E. Tuttle, 1989.

Suga Hidemi. "Gūsū to kisū—*Sennen no yuraku* o yomu." *Shūkan dokushojin* 20 (1992): 91–96.

Suzuki, Tomi. *Narrating the Self: Fictions of Japanese Modernity*. Stanford, CA: Stanford University Press, 1996.

Takazawa Shūji. *Hyōden Nakagami Kenji*. Tokyo: Shūeisha, 1998.

——. *Nakagami Kenji jiten: ronkō to shuzai nichiroku*. Tokyo: Kōbunsha, 2002.

Tanikawa Shuntarō. *Selected Poems*. Trans. Harold Wright. San Francisco, CA: North Point, 1983.

Tanizaki Jun'ichirō. *The Reed Cutter and Captain Shigemoto's Mother*. Trans. Anthony Chambers. New York: Knopf, 1993.

———. *Seven Japanese Tales*. Trans. Howard Hibbett. New York: Perigree, 1963.

Tamura Satoko. "Omoide no naka no Nakagami Kenji." *Nakagami Kenji tokushū: Kumano-shi* 39 (1995): 60–62.

Tansman, Alan. "History, Repetition, and Freedom in the Narratives of Nakagami Kenji." *Journal of Japanese Studies* 24 (1998): 257–88.

Treat, John Whittier. *Writing Ground Zero: Japanese Literature and the Atomic Bomb*. Chicago, IL: University of Chicago Press, 1995.

Tsushima Yūko. "Ani Nakagami Kenji no yume." *Shinchō* (September 1995): 339–54.

Turner, Victor. *The Forest of Symbols*. Ithaca, NY: Cornell University Press, 1967.

Twitchell, James B. *Forbidden Partners: The Incest Taboo in Modern Culture*. New York: Columbia University Press, 1987.

Ueda Akinari. *Ugetsu Monogatari: Tales of Moonlight and Rain*. Trans. Leon Zolbrod. Vancouver, BC: University of British Columbia Press, 1974.

Umezawa Toshihiko, Hirano Hidehisa, and Yamagishi Takashi, eds. *Bungaku no naka no hisabetsu buraku zō: sengohen*. Tokyo: Akashi shoten, 1982.

Ury, Marian, trans. *Tales of Time Now Past*. Berkeley, CA: University of California Press, 1979.

Usui, Yoshimi, ed. *Sengo bungaku ronsō. 2 Vol.* Tokyo: Banchō shobō, 1972.

Wakamatsu Tsukasa and Mizuuchi Toshio. "Wakayama-ken Shingū-shi ni okeru dōwa chiku no hen'yō to Nakagami Kenji." *Jinken mondai kenkyū* 1 (2001): 55–93.

Watanabe Naomi. *Nakagami Kenji ron: itoshisha ni tsuite*. Tokyo: Kawade shobō shinsha, 1996.

———. *Ninhon kindai bungaku to sabetsu*. Tokyo: Ōta shuppan, 1994.

———."Shijifosu no yō ni yamai to tawamurete." Interview with Nakagami Kenji. *Bungakukai* (March 1992): 204–19.

Weiner, Michael, ed. *Japan's Minorities: The Illusion of Homogeneity*. New York and London: Routledge, 1997.

White, Hayden. "The Value of Narrativity in the Representation of Reality." *Critical Inquiry* 7, no. 1 (1980): 5–27.

Woolf, Virgina. "*Jane Eyre* and *Wuthering Heights.*" In *The Common Reader*, 219–27. New York: Harcourt, 1925. Reprinted in *Wuthering Heights*, 422–23. The Modern Library Edition.

Yasuoka Shōtarō, Minakami Tsutomu, Kawamura Jirō, Kanai Mieko, and Suga Hidemi. "Nakagami Kenji tsuitō tokushū." *Kaien* 11 (October 1992): 158–68.

Yomota Inuhiko. *Kishu to tensei*. Tokyo: Shinchōsha, 1987.

——. "Nakagami Kenji to shoki no shi ni tsuite." Addendum to vol. 14. *Nakagami Kenji zenshū*. Ed. Karatani Kōjin, Asada Akira, Yomota Inuhiko, and Watanabe Naomi. 15 vols. Tokyo: Shūeisha, 1996.

Yomota Inuhiko and Nakagami Kenji. "Tensei, monogatari, tennō." In *Nakagami Kenji hatsugen shūsei*, vol. 2. Ed. Karatani Kōjin and Suga Hidemi, 265–310. Tokyo: Daisan bunmeisha, 1995.

Yoshino Hiroko. *Nihonjin no shiseikan*. Tokyo: Kōdansha, 1982.

Yoshikawa, Mako. "The New Face of Incest?: Race, Class and the Controversy over Kathryn Harrison's *The Kiss*." In *Incest and the Literary Imagination*, ed. Elizabeth Barnes, 358–76. Gainesville, FL: University of Florida Press, 2002.

Zimmerman, Eve. "Hell at Home: Nakagami Kenji and the Discovery of Rimbaud." In *Issues of Canonicity and Canon Formation in Japanese Literary Studies*, ed. Stephen D. Miller, 233–45. Proceedings of the Association for Japanese Literary Studies, West Lafayette, IN: Purdue University, 2000.

——. "In the Trap of Words: Nakagami Kenji and the Making of Degenerate Fictions." In *Ōe and Beyond: Fiction in Contemporary Japan*. Ed. Stephen Snyder and Philip Gabriel, 130–52. Honolulu, HI: University of Hawai'i Press, 1999.

——. "A Language of Rebellion: Myth, Violence and Identity in the Fiction of Nakagami Kenji." Ph.D. diss., Columbia University, 1997.

——. "Nakagami Kenji (1946–1992)." In *Modern Japanese Writers*, ed. Jay Rubin, 245–59. New York: Charles Scribner's Sons, 2001.

——. "Peinteddo bādo to sono hoka no rurōshatachi." Trans. Tomii Reiko. *Yurīka* 3 (1993): 104–12.

Index

Harvard East Asian Monographs
(*out-of-print)

*1. Liang Fang-chung, *The Single-Whip Method of Taxation in China*
*2. Harold C. Hinton, *The Grain Tribute System of China, 1845–1911*
3. Ellsworth C. Carlson, *The Kaiping Mines, 1877–1912*
*4. Chao Kuo-chün, *Agrarian Policies of Mainland China: A Documentary Study, 1949–1956*
*5. Edgar Snow, *Random Notes on Red China, 1936–1945*
*6. Edwin George Beal, Jr., *The Origin of Likin, 1835–1864*
7. Chao Kuo-chün, *Economic Planning and Organization in Mainland China: A Documentary Study, 1949–1957*
*8. John K. Fairbank, *Ching Documents: An Introductory Syllabus*
*9. Helen Yin and Yi-chang Yin, *Economic Statistics of Mainland China, 1949–1957*
10. Wolfgang Franke, *The Reform and Abolition of the Traditional Chinese Examination System*
11. Albert Feuerwerker and S. Cheng, *Chinese Communist Studies of Modern Chinese History*
12. C. John Stanley, *Late Ching Finance: Hu Kuang-yung as an Innovator*
13. S. M. Meng, *The Tsungli Yamen: Its Organization and Functions*
*14. Ssu-yü Teng, *Historiography of the Taiping Rebellion*
15. Chun-Jo Liu, *Controversies in Modern Chinese Intellectual History: An Analytic Bibliography of Periodical Articles, Mainly of the May Fourth and Post-May Fourth Era*
*16. Edward J. M. Rhoads, *The Chinese Red Army, 1927–1963: An Annotated Bibliography*
*17. Andrew J. Nathan, *A History of the China International Famine Relief Commission*
*18. Frank H. H. King (ed.) and Prescott Clarke, *A Research Guide to China-Coast Newspapers, 1822–1911*
*19. Ellis Joffe, *Party and Army: Professionalism and Political Control in the Chinese Officer Corps, 1949–1964*

48. Paul Richard Bohr, *Famine and the Missionary: Timothy Richard as Relief Administrator and Advocate of National Reform*
49. Endymion Wilkinson, *The History of Imperial China: A Research Guide*
50. Britten Dean, *China and Great Britain: The Diplomacy of Commercial Relations, 1860–1864*
51. Ellsworth C. Carlson, *The Foochow Missionaries, 1847–1880*
52. Yeh-chien Wang, *An Estimate of the Land-Tax Collection in China, 1753 and 1908*
53. Richard M. Pfeffer, *Understanding Business Contracts in China, 1949–1963*
*54. Han-sheng Chuan and Richard Kraus, *Mid-Ching Rice Markets and Trade: An Essay in Price History*
55. Ranbir Vohra, *Lao She and the Chinese Revolution*
56. Liang-lin Hsiao, *China's Foreign Trade Statistics, 1864–1949*
*57. Lee-hsia Hsu Ting, *Government Control of the Press in Modern China, 1900–1949*
*58. Edward W. Wagner, *The Literati Purges: Political Conflict in Early Yi Korea*
*59. Joungwon A. Kim, *Divided Korea: The Politics of Development, 1945–1972*
60. Noriko Kamachi, John K. Fairbank, and Chūzō Ichiko, *Japanese Studies of Modern China Since 1953: A Bibliographical Guide to Historical and Social-Science Research on the Nineteenth and Twentieth Centuries, Supplementary Volume for 1953–1969*
61. Donald A. Gibbs and Yun-chen Li, *A Bibliography of Studies and Translations of Modern Chinese Literature, 1918–1942*
62. Robert H. Silin, *Leadership and Values: The Organization of Large-Scale Taiwanese Enterprises*
63. David Pong, *A Critical Guide to the Kwangtung Provincial Archives Deposited at the Public Record Office of London*
*64. Fred W. Drake, *China Charts the World: Hsu Chi-yü and His Geography of 1848*
*65. William A. Brown and Urgrunge Onon, translators and annotators, *History of the Mongolian People's Republic*
66. Edward L. Farmer, *Early Ming Government: The Evolution of Dual Capitals*
*67. Ralph C. Croizier, *Koxinga and Chinese Nationalism: History, Myth, and the Hero*
*68. William J. Tyler, tr., *The Psychological World of Natsume Sōseki,* by Doi Takeo
69. Eric Widmer, *The Russian Ecclesiastical Mission in Peking During the Eighteenth Century*
*70. Charlton M. Lewis, *Prologue to the Chinese Revolution: The Transformation of Ideas and Institutions in Hunan Province, 1891–1907*
71. Preston Torbert, *The Ching Imperial Household Department: A Study of Its Organization and Principal Functions, 1662–1796*
72. Paul A. Cohen and John E. Schrecker, eds., *Reform in Nineteenth-Century China*
73. Jon Sigurdson, *Rural Industrialism in China*
74. Kang Chao, *The Development of Cotton Textile Production in China*

75. Valentin Rabe, *The Home Base of American China Missions, 1880–1920*
*76. Sarasin Viraphol, *Tribute and Profit: Sino-Siamese Trade, 1652–1853*
77. Ch'i-ch'ing Hsiao, *The Military Establishment of the Yuan Dynasty*
78. Meishi Tsai, *Contemporary Chinese Novels and Short Stories, 1949–1974: An Annotated Bibliography*
*79. Wellington K. K. Chan, *Merchants, Mandarins and Modern Enterprise in Late Ching China*
80. Endymion Wilkinson, *Landlord and Labor in Late Imperial China: Case Studies from Shandong by Jing Su and Luo Lun*
*81. Barry Keenan, *The Dewey Experiment in China: Educational Reform and Political Power in the Early Republic*
*82. George A. Hayden, *Crime and Punishment in Medieval Chinese Drama: Three Judge Pao Plays*
*83. Sang-Chul Suh, *Growth and Structural Changes in the Korean Economy, 1910–1940*
84. J. W. Dower, *Empire and Aftermath: Yoshida Shigeru and the Japanese Experience, 1878–1954*
85. Martin Collcutt, *Five Mountains: The Rinzai Zen Monastic Institution in Medieval Japan*
86. Kwang Suk Kim and Michael Roemer, *Growth and Structural Transformation*
87. Anne O. Krueger, *The Developmental Role of the Foreign Sector and Aid*
*88. Edwin S. Mills and Byung-Nak Song, *Urbanization and Urban Problems*
89. Sung Hwan Ban, Pal Yong Moon, and Dwight H. Perkins, *Rural Development*
*90. Noel F. McGinn, Donald R. Snodgrass, Yung Bong Kim, Shin-Bok Kim, and Quee-Young Kim, *Education and Development in Korea*
*91. Leroy P. Jones and Il SaKong, *Government, Business, and Entrepreneurship in Economic Development: The Korean Case*
92. Edward S. Mason, Dwight H. Perkins, Kwang Suk Kim, David C. Cole, Mahn Je Kim et al., *The Economic and Social Modernization of the Republic of Korea*
93. Robert Repetto, Tai Hwan Kwon, Son-Ung Kim, Dae Young Kim, John E. Sloboda, and Peter J. Donaldson, *Economic Development, Population Policy, and Demographic Transition in the Republic of Korea*
94. Parks M. Coble, Jr., *The Shanghai Capitalists and the Nationalist Government, 1927–1937*
95. Noriko Kamachi, *Reform in China: Huang Tsun-hsien and the Japanese Model*
96. Richard Wich, *Sino-Soviet Crisis Politics: A Study of Political Change and Communication*
97. Lillian M. Li, *China's Silk Trade: Traditional Industry in the Modern World, 1842–1937*
98. R. David Arkush, *Fei Xiaotong and Sociology in Revolutionary China*
*99. Kenneth Alan Grossberg, *Japan's Renaissance: The Politics of the Muromachi Bakufu*
100. James Reeve Pusey, *China and Charles Darwin*

101. Hoyt Cleveland Tillman, *Utilitarian Confucianism: Chen Liang's Challenge to Chu Hsi*
102. Thomas A. Stanley, *Ōsugi Sakae, Anarchist in Taishō Japan: The Creativity of the Ego*
103. Jonathan K. Ocko, *Bureaucratic Reform in Provincial China: Ting Jih-ch'ang in Restoration Kiangsu, 1867–1870*
104. James Reed, *The Missionary Mind and American East Asia Policy, 1911–1915*
105. Neil L. Waters, *Japan's Local Pragmatists: The Transition from Bakumatsu to Meiji in the Kawasaki Region*
106. David C. Cole and Yung Chul Park, *Financial Development in Korea, 1945–1978*
107. Roy Bahl, Chuk Kyo Kim, and Chong Kee Park, *Public Finances During the Korean Modernization Process*
108. William D. Wray, *Mitsubishi and the N.Y.K, 1870–1914: Business Strategy in the Japanese Shipping Industry*
109. Ralph William Huenemann, *The Dragon and the Iron Horse: The Economics of Railroads in China, 1876–1937*

*110. Benjamin A. Elman, *From Philosophy to Philology: Intellectual and Social Aspects of Change in Late Imperial China*

111. Jane Kate Leonard, *Wei Yüan and China's Rediscovery of the Maritime World*
112. Luke S. K. Kwong, *A Mosaic of the Hundred Days:. Personalities, Politics, and Ideas of 1898*

*113. John E. Wills, Jr., *Embassies and Illusions: Dutch and Portuguese Envoys to K'ang-hsi, 1666–1687*

114. Joshua A. Fogel, *Politics and Sinology: The Case of Naitō Konan (1866–1934)*

*115. Jeffrey C. Kinkley, ed., *After Mao: Chinese Literature and Society, 1978–1981*

116. C. Andrew Gerstle, *Circles of Fantasy: Convention in the Plays of Chikamatsu*
117. Andrew Gordon, *The Evolution of Labor Relations in Japan: Heavy Industry, 1853–1955*

*118. Daniel K. Gardner, *Chu Hsi and the "Ta Hsueh": Neo-Confucian Reflection on the Confucian Canon*

119. Christine Guth Kanda, *Shinzō: Hachiman Imagery and Its Development*

*120. Robert Borgen, *Sugawara no Michizane and the Early Heian Court*

121. Chang-tai Hung, *Going to the People: Chinese Intellectual and Folk Literature, 1918–1937*

*122. Michael A. Cusumano, *The Japanese Automobile Industry: Technology and Management at Nissan and Toyota*

123. Richard von Glahn, *The Country of Streams and Grottoes: Expansion, Settlement, and the Civilizing of the Sichuan Frontier in Song Times*
124. Steven D. Carter, *The Road to Komatsubara: A Classical Reading of the Renga Hyakuin*
125. Katherine F. Bruner, John K. Fairbank, and Richard T. Smith, *Entering China's Service: Robert Hart's Journals, 1854–1863*

126. Bob Tadashi Wakabayashi, *Anti-Foreignism and Western Learning in Early-Modern Japan: The "New Theses" of 1825*
127. Atsuko Hirai, *Individualism and Socialism: The Life and Thought of Kawai Eijirō (1891–1944)*
128. Ellen Widmer, *The Margins of Utopia: "Shui-hu hou-chuan" and the Literature of Ming Loyalism*
129. R. Kent Guy, *The Emperor's Four Treasuries: Scholars and the State in the Late Chien-lung Era*
130. Peter C. Perdue, *Exhausting the Earth: State and Peasant in Hunan, 1500–1850*
131. Susan Chan Egan, *A Latterday Confucian: Reminiscences of William Hung (1893–1980)*
132. James T. C. Liu, *China Turning Inward: Intellectual-Political Changes in the Early Twelfth Century*

*133. Paul A. Cohen, *Between Tradition and Modernity: Wang T'ao and Reform in Late Ching China*

134. Kate Wildman Nakai, *Shogunal Politics: Arai Hakuseki and the Premises of Tokugawa Rule*

*135. Parks M. Coble, *Facing Japan: Chinese Politics and Japanese Imperialism, 1931–1937*

136. Jon L. Saari, *Legacies of Childhood: Growing Up Chinese in a Time of Crisis, 1890–1920*
137. Susan Downing Videen, *Tales of Heichū*
138. Heinz Morioka and Miyoko Sasaki, *Rakugo: The Popular Narrative Art of Japan*
139. Joshua A. Fogel, *Nakae Ushikichi in China: The Mourning of Spirit*
140. Alexander Barton Woodside, *Vietnam and the Chinese Model: A Comparative Study of Vietnamese and Chinese Government in the First Half of the Nineteenth Century*

*141. George Elison, *Deus Destroyed: The Image of Christianity in Early Modern Japan*

142. William D. Wray, ed., *Managing Industrial Enterprise: Cases from Japan's Prewar Experience*

*143. T'ung-tsu Ch'ü, *Local Government in China Under the Ching*

144. Marie Anchordoguy, *Computers, Inc.: Japan's Challenge to IBM*
145. Barbara Molony, *Technology and Investment: The Prewar Japanese Chemical Industry*
146. Mary Elizabeth Berry, *Hideyoshi*
147. Laura E. Hein, *Fueling Growth: The Energy Revolution and Economic Policy in Postwar Japan*
148. Wen-hsin Yeh, *The Alienated Academy: Culture and Politics in Republican China, 1919–1937*
149. Dru C. Gladney, *Muslim Chinese: Ethnic Nationalism in the People's Republic*
150. Merle Goldman and Paul A. Cohen, eds., *Ideas Across Cultures: Essays on Chinese Thought in Honor of Benjamin L Schwartz*
151. James M. Polachek, *The Inner Opium War*
152. Gail Lee Bernstein, *Japanese Marxist: A Portrait of Kawakami Hajime, 1879–1946*

- *153. Lloyd E. Eastman, *The Abortive Revolution: China Under Nationalist Rule, 1927–1937*
- 154. Mark Mason, *American Multinationals and Japan: The Political Economy of Japanese Capital Controls, 1899–1980*
- 155. Richard J. Smith, John K. Fairbank, and Katherine F. Bruner, *Robert Hart and China's Early Modernization: His Journals, 1863–1866*
- 156. George J. Tanabe, Jr., *Myōe the Dreamkeeper: Fantasy and Knowledge in Kamakura Buddhism*
- 157. William Wayne Farris, *Heavenly Warriors: The Evolution of Japan's Military, 500–1300*
- 158. Yu-ming Shaw, *An American Missionary in China: John Leighton Stuart and Chinese-American Relations*
- 159. James B. Palais, *Politics and Policy in Traditional Korea*
- *160. Douglas Reynolds, *China, 1898–1912: The Xinzheng Revolution and Japan*
- 161. Roger R. Thompson, *China's Local Councils in the Age of Constitutional Reform, 1898–1911*
- 162. William Johnston, *The Modern Epidemic: History of Tuberculosis in Japan*
- 163. Constantine Nomikos Vaporis, *Breaking Barriers: Travel and the State in Early Modern Japan*
- 164. Irmela Hijiya-Kirschnereit, *Rituals of Self-Revelation: Shishōsetsu as Literary Genre and Socio-Cultural Phenomenon*
- 165. James C. Baxter, *The Meiji Unification Through the Lens of Ishikawa Prefecture*
- 166. Thomas R. H. Havens, *Architects of Affluence: The Tsutsumi Family and the Seibu-Saison Enterprises in Twentieth-Century Japan*
- 167. Anthony Hood Chambers, *The Secret Window: Ideal Worlds in Tanizaki's Fiction*
- 168. Steven J. Ericson, *The Sound of the Whistle: Railroads and the State in Meiji Japan*
- 169. Andrew Edmund Goble, *Kenmu: Go-Daigo's Revolution*
- 170. Denise Potrzeba Lett, *In Pursuit of Status: The Making of South Korea's "New" Urban Middle Class*
- 171. Mimi Hall Yiengpruksawan, *Hiraizumi: Buddhist Art and Regional Politics in Twelfth-Century Japan*
- 172. Charles Shirō Inouye, *The Similitude of Blossoms: A Critical Biography of Izumi Kyōka (1873–1939), Japanese Novelist and Playwright*
- 173. Aviad E. Raz, *Riding the Black Ship: Japan and Tokyo Disneyland*
- 174. Deborah J. Milly, *Poverty, Equality, and Growth: The Politics of Economic Need in Postwar Japan*
- 175. See Heng Teow, *Japan's Cultural Policy Toward China, 1918–1931: A Comparative Perspective*
- 176. Michael A. Fuller, *An Introduction to Literary Chinese*
- 177. Frederick R. Dickinson, *War and National Reinvention: Japan in the Great War, 1914–1919*

178. John Solt, *Shredding the Tapestry of Meaning: The Poetry and Poetics of Kitasono Katue (1902–1978)*
179. Edward Pratt, *Japan's Protoindustrial Elite: The Economic Foundations of the Gōnō*
180. Atsuko Sakaki, *Recontextualizing Texts: Narrative Performance in Modern Japanese Fiction*
181. Soon-Won Park, *Colonial Industrialization and Labor in Korea: The Onoda Cement Factory*
182. JaHyun Kim Haboush and Martina Deuchler, *Culture and the State in Late Chosŏn Korea*
183. John W. Chaffee, *Branches of Heaven: A History of the Imperial Clan of Sung China*
184. Gi-Wook Shin and Michael Robinson, eds., *Colonial Modernity in Korea*
185. Nam-lin Hur, *Prayer and Play in Late Tokugawa Japan: Asakusa Sensōji and Edo Society*
186. Kristin Stapleton, *Civilizing Chengdu: Chinese Urban Reform, 1895–1937*
187. Hyung Il Pai, *Constructing "Korean" Origins: A Critical Review of Archaeology, Historiography, and Racial Myth in Korean State-Formation Theories*
188. Brian D. Ruppert, *Jewel in the Ashes: Buddha Relics and Power in Early Medieval Japan*
189. Susan Daruvala, *Zhou Zuoren and an Alternative Chinese Response to Modernity*

*190. James Z. Lee, *The Political Economy of a Frontier: Southwest China, 1250–1850*

191. Kerry Smith, *A Time of Crisis: Japan, the Great Depression, and Rural Revitalization*
192. Michael Lewis, *Becoming Apart: National Power and Local Politics in Toyama, 1868–1945*
193. William C. Kirby, Man-houng Lin, James Chin Shih, and David A. Pietz, eds., *State and Economy in Republican China: A Handbook for Scholars*
194. Timothy S. George, *Minamata: Pollution and the Struggle for Democracy in Postwar Japan*
195. Billy K. L. So, *Prosperity, Region, and Institutions in Maritime China: The South Fukien Pattern, 946–1368*
196. Yoshihisa Tak Matsusaka, *The Making of Japanese Manchuria, 1904–1932*
197. Maram Epstein, *Competing Discourses: Orthodoxy, Authenticity, and Engendered Meanings in Late Imperial Chinese Fiction*
198. Curtis J. Milhaupt, J. Mark Ramseyer, and Michael K. Young, eds. and comps., *Japanese Law in Context: Readings in Society, the Economy, and Politics*
199. Haruo Iguchi, *Unfinished Business: Ayukawa Yoshisuke and U.S.-Japan Relations, 1937–1952*
200. Scott Pearce, Audrey Spiro, and Patricia Ebrey, *Culture and Power in the Reconstitution of the Chinese Realm, 200–600*
201. Terry Kawashima, *Writing Margins: The Textual Construction of Gender in Heian and Kamakura Japan*
202. Martin W. Huang, *Desire and Fictional Narrative in Late Imperial China*

203. Robert S. Ross and Jiang Changbin, eds., *Re-examining the Cold War: U.S.-China Diplomacy, 1954–1973*
204. Guanhua Wang, *In Search of Justice: The 1905–1906 Chinese Anti-American Boycott*
205. David Schaberg, *A Patterned Past: Form and Thought in Early Chinese Historiography*
206. Christine Yano, *Tears of Longing: Nostalgia and the Nation in Japanese Popular Song*
207. Milena Doleželová-Velingerová and Oldřich Král, with Graham Sanders, eds., *The Appropriation of Cultural Capital: China's May Fourth Project*
208. Robert N. Huey, *The Making of 'Shinkokinshū'*
209. Lee Butler, *Emperor and Aristocracy in Japan, 1467–1680: Resilience and Renewal*
210. Suzanne Ogden, *Inklings of Democracy in China*
211. Kenneth J. Ruoff, *The People's Emperor: Democracy and the Japanese Monarchy, 1945–1995*
212. Haun Saussy, *Great Walls of Discourse and Other Adventures in Cultural China*
213. Aviad E. Raz, *Emotions at Work: Normative Control, Organizations, and Culture in Japan and America*
214. Rebecca E. Karl and Peter Zarrow, eds., *Rethinking the 1898 Reform Period: Political and Cultural Change in Late Qing China*
215. Kevin O'Rourke, *The Book of Korean Shijo*
216. Ezra F. Vogel, ed., *The Golden Age of the U.S.-China-Japan Triangle, 1972–1989*
217. Thomas A. Wilson, ed., *On Sacred Grounds: Culture, Society, Politics, and the Formation of the Cult of Confucius*
218. Donald S. Sutton, *Steps of Perfection: Exorcistic Performers and Chinese Religion in Twentieth-Century Taiwan*
219. Daqing Yang, *Technology of Empire: Telecommunications and Japanese Expansionism, 1895–1945*
220. Qianshen Bai, *Fu Shan's World: The Transformation of Chinese Calligraphy in the Seventeenth Century*
221. Paul Jakov Smith and Richard von Glahn, eds., *The Song-Yuan-Ming Transition in Chinese History*
222. Rania Huntington, *Alien Kind: Foxes and Late Imperial Chinese Narrative*
223. Jordan Sand, *House and Home in Modern Japan: Architecture, Domestic Space, and Bourgeois Culture, 1880–1930*
224. Karl Gerth, *China Made: Consumer Culture and the Creation of the Nation*
225. Xiaoshan Yang, *Metamorphosis of the Private Sphere: Gardens and Objects in Tang-Song Poetry*
226. Barbara Mittler, *A Newspaper for China? Power, Identity, and Change in Shanghai's News Media, 1872–1912*
227. Joyce A. Madancy, *The Troublesome Legacy of Commissioner Lin: The Opium Trade and Opium Suppression in Fujian Province, 1820s to 1920s*

228. John Makeham, *Transmitters and Creators: Chinese Commentators and Commentaries on the Analects*
229. Elisabeth Köll, *From Cotton Mill to Business Empire: The Emergence of Regional Enterprises in Modern China*
230. Emma Teng, *Taiwan's Imagined Geography: Chinese Colonial Travel Writing and Pictures, 1683–1895*
231. Wilt Idema and Beata Grant, *The Red Brush: Writing Women of Imperial China*
232. Eric C. Rath, *The Ethos of Noh: Actors and Their Art*
233. Elizabeth Remick, *Building Local States: China During the Republican and Post-Mao Eras*
234. Lynn Struve, ed., *The Qing Formation in World-Historical Time*
235. D. Max Moerman, *Localizing Paradise: Kumano Pilgrimage and the Religious Landscape of Premodern Japan*
236. Antonia Finnane, *Speaking of Yangzhou: A Chinese City, 1550–1850*
237. Brian Platt, *Burning and Building: Schooling and State Formation in Japan, 1750–1890*
238. Gail Bernstein, Andrew Gordon, and Kate Wildman Nakai, eds., *Public Spheres, Private Lives in Modern Japan, 1600–1950: Essays in Honor of Albert Craig*
239. Wu Hung and Katherine R. Tsiang, *Body and Face in Chinese Visual Culture*
240. Stephen Dodd, *Writing Home: Representations of the Native Place in Modern Japanese Literature*
241. David Anthony Bello, *Opium and the Limits of Empire: Drug Prohibition in the Chinese Interior, 1729–1850*
242. Hosea Hirata, *Discourses of Seduction: History, Evil, Desire, and Modern Japanese Literature*
243. Kyung Moon Hwang, *Beyond Birth: Social Status in the Emergence of Modern Korea*
244. Brian R. Dott, *Identity Reflections: Pilgrimages to Mount Tai in Late Imperial China*
245. Mark McNally, *Proving the Way: Conflict and Practice in the History of Japanese Nativism*
246. Yongping Wu, *A Political Explanation of Economic Growth: State Survival, Bureaucratic Politics, and Private Enterprises in the Making of Taiwan's Economy, 1950–1985*
247. Kyu Hyun Kim, *The Age of Visions and Arguments: Parliamentarianism and the National Public Sphere in Early Meiji Japan*
248. Zvi Ben-Dor Benite, *The Dao of Muhammad: A Cultural History of Muslims in Late Imperial China*
249. David Der-wei Wang and Shang Wei, eds., *Dynastic Crisis and Cultural Innovation: From the Late Ming to the Late Qing and Beyond*
250. Wilt L. Idema, Wai-yee Li, and Ellen Widmer, eds., *Trauma and Transcendence in Early Qing Literature*
251. Barbara Molony and Kathleen Uno, eds., *Gendering Modern Japanese History*

252. Hiroshi Aoyagi, *Islands of Eight Million Smiles: Idol Performance and Symbolic Production in Contemporary Japan*
253. Wai-yee Li, *The Readability of the Past in Early Chinese Historiography*
254. William C. Kirby, Robert S. Ross, and Gong Li, eds., *Normalization of U.S.-China Relations: An International History*
255. Ellen Gardner Nakamura, *Practical Pursuits: Takano Chōei, Takahashi Keisaku, and Western Medicine in Nineteenth-Century Japan*
256. Jonathan W. Best, *A History of the Early Korean Kingdom of Paekche, together with an annotated translation of* The Paekche Annals *of the* Samguk sagi
257. Liang Pan, *The United Nations in Japan's Foreign and Security Policymaking, 1945–1992: National Security, Party Politics, and International Status*
258. Richard Belsky, *Localities at the Center: Native Place, Space, and Power in Late Imperial Beijing*
259. Zwia Lipkin, *"Useless to the State": "Social Problems" and Social Engineering in Nationalist Nanjing, 1927–1937*
260. William O. Gardner, *Advertising Tower: Japanese Modernism and Modernity in the 1920s*
261. Stephen Owen, *The Making of Early Chinese Classical Poetry*
262. Martin J. Powers, *Pattern and Person: Ornament, Society, and Self in Classical China*
263. Anna M. Shields, *Crafting a Collection: The Cultural Contexts and Poetic Practice of the* Huajian ji 花間集 *(Collection from Among the Flowers)*
264. Stephen Owen, *The Late Tang: Chinese Poetry of the Mid-Ninth Century (827–860)*
265. Sara L. Friedman, *Intimate Politics: Marriage, the Market, and State Power in Southeastern China*
266. Patricia Buckley Ebrey and Maggie Bickford, *Emperor Huizong and Late Northern Song China: The Politics of Culture and the Culture of Politics*
267. Sophie Volpp, *Worldly Stage: Theatricality in Seventeenth-Century China*
268. Ellen Widmer, *The Beauty and the Book: Women and Fiction in Nineteenth-Century China*
269. Steven B. Miles, *The Sea of Learning: Mobility and Identity in Nineteenth-Century Guangzhou*
270. Lin Man-houng, *China Upside Down: Currency, Society, and Ideologies, 1808–1856*
271. Ronald Egan, *The Problem of Beauty: Aesthetic Thought and Pursuits in Northern Song Dynasty China*
272. Mark Halperin, *Out of the Cloister: Literati Perspectives on Buddhism in Sung China, 960–1279*
273. Helen Dunstan, *State or Merchant? Political Economy and Political Process in 1740s China*
274. Sabina Knight, *The Heart of Time: Moral Agency in Twentieth-Century Chinese Fiction*